PowerNomics

Part I: Foundational Theories and Vision

Chapter 1: Introduction – Re-envisioning Socio-Economic Empowerment

In an era marked by rapid technological change, shifting global power structures, and increasingly complex socio-economic challenges, the traditional models of economic development and community organization are showing their limitations. Dr. Justin Goldston's integrated approach calls for a paradigm shift—a radical re-envisioning of socio-economic empowerment that harnesses the transformative potential of advanced science, technology, and systemic pedagogy. This chapter sets the stage for understanding the need for sustainable, decentralized communities built on a foundation of interdisciplinary innovation and collective action.

1.1 The Imperative for a New Paradigm

For decades, conventional economic systems have been driven by centralized models that often perpetuate inequalities and stifle local innovation. Despite significant progress in technology and communication, many communities continue to face persistent challenges: economic stagnation, resource concentration in urban centers, and disconnection between technological advances and everyday human needs. The limitations of these traditional structures have sparked a growing call for approaches that are not only adaptive but also inherently inclusive and resilient.

Dr. Goldston argues that sustainable empowerment requires a holistic framework—one that integrates elements of advanced scientific inquiry, cutting-edge technological tools, and innovative pedagogical methods. The goal is to transform community dynamics from passive recipients of top-down policies into active, self-governing entities capable of steering their own socio-economic destinies.

1.2 The Pillars of Dr. Goldston's Integrated Approach

Dr. Goldston's model is built upon three foundational pillars, each interlocking to form a robust structure for socio-economic empowerment:

Advanced Science

At the forefront of this integrated approach is a deep engagement with advanced science. The incorporation of breakthrough areas such as fusion plasma physics and cosmology is not merely for their intrinsic scientific value, but as metaphors and mechanisms for understanding and harnessing energy dynamics in socio-economic systems. Fusion plasma physics, for example, symbolizes the potential for generating abundant, sustainable energy—a metaphor for how communities can catalyze their own growth through self-reinforcing cycles of innovation and investment.

Cutting-Edge Technology

Technology is the engine that powers the transition from theory to practical implementation. Dr. Goldston's strategy leverages technologies such as blockchain, artificial intelligence (AI), and decentralized autonomous organizations (DAOs) to create transparent, resilient, and self-sustaining economic structures. Blockchain technology underpins the creation of secure, immutable records of transactions, while AI optimizes decision-making and resource allocation in real-time. Together, these technologies support the development of decentralized platforms where power is distributed among community members, rather than concentrated in a centralized authority.

Systemic Pedagogy

The third pillar of this approach is systemic pedagogy—a reimagined educational framework that prioritizes practical, real-world applications of knowledge over traditional, siloed academic disciplines. This pedagogy emphasizes the importance of integrating theoretical understanding with hands-on learning experiences. Through initiatives like the Gemach Pedagogy, the approach aims to cultivate a generation of leaders who are not only technically proficient but also deeply committed to community empowerment and systemic change.

1.3 Building Sustainable, Decentralized Communities

At its core, Dr. Goldston's vision is about creating communities that are self-sustaining, adaptive, and resilient in the face of global challenges. Decentralization is key: by redistributing power and resources across multiple nodes within a community, the model seeks to mitigate the vulnerabilities inherent in centralized systems. This decentralized framework supports the emergence of local hubs of innovation—environments where community members can engage in collective decision-making, share resources equitably, and collaborate on long-term projects that drive socio-economic progress.

The pilot study, set in a historically rich and evolving locale like Asheboro, NC, will serve as a demonstration project. While the pilot study is designed with inclusive principles that benefit all community members, its strategic foundations are informed by historical models of collective empowerment. By aligning advanced scientific principles, transformative technologies, and revolutionary pedagogical methods, the pilot project will serve as a replicable blueprint for decentralized empowerment that can be adapted to diverse contexts worldwide.

1.4 The Road Ahead: Integrating Disciplines for Holistic Change

This textbook embarks on a comprehensive exploration of the theories, technologies, and practices that underpin Dr. Goldston's integrated approach. Each chapter will delve into specific elements—from the technical nuances of blockchain and AI to the philosophical underpinnings of the Infinite Cycle Theory and the Hope Paradox. By synthesizing insights from multiple disciplines, the text offers a cohesive framework that empowers communities to reclaim economic agency and foster a more equitable and sustainable future.

As we journey through the subsequent chapters, readers will gain not only a deep theoretical understanding of each component but also practical guidance on how to implement these strategies in real-world settings. This integrated approach represents a bold re-imagination of socio-economic empowerment—one that is designed to catalyze change at the local level while contributing to a global movement towards resilience, inclusivity, and self-determination.

In summary, Chapter 1 lays the groundwork for a transformative exploration of socio-economic empowerment. Dr. Goldston's vision is clear: by marrying advanced science, state-of-the-art technology, and systemic pedagogy, we can create decentralized communities that are both resilient and innovative. This paradigm shift is not only a theoretical necessity but also a practical imperative for addressing the complex challenges of our modern world.

Chapter 1: Introduction – Re-envisioning Socio-Economic Empowerment

In an era defined by rapid technological advancement, shifting global power structures, and increasingly complex socio-economic challenges, traditional models of economic development and community organization are proving inadequate. Dr. Justin Goldston's integrated approach calls for a paradigm shift—one that leverages advanced science, cutting-edge technology, and systemic pedagogy to create sustainable, decentralized communities. This chapter lays the groundwork for understanding why a comprehensive re-envisioning of socio-economic empowerment is not only timely but also essential for building resilient, self-governing societies that can meet the demands of the modern world.

1.1 The Imperative for a New Paradigm

1.1.1 Limitations of Traditional Economic Models

For decades, centralized economic systems have concentrated power and resources in the hands of a few, often resulting in persistent inequalities and regional disparities. Conventional structures tend to favor established hierarchies, leaving communities with limited agency and minimal opportunities for self-directed growth. Despite technological progress and expanded communication channels, many areas continue to struggle with economic stagnation, resource extraction from localities, and a disconnect between technological innovations and community needs.

1.1.2 The Call for Integration and Inclusivity

Dr. Goldston posits that the future of socio-economic empowerment lies in an integrated framework that brings together disparate fields of knowledge. By combining advanced science with state-of-the-art technology and transformative educational strategies, communities can transition from being passive recipients of top-down policies to active architects of their own destiny. This integration is not merely additive; it creates a synergistic effect that multiplies the impact of each individual component, leading to a more dynamic and inclusive system of empowerment.

1.1.3 The Role of Decentralization

At the heart of this paradigm is the principle of decentralization. Decentralized systems distribute power and resources across multiple nodes, ensuring that communities are not at the mercy of distant, centralized authorities. This shift towards localized decision-making and self-sufficiency underpins the resilience of communities, making them better equipped to respond to economic disruptions and social challenges. The emerging technologies of blockchain and artificial intelligence (AI) serve as critical enablers of this decentralization, offering tools for transparency, efficiency, and collective governance.

1.2 Pillars of Dr. Goldston's Integrated Approach

Dr. Goldston's model is built on three interlocking pillars—each essential for fostering a new era of socio-economic empowerment. These pillars form the foundation for constructing decentralized communities that are not only sustainable but also adaptive to future challenges.

1.2.1 Advanced Science: Energy, Cosmology, and Systemic Dynamics

Advanced science is more than a theoretical pursuit; it is a practical tool for reimagining how communities generate and harness energy. Dr. Goldston draws on breakthroughs in fusion plasma physics—not only as a source of nearly limitless clean energy but also as a metaphor for self-sustaining growth. The study of cosmology further enriches this perspective, offering insights into the interconnectedness of all systems. The vast, cyclical processes of the universe serve as a model for the kind of regenerative, feedback-driven economic systems that can propel communities forward. This pillar lays the groundwork for understanding natural cycles of energy and matter, which can be mirrored in socio-economic systems to foster resilience and continuous innovation.

1.2.2 Cutting-Edge Technology: Blockchain, AI, and Decentralized Autonomous Organizations

Technology is the engine driving the transition from theoretical frameworks to real-world applications. Central to this pillar is blockchain technology, which offers a secure, transparent, and decentralized means of recording transactions and managing resources. Blockchain is complemented by AI, which provides advanced analytical capabilities to optimize decision-making and resource allocation in real time. The creation of Decentralized Autonomous Organizations (DAOs) further reinforces this pillar by enabling communities to govern themselves democratically. DAOs empower members to participate directly in decision-making processes, ensuring that economic growth is inclusive and benefits all stakeholders. Together, these technologies underpin the creation of robust, scalable infrastructures that can support the ambitions of a decentralized community.

1.2.3 Systemic Pedagogy: Transformative Education for Real-World Impact

Traditional education often falls short when it comes to preparing individuals for the challenges of modern socio-economic landscapes. Dr. Goldston's systemic pedagogy reimagines learning by integrating academic theory with practical, hands-on experiences. This approach—embodied in initiatives like the Gemach Pedagogy—prioritizes experiential learning, critical thinking, and community engagement. By aligning curricula with the demands of a decentralized, technology-driven economy, systemic pedagogy cultivates a new generation of leaders who are as adept in digital fluency as they are in traditional academic disciplines. The focus is not only on technical proficiency but also on cultivating the mindset needed to drive systemic change and foster community empowerment.

1.3 Building Sustainable, Decentralized Communities

1.3.1 The Concept of Decentralization in Practice

Decentralization is more than a theoretical construct; it is a practical strategy for building resilient communities. By distributing power and resources across multiple nodes, communities can create self-sustaining ecosystems that are less vulnerable to external shocks. In a decentralized system, local hubs of innovation emerge—each acting as a center for economic, educational, and technological advancement. This approach mitigates the risks associated with centralized control and ensures that decision-making is both participatory and reflective of local needs.

1.3.2 Interdisciplinary Synergy: Science, Technology, and Pedagogy

A key innovation of Dr. Goldston's approach is the integration of interdisciplinary knowledge. Advanced science, cutting-edge technology, and systemic pedagogy do not operate in isolation; they interact dynamically to produce a robust framework for empowerment. For example, breakthroughs in fusion plasma physics provide a metaphor for generating self-sustaining energy cycles, while blockchain and AI offer the technical means to manage these cycles in a decentralized manner. Simultaneously, systemic pedagogy ensures that individuals are equipped with the skills and mindset necessary to harness these innovations for collective benefit. This synergy is what makes the model not only innovative but also practically viable.

1.3.3 Case Study: The Pilot Study in Asheboro, NC

To illustrate the practical application of these concepts, a pilot study is proposed in Asheboro, NC. This community serves as a fertile ground for testing the integrated approach due to its historical legacy of resilience and its potential for inclusive growth. The Asheboro pilot is designed to function as an experimental hub where the principles of decentralized empowerment are put into practice. By leveraging local institutions, establishing cooperative economic networks, and deploying advanced technologies, the pilot project aims to demonstrate how a community can transform itself into a self-sustaining, innovative hub of economic and social progress. Although the pilot is designed with inclusive principles that benefit all members, its strategic foundations draw on historical models of collective empowerment to generate reparative impact.

1.4 Theoretical Underpinnings and Philosophical Foundations

1.4.1 The Infinite Cycle Theory: A Framework for Regeneration

The Infinite Cycle Theory posits that progress is not linear but cyclical. Social and economic systems, much like natural ecosystems, undergo phases of growth, maturity, and renewal. This theory provides a framework for understanding how communities can continuously regenerate their resources and capacities. It emphasizes the importance of feedback loops, where investment in one cycle leads to returns that fuel the next. Dr. Goldston uses this theory to argue that with the right structures in place, communities can achieve perpetual renewal—ensuring long-term sustainability and adaptability.

1.4.2 The Hope Paradox: Harnessing Optimism as a Catalyst for Change

The Hope Paradox explores the dual role of hope in driving transformation. While hope can be a powerful motivator, it can also lead to complacency if not paired with actionable strategies. Dr. Goldston's approach harnesses hope as a catalyst for change by coupling it with practical frameworks that translate optimism into measurable outcomes. This concept is integral to motivating communities to embrace new technologies and educational models, ensuring that hope is sustained through concrete achievements and continuous progress.

1.4.3 Web3 Systems Thinking and G-Theory: Reconstructing Socio-Economic Models

Web3 Systems Thinking represents a departure from traditional economic models by emphasizing decentralization, transparency, and distributed control. It provides a lens through which to view economic interactions as interconnected networks rather than isolated transactions. Complementing this is G-Theory, an integrative framework that synthesizes insights from economics, physics, philosophy, and technology. Together, these theories offer a comprehensive blueprint for constructing socio-economic systems that are adaptive, resilient, and equitable. They challenge conventional wisdom by proposing that true empowerment comes from reconfiguring the very foundations of how communities organize and interact.

1.5 Technological Enablers and the Path to Implementation

1.5.1 Blockchain as the Backbone of Decentralized Economies

Blockchain technology is central to the creation of decentralized systems. Its inherent properties of transparency, security, and immutability make it an ideal tool for recording transactions, managing resources, and ensuring accountability within a community. In Dr. Goldston's model, blockchain is not only a technological innovation but a symbol of trust and collective ownership. It enables the creation of decentralized autonomous organizations (DAOs), which democratize decision-making and empower individuals to participate in the governance of their community's resources.

1.5.2 Artificial Intelligence: Optimizing Decision-Making and Resource Allocation

Artificial intelligence plays a pivotal role in managing the complexity of decentralized systems. By leveraging AI-driven analytics, communities can optimize resource allocation, forecast future trends, and make informed decisions in real time. AI complements blockchain by processing vast amounts of data, identifying patterns, and suggesting strategies that maximize collective benefit. This technological synergy ensures that the community remains agile and responsive to both challenges and opportunities.

1.5.3 The Role of Decentralized Autonomous Organizations (DAOs)

DAOs are innovative organizational structures that embody the principles of decentralized governance. In a DAO, decision-making is distributed among all stakeholders, eliminating traditional hierarchies and enabling a more participatory form of management. Dr. Goldston's model incorporates DAOs to ensure that economic, educational, and technological initiatives are collectively governed. This structure not only fosters transparency but also builds a sense of shared responsibility and ownership—key ingredients for long-term socio-economic empowerment.

1.6 Systemic Pedagogy: Transformative Education for a New Era

1.6.1 Rethinking Traditional Education

The conventional education system often emphasizes theoretical knowledge without sufficient emphasis on practical application. Dr. Goldston's systemic pedagogy challenges this model by integrating hands-on learning, real-world problem solving, and community engagement into the curriculum. This approach prepares learners not just to participate in the economy but to actively shape it. The aim is to cultivate critical thinkers and innovators who are well-versed in both traditional academic disciplines and the skills needed to thrive in a decentralized, technology-driven society.

1.6.2 The Gemach Pedagogy: Bridging Theory and Practice

A cornerstone of this transformative educational model is the Gemach Pedagogy. This innovative framework transforms learning into a participatory, experiential process where academic insights are directly applied to community-based projects. Through collaborative initiatives, students and community members alike engage in practical exercises that reinforce theoretical concepts. The Gemach Pedagogy is designed to nurture a mindset of empowerment, encouraging learners to view themselves as both beneficiaries and active contributors to the community's economic and social progress.

1.6.3 Building Future Leaders Through Inclusive, Practical Learning

In this re-envisioned educational landscape, institutions such as SydTek University play a pivotal role. By integrating advanced technologies, interdisciplinary research, and community engagement, these institutions serve as incubators for the next generation of leaders. Students are trained to think systemically, to leverage digital tools like blockchain and AI, and to implement innovative solutions in real-world contexts. This holistic approach ensures that graduates are not only academically accomplished but also equipped with the practical skills necessary to drive systemic change.

1.7 From Pilot Study to Global Blueprint

1.7.1 The Asheboro Model: A Real-World Testbed

The envisioned pilot study in Asheboro, NC, represents a tangible application of Dr. Goldston's integrated framework. Asheboro has been chosen as an ideal testbed due to its rich history of community resilience and its potential as a microcosm for broader socio-economic transformation. The pilot project will implement decentralized governance structures, cooperative economic models, and systemic pedagogical strategies to demonstrate how a community can evolve into a self-sustaining, innovative hub. This initiative serves as a proof of concept, offering valuable insights and scalable models that can be adapted to diverse contexts around the globe.

1.7.2 Metrics for Success and Continuous Feedback

A robust framework for evaluation is essential to gauge the success of the pilot study. Key performance indicators (KPIs) will be established to monitor progress in areas such as economic growth, educational outcomes, technological adoption, and community engagement. Continuous feedback loops, inspired by the Infinite Cycle Theory, will ensure that the system remains dynamic and responsive to emerging challenges. By analyzing data in real time, decision-makers can adapt strategies, optimize resource allocation, and reinforce the system's resilience.

1.7.3 Scaling and Replicating the Model

While the pilot study is localized, its underlying principles are universally applicable. Once validated, the model can be scaled and replicated in other communities, both nationally and internationally. The blueprint developed in Asheboro will serve as a template for building decentralized, self-sustaining ecosystems that promote economic empowerment, foster technological innovation, and drive systemic educational reform. This scalability is one of the model's most powerful attributes, offering a pathway to global socio-economic transformation.

1.8 Challenges, Opportunities, and Future Directions

1.8.1 Navigating Technological and Institutional Barriers

The path to re-envisioned socio-economic empowerment is fraught with challenges. Technological integration, particularly in the realms of blockchain and AI, requires overcoming issues related to scalability, security, and regulatory compliance. Institutional inertia and resistance to change can also hinder the adoption of decentralized governance models. This chapter acknowledges these challenges while emphasizing that they are not insurmountable. Through strategic planning, continuous innovation, and collaborative problem-solving, communities can navigate these barriers and turn potential obstacles into opportunities for growth.

1.8.2 The Promise of Interdisciplinary Synergy

The convergence of advanced science, technology, and systemic pedagogy presents unprecedented opportunities for innovation. By breaking down traditional silos and fostering interdisciplinary collaboration, communities can unlock new sources of economic and social capital. This synergy not only drives technological progress but also cultivates a culture of lifelong learning and collective empowerment. The integrated approach serves as a catalyst for holistic transformation, paving the way for a future where decentralized communities thrive on their own terms.

1.8.3 Future Research and Policy Implications

As the model evolves, future research will be critical in refining theoretical frameworks and testing practical applications. The insights gained from the Asheboro pilot and subsequent implementations will inform policy decisions at local, national, and global levels. Policymakers will need to adapt regulatory frameworks to support decentralized technologies and innovative governance structures. This research agenda will also explore the long-term socio-economic impacts of systemic empowerment and provide guidance on how best to scale successful initiatives.

1.9 Conclusion: A Bold Vision for the Future

This introductory chapter has set the stage for an ambitious journey—a journey toward re-envisioning socio-economic empowerment through an integrated framework that harnesses the power of advanced science, cutting-edge technology, and transformative pedagogy. Dr. Goldston's approach challenges us to rethink the very foundations of how communities are organized and empowered, shifting from centralized, top-down models to decentralized, self-sustaining ecosystems.

The principles outlined in this chapter form the backbone of a comprehensive strategy aimed at building resilient, inclusive, and dynamic communities. By drawing inspiration from natural cycles, harnessing the potential of digital technologies, and reimagining education as a tool for systemic change, this framework offers a roadmap for the future—a future where every community has the capacity to thrive, innovate, and lead.

As we move forward through the subsequent chapters, readers will delve deeper into the specific components that make up this integrated approach. From the technical nuances of blockchain and AI to the philosophical insights of the Infinite Cycle Theory and the Hope Paradox, each chapter will contribute to a holistic understanding of how decentralized empowerment can reshape our socio-economic landscape.

The vision is bold, the challenges are significant, and the opportunities are boundless. The journey begins here—in the theoretical, practical, and transformative exploration of a new socio-economic order. This is not merely an academic exercise; it is a call to action for communities around the world to reclaim their power, reimagine their futures, and build a society that is both sustainable and just.

In summary, Chapter 1 has provided an extensive overview of the need for a paradigm shift in socio-economic empowerment. By integrating advanced scientific insights, state-of-the-art technological tools, and revolutionary pedagogical strategies, Dr. Goldston's framework offers a transformative vision for building decentralized communities capable of addressing modern challenges while fostering long-term, inclusive growth. The path ahead is complex, yet filled with promise—and it all begins with re-envisioning our approach to empowerment in an interconnected, rapidly evolving world.

Chapter 2: Historical Paradigms & Lessons Learned

This chapter embarks on an extensive exploration of historical experiments in collective economics and self-sufficiency, analyzing centuries-old systems of communal empowerment across diverse cultures and eras. By deeply examining successes, failures, and transformative moments in communal organization, we lay the groundwork for developing a modern, inclusive strategy that integrates decentralized governance, advanced technologies, and innovative pedagogy. The lessons from the past do not merely serve as nostalgic reflections; they are active ingredients in designing dynamic future systems, allowing us to build upon proven strategies and avoid historical pitfalls.

2.1 Early Communal Practices and Collective Economics

2.1.1 Agrarian Societies and Collective Resource Management

Long before industrialization, human communities thrived under models of communal resource management. Agrarian societies across continents developed intricate systems that balanced shared labor with equitable distribution of resources:

- **Collective Decision-Making:**
  Early villages frequently adopted councils or communal assemblies to decide on agricultural practices, land use, and irrigation schedules. This ensured that risk was shared during harvest failures, and rewards were distributed fairly during times of plenty. Rituals, seasonal festivals, and oral storytelling were often used to reinforce these decisions as part of the community's collective memory.

- **Resource Pooling and Labor Sharing:**
  Communities pooled essential resources such as seeds, tools, and manpower. Labor-sharing arrangements were vital; for instance, in certain Asian and African societies, community members would come together during planting and harvest periods. This cooperation enabled them to overcome environmental uncertainties and demonstrate remarkable resilience in the face of famine or drought.

- **Reciprocity and Social Contracts:**
  Underlying these practices were social contracts anchored in reciprocity. Customary laws and moral codes reinforced mutual aid, ensuring that those who contributed to communal efforts would receive support in times of personal or collective need. This system of informal insurance was critical in maintaining social cohesion and ensuring survival.

2.1.2 Indigenous and Tribal Models of Collective Organization

Indigenous communities across the globe have long practiced systems of collective economics that emphasize stewardship of natural resources and community well-being:

- **Communal Land Ownership:**
  Among many Native American tribes, land was not owned in the Western sense, but managed as a communal asset. Land was considered sacred, and its stewardship was entrusted to community elders and councils who made decisions based on consensus and long-term sustainability rather than short-term profit.

- **Resource Sharing and Subsistence Strategies:**
  Tribes in Africa, South America, and Oceania developed communal strategies for hunting, gathering, and later, small-scale farming. These communities negotiated resource access through intricate networks of reciprocal relationships, ensuring that no individual was marginalized, and that the group as a whole remained resilient against external shocks.

- **Cultural Rituals and Collective Identity:**
  Collective identity was reinforced by cultural rituals, myths, and storytelling traditions that underscored the interconnectedness of all members. These narratives often celebrated heroes who exemplified the virtues of collective

effort and self-sacrifice, thereby embedding the ethos of communal responsibility into the cultural fabric.

2.1.3 Guild Systems and the Rise of Cooperative Networks

As societies evolved beyond purely agrarian models, the emergence of specialized trades necessitated the formation of guilds, which operated as early cooperatives:

- **Medieval European Guilds:**
  In medieval Europe, guilds became the cornerstone of urban economic life. They standardized practices, ensured quality through apprenticeships, and provided social safety nets for members. Guilds regulated production and trade, often prohibiting undercutting within their ranks to preserve collective prosperity.

- **Trade Networks and Mutual Support:**
  Guilds extended their influence through regional networks that collaborated with one another to share best practices, expand markets, and protect members' interests in the face of external competition. These associations functioned as early examples of vertical integration, ensuring that production, distribution, and trade were managed within a regulated framework.

- **Cultural Significance and Legacy:**
  The guild system also played a vital role in fostering a sense of professional identity and community pride. The ceremonial aspects—such as guild halls, initiation rituals, and commemorative art—served to reinforce collective memory and continuity across generations, an element that modern decentralized models can adapt to build lasting cultural capital.

2.2 The Industrial Age and the Cooperative Movement

2.2.1 Early Industrialization: Workers, Cooperatives, and the Birth of Urban Solidarity

The transition from agrarian to industrial economies in the 18th and 19th centuries brought profound social transformations. Urbanization, while offering new opportunities, also generated harsh working conditions that spurred collective action among industrial laborers:

- **Worker Cooperatives and Trade Unions:**
  Industrial workers, facing long hours, unsafe conditions, and exploitative labor practices, began forming cooperatives as a means to reclaim control over their labor. Early cooperatives provided platforms for collective bargaining, economic self-help, and even shared ownership of production facilities.

- **Financial Cooperatives: Banks and Credit Unions:**
  The establishment of cooperative banks and credit unions emerged as a counterforce to exploitative financial institutions. These cooperatives enabled workers and local entrepreneurs to access capital under fair terms, invest in community projects, and foster local economic growth. They served as precursors to modern decentralized financial systems, emphasizing transparency and equitable access.

- **Mutual Aid and Community Insurance Schemes:**
  Faced with the risks inherent in rapid industrialization, many urban workers organized mutual aid societies and insurance schemes. Such arrangements provided a safety net for illness, injury, and unemployment, reinforcing the principle

that collective solidarity is essential for mitigating systemic vulnerabilities.

2.2.2 Utopian Communities and Experimental Models of Self-Sufficiency

The modern era has witnessed numerous experiments in intentional community-building, driven by ideals of equality, sustainability, and shared prosperity:

- **New Harmony and Early American Communal Experiments:**
  Founded in the early 19th century by social reformers, New Harmony was an ambitious experiment in communal living and shared wealth. Although its lifespan was short-lived, New Harmony's emphasis on collective education, resource sharing, and participatory governance left a lasting legacy that informs modern community planning.

- **The Kibbutz Movement in Israel:**
  Perhaps the most enduring example of communal economics is found in the kibbutzim of Israel. These self-contained, agrarian communities were founded on egalitarian principles and have evolved to include modern industrial and technological enterprises while maintaining a robust commitment to collective responsibility and shared ownership.

- **Modern Eco-villages and Intentional Communities:**
  In recent decades, eco-villages and intentional communities have proliferated around the world. These modern iterations draw on ancient practices of communal living while incorporating sustainable technology, permaculture, and digital tools to enhance collaboration. Such models not only pursue environmental sustainability but also aim to create economic systems that are resilient to global market

fluctuations.

2.2.3 Comparative Case Studies: Successes and Failures in Collective Models

Evaluating historical models requires a nuanced understanding of both their achievements and shortcomings:

- **Successful Adaptations:**
  Successful models, such as certain guilds, kibbutzim, and cooperatives, have demonstrated remarkable resilience by evolving over time. Their ability to adapt to new economic realities, integrate technological innovations, and maintain a robust sense of community identity has allowed them to endure where others have failed.

- **Structural Failures and Lessons Learned:**
  Other experiments, despite their idealism, have faltered due to a lack of economic realism or internal conflict. For example, some utopian communes dissolved when resource scarcity or ideological differences led to fragmentation. These failures highlight the critical importance of balancing communal ideals with robust economic planning and conflict resolution mechanisms—a balance that must be central to modern strategies.

2.3 Lessons from Historical Paradigms: Bridging the Past and the Future

2.3.1 Key Success Factors in Historical Models

The following elements are consistently found in successful historical communal models:

- **Inclusive, Democratic Governance:**
  The success of communal systems often hinged on inclusive decision-making processes where every member's voice contributed to shaping policies and practices. This democratic ethos is vital in establishing systems that are resilient to internal power imbalances.

- **Resilience and Adaptability:**
  Communities that thrived were those able to adapt to changing circumstances—be it economic downturns, environmental crises, or social upheavals. Flexibility in governance and resource management allowed these communities to reinvent themselves in the face of external pressures.

- **Strong Social Bonds and Shared Narratives:**
  A unifying cultural narrative and robust social capital were central to many successful models. Shared rituals, communal gatherings, and collective storytelling created a sense of identity and belonging that sustained cooperation over time.

- **Integrated Economic Structures:**
  Success was also found in systems that integrated various economic functions—from production to distribution—within the community. Vertical integration ensured that wealth remained internal, promoting reinvestment and sustained growth.

2.3.2 Challenges and Pitfalls: Cautionary Tales from History

Historical models offer as much caution as they do inspiration:

- **Over-Idealism Without Pragmatism:**
  Several utopian experiments collapsed when lofty ideals were not matched by practical economic systems. The tension between idealism and economic viability serves as a reminder that a balance must be struck between visionary goals and the imperatives of sustainable finance.

- **Internal Division and Leadership Conflicts:**
  Internal dissent, often fueled by diverging visions or inequitable power distribution, has undermined many communal experiments. Robust conflict resolution mechanisms and transparent governance are essential to preventing fragmentation.

- **External Exploitation and Economic Pressures:**
  Communities have historically faced challenges from external forces—be it exploitative market pressures or hostile political regimes—that disrupted internal stability. Protecting communal autonomy in the face of external economic and regulatory pressures is a critical lesson for modern systems.

2.3.3 Synthesis and Translation to Modern Systems

The synthesis of historical lessons provides a rich template for contemporary models:

- **Decentralization as a Consistent Thread:**
  From early agrarian collectives to urban cooperatives, decentralization has proven to be an effective strategy for distributing power and safeguarding resources. Modern technologies such as blockchain and decentralized autonomous organizations (DAOs) translate these age-old principles into scalable, transparent systems.

- **Interdisciplinary Integration:**
  Historical successes were rarely confined to economic strategies alone; they integrated cultural, social, and environmental dimensions. Today's model must reflect this holistic perspective by combining advanced scientific research, state-of-the-art technology, and transformative education to create dynamic, multifaceted empowerment strategies.

- **Adaptability and Continuous Innovation:**
  The need for continuous adaptation in historical models underscores the importance of building systems that are flexible and responsive. Modern strategies must incorporate mechanisms for real-time feedback and iterative improvement, ensuring that communities can pivot in response to technological innovation and market shifts.

2.4 The Emergence of a New Inclusive Strategy

2.4.1 Defining Modern Self-Sufficiency

Modern self-sufficiency extends traditional communal practices into a framework that supports economic, cultural, and technological sustainability:

- **Holistic Economic Independence:**
  Rather than a narrow focus on wealth accumulation, modern self-sufficiency emphasizes a balanced approach that fosters economic independence, environmental stewardship, and social well-being. This involves creating closed-loop economic systems where resources are

continuously reinvested within the community.

- **Cultural and Educational Renewal:**
  The principles of self-sufficiency now incorporate reinvention in education and cultural expression. Programs like the Gemach Pedagogy facilitate experiential learning that connects traditional communal wisdom with digital literacy and modern entrepreneurial skills.

- **Technological Empowerment:**
  Empowerment is achieved through advanced technology that ensures equitable access to information, resources, and decision-making tools. The integration of AI, blockchain, and decentralized digital infrastructures provides not only transparency but also a scalable method to coordinate collective action and preserve communal autonomy.

2.4.2 Constructing an Inclusive, Scalable Blueprint

Drawing on historical paradigms, the development of an inclusive, modern blueprint focuses on broad participation and adaptive structures:

- **Broad Participation Through Digital Platforms:**
  The democratization of decision-making is enhanced by digital platforms that enable broad-based participation. By leveraging technologies like DAOs and secure blockchain networks, communities can ensure that every member, regardless of background, has a stake in their collective future.

- **Vertical Integration in Community Ventures:**
  Emulating the guild systems and cooperative networks of the past, modern strategies propose vertical integration that spans production, distribution, and service delivery. This ensures that economic benefits are internalized, fostering

long-term resilience and reducing dependency on external markets.

- **Policy Innovation and Adaptive Regulation:**
  Constructing an inclusive blueprint requires supportive policy frameworks that encourage innovation while safeguarding community interests. Modern strategies must advocate for adaptive regulation that accommodates decentralized models and incentivizes sustainable practices at local, national, and international levels.

2.4.3 Case Applications and Future Possibilities

Historical paradigms inspire a wide range of contemporary applications:

- **Urban Regeneration and Smart City Initiatives:**
  Urban centers facing socio-economic decline can adopt decentralized models to revitalize local economies. By integrating cooperative housing, community-owned energy solutions, and localized digital marketplaces, cities can foster inclusive growth and counteract urban gentrification.

- **Rural Empowerment and Sustainable Agriculture:**
  Rural regions can draw on centuries of agrarian collective practices combined with modern technology to enhance food security, promote eco-friendly farming methods, and build robust local supply chains. This model not only preserves traditional practices but also leverages modern innovations to improve productivity and sustainability.

- **Global Digital Communities and Cross-Border Cooperatives:**
  The digital age enables the formation of global communities based on shared economic interests and cultural values. Decentralized autonomous organizations (DAOs) can

coordinate transnational efforts, facilitating cross-border trade, global resource management, and collective innovation on a worldwide scale.

2.5 Comparative Regional Case Studies

2.5.1 Indigenous Cooperatives in Latin America

Throughout Latin America, indigenous communities have implemented models of shared resource management that combine traditional practices with modern cooperative techniques. These case studies reveal:

- **Preservation of Cultural Heritage:**
  Initiatives that fuse modern cooperative practices with indigenous cultural traditions have led to the sustainable management of natural resources while protecting cultural identities. The integration of local wisdom with contemporary economic strategies offers a blueprint for rural empowerment.

- **Success Amidst Global Pressures:**
  Facing the pressures of globalization and market infiltration, many indigenous cooperatives have relied on community solidarity and decentralized decision-making to maintain autonomy. Their experiences demonstrate the potential of localized power structures to resist external economic exploitation.

2.5.2 Cooperative Networks in Eastern Europe and Asia

In regions of Eastern Europe and Asia, post-communist transformations have given rise to innovative cooperative models:

- **Transitioning Economies:**
  Countries in Eastern Europe, dealing with the aftermath of centrally planned economies, have experimented with cooperatives as vehicles for economic revival. These initiatives blend historical communal practices with modern entrepreneurial strategies to foster economic resilience and local self-reliance.

- **Technological Integration in Asia:**
  In parts of Asia, communities have effectively integrated technology into their cooperative models. Advanced mobile payment systems, digital farming platforms, and community-run tech incubators exemplify how modern tools can transform age-old collective practices into dynamic economic engines.

2.6 Global Perspectives: Cross-Cultural Cooperation and Economic Models

2.6.1 Lessons from the Global South

The Global South offers a wealth of insights into the resilience of communal models under challenging circumstances:

- **Adaptive Strategies in Resource-Constrained Environments:**
  Nations in Africa, South Asia, and Latin America often face adverse environmental and economic conditions. Yet, communal resource management and cooperative finance have enabled these regions to build adaptive strategies that

counteract external market pressures.

- **Empowerment Through Grassroots Movements:**
  Grassroots organizations in the Global South have frequently spearheaded efforts to reclaim economic agency through community-driven development projects. These initiatives emphasize the importance of localized decision-making and have successfully integrated traditional practices with contemporary cooperative techniques.

2.6.2 Cross-Cultural Exchange and the Future of Collective Economics

Globalization provides an unprecedented opportunity to share successful models and foster cross-cultural cooperation:

- **Knowledge Transfer and Collaborative Networks:**
  In an interconnected world, successful models from diverse regions can be adapted and scaled to suit local conditions in entirely different cultural contexts. Digital platforms and international forums facilitate the exchange of ideas, enabling communities to learn from one another and collectively innovate in areas such as sustainable agriculture, renewable energy, and decentralized finance.

- **Creating a Global Commons:**
  The future of collective economics envisions the establishment of a global commons—a decentralized, shared space where communities worldwide can collectively manage resources, share innovations, and co-develop solutions to global challenges. This vision draws inspiration from historical precedents and modern technologies alike, creating a bridge between local practices and global interdependence.

2.7 Socio-Political Ramifications and the Role of Collective Narratives

2.7.1 The Power of Narrative in Shaping Collective Identity

Historical models of communal empowerment were often sustained not only by economic mechanisms but also by powerful narratives that united people:

- **Myth, Memory, and Identity:**
  Stories of shared struggle and triumph have the power to inspire and mobilize communities. The narratives constructed around medieval guilds, utopian communes, and indigenous cooperatives have helped embed a sense of purpose and belonging. These stories continue to resonate today, providing a cultural foundation for modern decentralized movements.

- **Transformative Narratives for the Modern Era:**
  As modern communities navigate the complexities of globalization and technological disruption, crafting new, inclusive narratives becomes essential. These narratives must draw on historical precedents while articulating a bold vision for future empowerment that transcends traditional economic paradigms.

2.7.2 Political Implications of Collective Organization

The political landscape is deeply influenced by the organization of economic power. Historical and contemporary models alike suggest:

- **Empowering Local Governance:**
  Decentralized economic models inherently support local governance structures that are more attuned to the needs of the community. The integration of decentralized technologies like DAOs has the potential to reshape political participation, making governance more inclusive and responsive.

- **Challenging Centralized Power:**
  The historical successes of cooperative movements underscore the potential for grassroots initiatives to challenge dominant political and economic systems. Modern movements drawing on historical lessons aim not only to generate wealth but also to recalibrate power relations—shifting decision-making authority back to the community level.

2.8 Historical Relevance to Modern Decentralized Models

2.8.1 The Evolution from Centralization to Decentralization

The shift from centralized power structures to decentralized models has deep historical roots:

- **From Feudalism to Modern Cooperatives:**
  The evolution from feudal systems—where wealth and power were concentrated in the hands of a few—to decentralized guilds and cooperatives illustrates the human drive for more equitable systems. Each historical phase has contributed to the gradual decentralization of economic power, a process that modern digital technologies now

accelerate.

- **Translating Historical Insights into Digital Frameworks:**
  The principles of decentralization observed in historical models are mirrored in the design of blockchain technologies and DAOs. These digital frameworks encapsulate the lessons of inclusivity and shared governance, providing a contemporary platform to reimagine collective empowerment on a global scale.

2.8.2 Aligning Past Strategies with Future Innovations

Modern decentralized strategies are not created in a vacuum; they are deeply informed by historical practice:

- **Interdisciplinary Integration:**
  The integration of disparate historical experiences—ranging from indigenous communal practices to medieval guilds—offers a rich tapestry upon which modern strategies can be built. This interdisciplinary approach ensures that technological innovations are grounded in the social, cultural, and economic insights of past generations.

- **Creating Resilient, Iterative Systems:**
  Historical models demonstrate that resilience often emerges from iterative cycles of innovation and adaptation. The concept of the Infinite Cycle Theory, which posits that progress is regenerative rather than linear, draws directly from this historical understanding. Modern decentralized models, by harnessing continuous feedback loops and agile methodologies, embody these principles and extend them into the digital age.

2.9 Future Directions and Synthesis

2.9.1 Translating Historical Lessons into Actionable Strategies

The historical paradigms discussed in this chapter do more than inform—they provide actionable insights for constructing modern, decentralized models:

- **Hybrid Models:**
  The lessons drawn from past communal systems encourage the creation of hybrid models that combine digital innovation with traditional cooperative practices. These systems can be tailored to suit varied contexts, from small rural communities to expansive urban centers, ensuring flexibility and scalability.

- **Institutional Frameworks:**
  By integrating the strengths of historical institutions—such as guilds and indigenous councils—with modern governance technologies, we can develop institutional frameworks that are both robust and adaptive. These frameworks serve as the bedrock for economic systems that are self-sustaining and community-driven.

2.9.2 Continuous Innovation and the Road Ahead

As we look toward the future, continuous innovation and adaptation remain paramount:

- **Dynamic Policy and Governance:**
  Modern decentralized models must include mechanisms for agile policy-making and adaptive governance. Historical experiences highlight the danger of rigid institutions; modern systems must incorporate real-time feedback loops to

remain responsive to societal changes.

- **Scalability and Global Replication:**
  The scalability of successful historical models—demonstrated by the enduring nature of the kibbutzim, cooperatives, and guilds—provides a hopeful blueprint for future initiatives. By leveraging digital platforms, these models can be replicated and adapted worldwide, fostering a global network of resilient, community-led economies.

2.10 Concluding Insights: Bridging History and Modern Innovation

Historical paradigms of collective economics and self-sufficiency offer a multifaceted reservoir of knowledge that is directly applicable to modern challenges. The enduring themes of shared governance, resilience, and interdisciplinary integration have sustained communities through crises and transformations throughout the centuries. The journey from agrarian collectives to digital DAOs is not a radical departure from the past—it is a natural evolution fueled by the same human desire for equity, belonging, and empowerment.

By critically examining historical lessons—from indigenous communalism and medieval guilds to industrial cooperatives and utopian experiments—we gain a profound understanding of the principles that underpin effective collective organization. These principles inform our modern strategies, guiding us as we construct decentralized, inclusive frameworks that embody the full spectrum of human ingenuity.

As we synthesize these lessons into actionable strategies, the challenge and opportunity lie in re-imagining socio-economic empowerment for an interconnected, technologically advanced future. This chapter has laid a comprehensive foundation that underscores the relevance of historical paradigms. The models of the past do not simply echo in the corridors of history; they serve as dynamic blueprints for the innovative systems of tomorrow.

In sum, the historical journey through communal empowerment has revealed a continuum of evolving strategies that have continually adapted to meet the challenges of their times. Today's decentralized models—grounded in advanced technology, innovative pedagogy, and a deep respect for collective memory—are the natural successors of these historical traditions. They promise not only economic resilience and sustainability but also a more inclusive, participatory society where every individual has the power to shape their destiny.

This chapter, by mapping the intricate tapestry of historical paradigms, provides both inspiration and direction. It invites us to view history not as a static record of what once was, but as a living, dynamic force that informs the creation of a future where empowerment is shared, sustainability is paramount, and the collective potential of communities is realized in innovative, transformative ways.

Chapter 3: The Infinite Cycle Theory – A Framework for Regeneration

The Infinite Cycle Theory offers a transformative framework for understanding how social and economic progress unfolds—not as a linear, one-directional march toward an end state, but as a series of recurring, regenerative cycles. This theory contends that innovation, cultural shifts, and economic transformation are driven by natural feedback mechanisms and iterative processes that promote continual renewal and evolution. In this chapter, we delve exhaustively into the theoretical underpinnings, detailed feedback loops, mechanisms of regeneration, and the pivotal role of cyclical innovation. We establish a model that elucidates how dynamic systems, ranging from ecological networks to human institutions, can perpetually regenerate and transform themselves.

3.1 Conceptual Foundations: Beyond Linear Progress

3.1.1 Moving Away from Linear Paradigms

Traditional models of progress tend to evoke the image of a straight line—a continuous, unidirectional trajectory from an initial state to some ever-higher plateau. In these models, advancements accumulate steadily over time, and obstacles are seen as deviations or setbacks along an otherwise upward path. However, such linear paradigms fall short when describing complex systems in which growth is erratic, punctuated, and often non-monotonic.

- **Nature as a Template:**
  Consider the cyclical nature of the seasons: spring brings renewal after the dormancy of winter; summer, with its vibrancy, is eventually succeeded by the cooling, introspective phase of autumn. Similarly, biological life cycles—where organisms are born, mature, and eventually regenerate through reproduction—illustrate that progress is not strictly linear. Instead, it is characterized by repetitive cycles in which each cycle builds upon the learnings and resources of the previous one while also responding to environmental changes.

- **Dynamic Equilibrium:**
  In dynamic systems, equilibrium is not a static point but a

state of continuous adjustment. Rather than settling at a final "end state," systems remain in flux—constantly assimilating external shocks, internal innovations, and random variations. The Infinite Cycle Theory thus shifts our perspective from an expectation of continuous, one-way advancement to an appreciation of iterative, regenerative patterns.

- **Beyond Incrementalism:**
  The linear view often supports incremental change, but it underestimates the potential of transformative leaps that can occur once a cycle reaches a critical threshold. In the Infinite Cycle framework, these leaps are not anomalies but essential features of the process, driven by the accumulation and eventual release of built-up potential.

3.1.2 The Nature of Cycles in Human History

Throughout human history, civilizations have risen, matured, experienced periods of decline, and then reinvented themselves through cycles of innovation and reform. These cycles are evident across various domains:

- **Economic and Financial Cycles:**
  Economic booms and busts—such as those seen in the 19th-century industrialization waves, the Great Depression, or the cyclical nature of modern recessions—illustrate how economies periodically collapse, reorganize, and emerge with new foundations of growth. Each downturn forces a reassessment of financial practices and regulatory frameworks, setting the stage for subsequent periods of expansion.

- **Political and Social Upheavals:**
  Revolutions and reform movements (e.g., the French Revolution, the Civil Rights Movement, and recent global protests for democratic reforms) are emblematic of cycles in

political consciousness. Social upheaval often marks the end of one regime, but it also generates the necessary energy for reformed governance systems to take shape—a process that is repeated in various forms throughout history.

- **Cultural and Intellectual Renaissances:**
  Cultural renaissances, like the European Renaissance or the Harlem Renaissance, underscore the recurring nature of intellectual and artistic rebirth. These periods are characterized by a renewed interest in learning, creativity, and philosophy, often emerging after prolonged periods of stagnation or suppression.

The Infinite Cycle Theory integrates these historical dynamics, arguing that each phase—whether of prosperity or of crisis—is imbued with the seeds of its successor. Rather than viewing decline solely as regression, it is reframed as the precursor to a new period of innovation and vibrancy.

3.1.3 Regeneration as an Inherent Feature of Systems

Central to the Infinite Cycle Theory is the notion of regeneration. This concept suggests that every system—biological, economic, cultural, or political—has an intrinsic capacity to absorb past experiences, learn from them, and transform its structure to meet new challenges.

- **Evolutionary Learning:**
  Just as organisms evolve by passing genetic information from one generation to the next with modifications that better suit them to their environment, institutions and societies evolve through the accumulation of historical knowledge. This evolutionary process is reinforced by institutional memory, cultural narratives, and the lessons embedded in past cycles.

- **Adaptive Resilience:**
  Systems that regenerate are not frozen in time; they actively adjust to changes. For example, a forest that experiences a wildfire may suffer immediate loss, yet the clearing of old growth paves the way for a more diverse and resilient ecosystem. Similarly, businesses that undergo "creative destruction" shed outdated practices to make room for innovative models that are better adapted to current market conditions.

- **Cumulative Wisdom:**
  Every cycle builds on the accumulated wisdom of previous iterations, ensuring that subsequent cycles are not mere repetitions but rather refinements and evolutions that address emergent problems while capitalizing on established strengths. This cumulative effect is central to sustainable progress.

3.2 Feedback Loops: Engines of Cyclical Transformation

3.2.1 Understanding Feedback Mechanisms

Feedback loops are the essential mechanisms through which systems self-regulate and evolve. They involve the return of outputs from a process into the system as inputs, thereby shaping subsequent outcomes.

- **Positive Feedback Loops:**
  In a positive feedback loop, an initial change is amplified by the system's response. For instance, a breakthrough in technology may spur additional research and development, creating a virtuous cycle of innovation. When applied to

socio-economic systems, positive feedback can result in rapid growth and creative energy, driving communities to exceed their previous limits.

- **Negative Feedback Loops:**
  In contrast, negative feedback loops act to stabilize a system by counteracting deviations from a desired state. For example, when an economy overheats, regulatory mechanisms such as interest rate adjustments can dampen exuberance and prevent runaway inflation. Negative feedback loops are critical for maintaining balance and preventing systemic collapse.

- **Feedback in Complex Systems:**
  In systems characterized by complexity, feedback loops are interwoven and multifaceted. They can operate simultaneously on different timescales and in various directions, creating oscillations, convergences, and sometimes chaotic behavior. Understanding these interactions is key to harnessing them for regenerative purposes.

3.2.2 Feedback Loops in Natural and Social Systems

Feedback loops are not a phenomenon confined to abstract theory; they are observable in nearly every natural and social process:

- **Ecological Feedback:**
  In natural ecosystems, the water cycle is a classic example of a feedback loop. Evaporation, condensation, and precipitation form a continuous and self-sustaining process that is vital for life. Other examples include predator-prey dynamics, where the fluctuation in populations of each influences the other's growth, thereby keeping the ecosystem in check.

- **Economic Feedback:**
  Economic systems exhibit feedback loops through the interplay of supply and demand, investment and returns, and regulatory responses to market conditions. For instance, a surge in consumer confidence can lead to increased spending, which in turn boosts production and employment. However, if the growth becomes excessive, corrective measures such as interest rate hikes may be deployed to prevent inflation.

- **Social and Political Feedback:**
  In the realm of governance and societal change, feedback loops manifest in the cyclical nature of public sentiment and policy reform. Social movements build momentum as their successes encourage further participation, yet as change becomes institutionalized, complacency or resistance may set in, prompting a need for renewed activism.

3.2.3 The Role of Feedback in Socio-Economic Progress

Feedback loops are fundamental to spurring progress and maintaining the dynamism of socio-economic systems:

- **Driving Innovation:**
  Positive feedback loops in innovation ensure that initial successes generate further ideas and advancements. A breakthrough in one area, such as renewable energy technology, can attract further investment, inspire competing innovations, and ultimately drive an entire sector forward.

- **Maintaining Equilibrium:**
  Negative feedback loops function as a check against runaway processes. In economic policy, these loops help moderate boom-bust cycles by reinvesting profits during growth phases and reining in excesses during downturns.

This self-regulating behavior is crucial for long-term stability.

- **Facilitating Adaptation:**
  Continuous feedback allows systems to adapt to changing circumstances. Organizations that monitor performance metrics and internalize lessons from past cycles can pivot more effectively when encountering new challenges, thus maintaining their relevance and competitive edge.

3.3 Mechanisms of Regeneration and Renewal

3.3.1 Regeneration in Natural Ecosystems

Biological systems are masters of regeneration, and their processes offer profound insights into how socio-economic systems might replicate such dynamism:

- **Ecological Succession:**
  When a forest experiences a disturbance—whether from a wildfire, storm, or pest invasion—its ecosystem undergoes a process known as ecological succession. Early colonizers, or pioneer species, quickly repopulate the cleared area, modifying the environment (for example, by enriching the soil) and paving the way for more complex species. This sequential regeneration results in a resilient ecosystem that is more diverse and better adapted to environmental pressures.

- **Regenerative Cycles in Marine Ecosystems:**
  Coral reefs, for example, exhibit striking regenerative properties. After periods of bleaching or damage, these structures can recover if given time and conducive

environmental conditions. The cycle of destruction and renewal in these ecosystems demonstrates that resilience is not the absence of failure, but the capacity to rebuild more robustly afterward.

- **Lessons for Human Systems:**
  The regeneration seen in nature teaches us that recovery does not mean a simple return to the status quo. Instead, it signals a dynamic process where past limitations are overcome, and new, more efficient systems arise—principles that can be emulated in economic, social, and political arenas.

3.3.2 Regenerative Processes in Human Institutions

Human institutions and organizations, though subject to different dynamics than natural ecosystems, exhibit analogous processes of regeneration:

- **Creative Destruction in Business:**
  Economic historian Joseph Schumpeter coined the term "creative destruction" to describe how outdated business models and technologies are supplanted by innovations that provide improved efficiency and performance. This process, though often disruptive in the short term, ultimately leads to a more dynamic, competitive, and resilient economic landscape.

- **Institutional Reforms in Governance:**
  Democracies and other forms of governance regularly undergo processes of reform and reinvention. Constitutional amendments, electoral reforms, and public policy overhauls are analogous to natural regenerative cycles—resetting and recalibrating power structures to better serve the evolving needs of society.

- **Community Resilience:**
  Social institutions—such as local governance bodies, non-profits, and educational establishments—exhibit resilience by institutionalizing lessons from past crises. By maintaining an adaptive organizational memory through documented practices, cultural traditions, and continuous learning, communities are better equipped to regenerate in the face of rapid change.

3.3.3 Learning and Adaptation as Regenerative Drivers

The capacity of systems to learn from experience is a critical driver of regeneration:

- **Institutional Memory and Cultural Learning:**
  Organizations that can capture historical data, institutional narratives, and cultural experiences create repositories of wisdom that guide future decisions. Such learning mechanisms allow for the refinement of processes and the avoidance of past mistakes, ensuring that each cycle of regeneration is better informed than the last.

- **Adaptive Leadership and Organizational Agility:**
  Leadership that embraces change and fosters an environment of experimentation contributes to an organization's ability to regenerate. Adaptive leadership models emphasize flexibility, continuous improvement, and the solicitation of diverse viewpoints, all of which are essential for thriving through cycles of change.

- **Technological and Educational Feedback:**
  Modern systems increasingly rely on real-time data collection, analytics, and feedback loops to adjust strategies quickly. In education, for instance, innovative pedagogies and digital learning platforms can rapidly disseminate new

knowledge, ensuring that learners—and by extension, the institutions that serve them—are continually evolving.

3.3.4 Cycles of Renewal in Innovation and Creativity

The process of creative destruction and renewal is observable across industries and cultural phenomena:

- **Technological Innovations:**
  The introduction of disruptive technologies often upends established industries, leading to periods of instability followed by rapid reorganization. For example, the advent of the internet transformed traditional media, commerce, and communication, triggering a period of turbulent change that eventually paved the way for a digitally integrated global economy.

- **Social Movements and Cultural Shifts:**
  Periods of social unrest and transformation, such as the civil rights movement or the digital revolution in music and art, demonstrate how disruption can create fertile ground for renewal. The initial breakdown of entrenched systems creates a vacuum that is subsequently filled by new ideas and practices, enriching the cultural tapestry of society.

- **Innovation Ecosystems:**
  In business and technology hubs like Silicon Valley, cycles of startup formation, growth, consolidation, and disruption occur in a continuous loop. Each cycle of innovation builds upon the infrastructure, talent, and market dynamics established in previous cycles, driving an ongoing evolution that reinforces economic resilience and creative dynamism.

3.4 Cyclical Innovation: The Catalyst for Transformation

3.4.1 Defining Cyclical Innovation

Cyclical innovation refers to the patterned emergence of successive waves of creative breakthroughs, technological advancements, and organizational reforms. It is characterized by:

- **Burst Phases:**
  Periods of intense innovation that generate rapid, significant changes across multiple domains—often triggered by a confluence of technological breakthroughs, shifts in consumer behavior, or regulatory changes.

- **Consolidation Phases:**
  Followed by periods in which innovations are integrated into existing systems, standards are established, and disruptive forces are neutralized. These phases allow for stabilization and resource allocation that support long-term growth.

- **Predictable Yet Dynamic Patterns:**
  While the specific innovations are unique to each cycle, the overall rhythm—marked by phases of explosive change followed by consolidation—remains observable. This regularity provides a heuristic framework for anticipating future transformations.

3.4.2 Historical Cycles of Innovation

History provides compelling examples of cyclical innovation across different spheres:

- **The Industrial Revolution:**
  A dramatic sequence of technological breakthroughs in

manufacturing, transportation, and energy production reshaped society. This period was marked by rapid industrial growth followed by regulatory and social adjustments that integrated these innovations into daily life.

- **Digital Transformation:**
  The late 20th century witnessed the birth of personal computing and the internet, triggering an innovation cascade that redefined information exchange, communication, and economic activities. The subsequent maturation of digital technologies established new business models and societal norms.

- **Cultural Renaissance:**
  The European Renaissance exemplifies how artistic and scientific revivals occur cyclically, injecting societies with renewed intellectual and creative energy that reverberates through subsequent generations.

3.4.3 Generational Dynamics and Innovation Cycles

Generational turnover plays a vital role in fueling cyclical innovation:

- **Youthful Disruption:**
  Younger generations, often less constrained by traditional paradigms and endowed with fresh perspectives, are more inclined to challenge the status quo. Their willingness to experiment lays the groundwork for the next cycle of innovation.

- **Maturation and Institutional Integration:**
  As these innovative ideas gain traction, they are absorbed into the fabric of society. Institutions gradually integrate these new paradigms—until a point of stagnation is reached, precipitating the need for another wave of disruptive

creativity.

- **Intergenerational Synergy:**
  The interplay between youthful exuberance and experienced prudence creates a dynamic tension that underpins cyclical renewal. This synergy ensures that while innovative breakthroughs are pursued, they are also tempered by the wisdom derived from previous cycles.

3.4.4 The Role of Decentralized Technologies in Accelerating Cycles

Modern technologies, especially those grounded in decentralization, act as powerful accelerators of cyclical innovation:

- **Blockchain and DAOs:**
  By decentralizing decision-making and resource allocation, blockchain technologies and decentralized autonomous organizations (DAOs) minimize the friction typically associated with hierarchical structures. This creates an environment in which innovation can spread rapidly and inclusively.

- **Artificial Intelligence and Machine Learning:**
  AI systems provide real-time insights and predictive analytics that help identify trends and optimize resource distribution. Such technologies facilitate faster feedback loops and enable organizations to adapt swiftly to emerging opportunities and challenges.

- **Digital Communication Platforms:**
  Global connectivity, enabled by high-speed internet and social media, allows ideas to proliferate quickly across borders. This rapid dissemination of information further compresses innovation cycles, fostering a global

environment of continuous renewal.

3.5 A Systems Theory and Mathematical Perspective

3.5.1 Nonlinear Dynamics and Complex Systems

The Infinite Cycle Theory finds strong resonance in systems theory, which examines how complex systems behave under nonlinear conditions:

- **Complexity and Emergence:**
  Complex systems are characterized by myriad interacting components whose collective behavior cannot be understood merely by examining individual parts. Nonlinear dynamics lead to emergent phenomena—patterns and behaviors that arise spontaneously from the interplay of system elements.

- **Chaos Theory:**
  Elements of chaos theory reveal that even highly sensitive and seemingly unpredictable systems can exhibit underlying patterns and tendencies toward cyclical behavior. Small changes in initial conditions, known as the butterfly effect, can precipitate significant, yet patterned, transformations over time.

3.5.2 Mathematical Modeling of Infinite Cycles

Mathematical models provide a quantitative framework for understanding cyclical progress:

- **Attractors and Bifurcations:**
  In nonlinear dynamics, attractors are states toward which a system converges. Bifurcation theory studies how small changes in parameters can cause a sudden qualitative change in a system's behavior, leading to the emergence of new cycles.

- **Logistic Maps and Iterative Functions:**
  The logistic map—a simple nonlinear recurrence relation—demonstrates how iterative functions can lead to cycles, chaos, and self-similarity. Such mathematical constructs model how simple rules can produce complex, recurring patterns.

- **Fractal Geometry:**
  Fractals, with their intrinsic self-similarity across scales, offer a visual and mathematical representation of the Infinite Cycle Theory. The repeated patterns at every scale echo the notion that regeneration and cyclicality are inherent features of both natural and socio-economic systems.

3.5.3 Fractal Structures and Self-Similarity

Fractal analysis enriches our understanding of cyclical processes:

- **Natural Fractals:**
  In nature, patterns such as branching trees, river networks, and coastlines exhibit fractal behavior. These self-similar structures demonstrate that cyclical processes repeat on many scales—from micro to macro.

- **Economic and Social Analogues:**
  Analogously, economic and social systems show fractal characteristics, where patterns of consumer behavior, market fluctuations, and even urban development repeat across different scales. Recognizing these fractal patterns

helps identify invariant structures that drive regeneration.

- **Implications for Policy and Design:**
  Understanding fractal dimensions in socio-economic systems allows policymakers to design interventions that work coherently at multiple levels—local, regional, and global—thereby fostering sustainable, integrated cycles of growth.

3.5.4 Attractors and Equilibrium States

Equilibrium states and attractors are essential for understanding how systems settle into recurring cycles:

- **Dynamic Equilibrium:**
  In dynamic systems, equilibrium is not static but is constantly maintained by feedback interactions. Systems may oscillate around a stable state, and these oscillations themselves are the essence of cyclical progress.

- **Harnessing Attractors:**
  By identifying attractor states—whether in market behavior, cultural norms, or technological adoption—community leaders and policymakers can steer development in desired directions, reinforcing cycles of renewal that support long-term sustainability.

3.6 Applications of the Infinite Cycle Theory in Social and Economic Systems

3.6.1 Economic Boom-and-Bust Cycles as Regenerative Processes

The traditional narrative of boom and bust cycles is reinterpreted through the lens of regeneration:

- **Reframing Recessions:**
  Economic downturns are often viewed solely as failures, but the Infinite Cycle Theory suggests that they also serve as opportunities for recalibration. For example, the Great Depression, while devastating, catalyzed significant regulatory reforms and technological advancements that laid the groundwork for future prosperity.

- **Market Corrections:**
  In capitalist economies, periodic corrections purge inefficiencies and recalibrate resource allocations. These adjustments enable the subsequent growth phase to be more robust, highlighting how downturns are integral to the cycle of sustainable progress.

- **Case Study – The 2008 Financial Crisis:**
  The crisis led to comprehensive reforms in financial regulation and risk management. These reforms, in turn, spurred innovation in financial technologies (fintech) and more resilient economic practices that have since stabilized markets, demonstrating the regenerative potential inherent in economic cycles.

3.6.2 Political and Social Movements

Political and social transformations also occur cyclically, driven by waves of activism and reform:

- **Social Reform Waves:**
  Historical movements—from the suffrage movements to contemporary struggles for environmental justice—follow cyclical patterns. Initial breakthroughs often give way to periods of consolidation, which eventually lead to renewed

efforts as unresolved issues resurface.

- **Political Realignment:**
  Political systems periodically undergo realignment as voters and leaders reconfigure their priorities. Cyclical shifts in public opinion can lead to transformative policy changes, reflecting the iterative process of societal evolution.

- **Case Study – Civil Rights Movement:**
  The civil rights movement in the United States not only reformed legal frameworks but also created a sustained culture of activism that continues to influence contemporary social justice initiatives, underscoring how cyclical pressures can foster enduring transformation.

3.6.3 Innovation Ecosystems and Technological Progress

Technological progress is perhaps the most visible manifestation of cyclical innovation:

- **Startup Culture and Disruption:**
  Innovation ecosystems, such as Silicon Valley, embody the cycle of creative destruction. Startups emerge rapidly, disrupt established industries, and eventually consolidate their innovations into the mainstream economy. This cycle fuels continuous technological advancement.

- **Digital Transformation:**
  The emergence of digital platforms, cloud computing, and AI exemplifies how technology can catalyze successive waves of innovation. Each phase of digital transformation builds on the foundational breakthroughs of previous cycles, creating an ongoing loop of renewal.

- **Impacts on Global Competitiveness:**
  Nations and corporations that harness these cycles effectively gain a competitive edge. By fostering environments that encourage iterative experimentation and rapid scaling, economies can maintain a dynamic pace of innovation that underpins long-term growth.

3.6.4 Educational and Cultural Renewal

The renewal of education and culture is an essential aspect of societal regeneration:

- **Evolution of Educational Paradigms:**
  Education systems have historically evolved in response to changing societal needs. The integration of digital tools, interdisciplinary curricula, and experiential learning models reflects a cycle of renewal that prepares communities for future challenges.

- **Cultural Renaissance:**
  Periods of cultural renewal—such as the Renaissance or the digital age's creative renaissance—demonstrate how artistic and intellectual pursuits can be cyclically revitalized. This infusion of fresh ideas inspires innovation across all sectors of society.

- **Community Engagement and Lifelong Learning:**
  Modern educational models promote lifelong learning and continuous engagement with cultural heritage. By fostering an environment where learning is iterative and community-oriented, education becomes a catalyst for broader societal regeneration.

3.7 Challenges and Limitations of a Cyclical Framework

3.7.1 Potential Disruptions and Nonconformity

While the Infinite Cycle Theory provides a robust explanatory framework, real-world systems may not always adhere neatly to cyclical patterns:

- **External Shocks:**
  Unpredictable events such as natural disasters, pandemics, or geopolitical conflicts can abruptly interrupt or reset cycles. Although these shocks can serve as catalysts for deeper transformation, they also pose significant risks that require robust resilience planning.

- **Systemic Nonconformity:**
  Not every disturbance leads to a beneficial cycle of renewal. In some cases, feedback loops may trigger pathological cycles that are self-destructive. Recognizing the signs of such disruptions is essential for devising corrective measures.

3.7.2 Managing Feedback Overload and Systemic Fragility

As systems become more interconnected, the potential for rapid, excessive feedback increases:

- **Digital Overload:**
  In an age dominated by digital communication and real-time data, systems can experience feedback overload. Uncontrolled amplification of information—such as in social media echo chambers or financial trading algorithms—can

lead to systemic instability.

- **Thresholds and Tipping Points:**
  Identifying the thresholds at which feedback becomes destructive rather than regenerative is a critical challenge. Mathematical models and real-world experiments are needed to quantify these thresholds and design safeguards accordingly.

- **Resilience Mechanisms:**
  Building buffers, redundancies, and negative feedback systems into the structure of organizations and economies is essential. These mechanisms help prevent runaway processes and ensure that cycles remain constructive rather than chaotic.

3.7.3 Ensuring Inclusivity in Cyclical Renewal

One potential pitfall in cyclic processes is the risk of reinforcing established power structures:

- **Dominant Narratives:**
  In some cycles, dominant groups may capture the feedback loops, thereby narrowing the range of ideas and perpetuating inequitable outcomes. Ensuring that every cycle incorporates a broad spectrum of perspectives is vital for genuine regeneration.

- **Intentional Design:**
  To mitigate these risks, systems must be designed intentionally to foster inclusivity and equitable participation. This involves creating platforms for underrepresented voices, instituting democratic decision-making processes, and embracing diverse cultural inputs.

- **Monitoring and Adaptation:**
  Continuous monitoring of cyclical processes and open channels for feedback are necessary to ensure that the regenerative process remains inclusive. This involves periodic audits, stakeholder consultations, and agile governance structures that can recalibrate when necessary.

3.8 Synthesizing the Infinite Cycle Theory with Modern Empowerment Strategies

3.8.1 Integrating Cyclical Models into Decentralized Systems

The principles of the Infinite Cycle Theory align seamlessly with the ethos of decentralized systems:

- **Blockchain and Distributed Governance:**
  Decentralized technologies, such as blockchain and DAOs, enable transparent, iterative feedback mechanisms. By decentralizing decision-making and resource management, these systems embody the cyclical model of continuous renewal and adaptive improvement.

- **Real-Time Data and Adaptive Management:**
  Leveraging AI-driven analytics and real-time monitoring tools, organizations can actively track feedback loops and dynamically adjust their strategies. This level of adaptive management ensures that each cycle of regeneration is optimized for current conditions.

- **Community-Driven Innovation:**
  Decentralized platforms foster environments where collective input shapes the direction of innovation. This participatory approach ensures that regenerative cycles are enriched by diverse perspectives, making them more robust and inclusive.

3.8.2 Policy Implications and Strategic Roadmapping

The cyclical nature of progress necessitates new approaches to policy and strategic planning:

- **Proactive Crisis Management:**
  Policy frameworks should be designed to anticipate downturns and prepare communities for the regenerative cycles ahead. This involves developing contingency plans, flexible regulatory environments, and adaptive economic policies that can absorb shocks and catalyze recovery.

- **Long-Term Vision with Short-Term Adaptability:**
  Strategic roadmaps must balance long-term objectives with short-term adaptability. Recognizing the cyclical rhythm of innovation and renewal, policymakers can create mechanisms for scheduled review, feedback incorporation, and policy adjustment.

- **Incentivizing Regenerative Practices:**
  Governments and institutions can further foster cyclical renewal by incentivizing innovation, research and development, and community-based projects. Tax incentives, grants, and public–private partnerships are examples of tools that can accelerate each cycle's positive outputs.

3.8.3 Cultivating a Regenerative Mindset

A transformative cultural shift is necessary to fully embrace the Infinite Cycle Theory:

- **Educational Reforms:**
  Integrating the principles of cyclical thinking into educational curricula fosters a mindset that views setbacks as opportunities for renewal. Programs such as the Gemach Pedagogy aim to instill a resilient, adaptive outlook that is crucial for navigating cyclical change.

- **Community Engagement:**
  Grassroots initiatives and community forums provide platforms for sharing experiences, celebrating cyclical successes, and collaboratively addressing challenges. These platforms create a culture of continuous learning and regeneration.

- **Leadership and Cultural Narratives:**
  Leaders who embrace regenerative principles can inspire collective action by articulating narratives that frame challenges as integral parts of a larger cycle of growth. Overcoming adversity becomes not an endpoint but a vital step in a cycle that ultimately leads to greater resilience and capability.

3.9 Conclusion: Embracing Cycles for Enduring Transformation

The Infinite Cycle Theory provides a powerful lens through which to view social and economic progress. By recognizing that innovation, renewal, and regeneration are not linear but part of an ongoing, self-sustaining loop, we can design systems that are both resilient and adaptive.

This chapter has examined in exhaustive detail the theoretical foundations of the theory, the complex interplay of feedback loops, the mechanisms underpinning natural and institutional regeneration, and the role of cyclical innovation as the catalyst for transformation. From nonlinear dynamics and fractal self-similarity to the practical applications in economic, political, technological, and cultural domains, every phase of growth and renewal is part of a larger tapestry of progress.

Incorporating the Infinite Cycle Theory into modern empowerment strategies provides a framework for building decentralized, inclusive systems capable of withstanding external shocks while continually reinventing themselves from within. By leveraging advanced technologies like blockchain, AI, and distributed governance, and by fostering a cultural shift toward proactive renewal, communities can navigate the unpredictable currents of change with confidence and resilience.

As we move forward within Dr. Goldston's integrated framework, the Infinite Cycle Theory serves as a foundational element—a reminder that every ending is merely a precursor to a new beginning, and that sustainable progress is achieved through the harmonious interplay of cycles, feedback, and regeneration. Embracing these cyclical principles not only positions communities to survive challenges but empowers them to thrive, innovate, and shape a future defined by continuous, inclusive transformation.

In summary, the Infinite Cycle Theory challenges us to reframe our understanding of progress, urging us to view setbacks as essential catalysts for renewal, and to harness the power of recurring feedback loops to drive enduring, transformative change. This cyclical perspective is not only a theoretical construct but a practical blueprint for constructing resilient socio-economic systems that are adaptable, inclusive, and forever regenerating.

Chapter 4: The Hope Paradox – Optimism Amid Systemic Challenges

The Hope Paradox examines how hope serves as both a potent motivator and a transformative force in environments fraught with systemic challenges. It is a multifaceted construct that catalyzes change even when entrenched obstacles seem insurmountable. In this chapter, we delve into the theoretical, psychological, sociocultural, and technological dimensions of hope. We explore how hope emerges from and interacts with adversity, how it drives collective action, and the ways in which it can be harnessed to foster regeneration and inclusive innovation. By analyzing historical and contemporary case studies, we demonstrate that hope is not merely an abstract ideal but an essential ingredient for sustainable progress in societies undergoing continuous cycles of change.

4.1 Introduction: Defining the Dual Nature of Hope

4.1.1 Understanding the Concept of Hope

- **Emotional and Cognitive Dimensions:**
  Hope operates on two intertwined levels. Emotionally, it provides comfort and a sense of possibility during difficult times. For instance, the feeling of hope can soften the emotional pain associated with loss or failure, offering a psychological buffer against despair. Cognitively, hope involves the mental processes that allow individuals to visualize potential futures, set goals, and devise plans to achieve them. This dual action means that hope is not just a

passive expectation of better times but an active process that mobilizes mental energy and resources. For example, when a community faces economic decline, hope can inspire local entrepreneurs to brainstorm innovative solutions, reframe challenges as opportunities, and work toward re-establishing a robust local economy.

- **Hope Versus Optimism:**
  While optimism generally refers to a positive outlook or expectation that things will improve, hope is more structured and action-oriented. Optimism might simply be a belief that "everything will work out," whereas hope involves an active engagement with possible strategies to reach a better outcome. In practical terms, an optimistic person might rely on fate or good fortune, while a hopeful person often starts planning and taking deliberate steps to effect change. This distinction is critical when designing systems or policies because fostering hope means encouraging people not only to believe in the future but also to be proactive in shaping it.

4.1.2 The Paradoxical Nature of Hope

- **Empowerment Through Aspirational Vision:**
  Hope serves as a catalyst by creating a vivid, aspirational vision that galvanizes individuals and communities to strive beyond their immediate circumstances. When people have a clear picture of a desired future—a future that includes equitable opportunities, improved living conditions, and systemic fairness—they are more likely to mobilize resources and commit to long-term change. This aspirational vision becomes a rallying cry that unites diverse groups under a common cause, such as when a community unites to build local infrastructure or reform public policies through social movements.

- **Risks of Complacency and Illusory Comfort:**
  However, there is an inherent risk when hope is not paired with realistic assessments. In some cases, excessive hope or wishful thinking can lead to complacency. For example, if policymakers assume that economic recovery will occur without intervention solely because of an optimistic outlook, they may delay necessary reforms. This complacency can mask systemic issues and lead to a false sense of security, ultimately stalling progress. The challenge is ensuring that hope does not become a substitute for critical analysis but instead acts as a bridge to constructive action.

- **Balancing Act:**
  The key lies in balancing aspirational hope with pragmatic strategies. Successful systems harness hope by converting inspiring visions into concrete plans with measurable outcomes. This means establishing clear goals and feedback mechanisms so that hopeful ideals are continuously aligned with real-world performance. For instance, a city initiative might set a hopeful vision of transforming urban spaces into green, thriving communities, but this vision is coupled with detailed plans, funding strategies, and periodic reviews to ensure that progress is both tangible and sustainable.

4.2 The Theoretical Underpinnings of the Hope Paradox

4.2.1 Philosophical Foundations

- **Existential and Humanistic Perspectives:**
  Philosophers such as Viktor Frankl and Albert Camus have explored how hope provides meaning in the face of

existential uncertainty. Frankl's work, for example, emphasizes that even in the direst circumstances, the pursuit of a purpose can sustain life. This philosophical stance underlines that hope is not just a psychological state but a fundamental aspect of human existence. It provides the impetus to endure hardship and build meaning, suggesting that hope is essential for both survival and transformation.

- **Critical Theory and Social Justice:**
  Critical theorists argue that hope fuels resistance and collective action in oppressive contexts. At the same time, they warn that hope must be critically examined; without proper scrutiny, it can sustain the status quo. For example, if marginalized groups are encouraged to remain hopeful without concrete plans for change, they risk enduring systemic injustices indefinitely. Thus, a dialectical approach is necessary—hope must empower action while constantly challenging existing power structures.

- **Dialectical Synthesis:**
  The reconciliation of hope and critical inquiry is achieved through a dialectical process where hope is continuously refined by evaluating outcomes and incorporating lessons learned. This dynamic synthesis ensures that hope remains an active force that is sensitive to both inspirational visions and the practicalities of implementation.

4.2.2 Psychological Models of Hope

- **Snyder's Hope Theory – Agency and Pathways:**
  Snyder's model articulates hope as comprising two interrelated components: agency (the drive and motivation to pursue goals) and pathways (the perceived strategies to achieve these goals). This model emphasizes that hope is a structured cognitive process that influences how individuals

plan, work, and persevere. For example, a student facing academic challenges who has a high level of hope will not only believe they can succeed (agency) but will also identify specific strategies—such as tutoring, enhanced study techniques, or time management (pathways)—to overcome obstacles.

- **Neural Correlates and Functional Implications:**
  Neuroscientific research indicates that hope activates particular brain regions associated with reward processing and goal-oriented behavior. This suggests that hope has a physiological foundation and that it can enhance cognitive functions like decision-making, planning, and problem-solving. These insights support interventions in educational or organizational settings where hope is fostered to improve performance and adaptability.

- **Behavioral Outcomes and Resilience:**
  Empirical studies have consistently shown that individuals with higher levels of hope are better equipped to handle stress, demonstrate persistence, and ultimately achieve their objectives. The link between hope and resilience underscores its importance as a psychological resource, enabling individuals to transform challenges into opportunities for growth.

4.2.3 Sociocultural Dimensions of Hope

- **Collective Narratives and Cultural Identity:**
  Societies construct and perpetuate hope through shared narratives, myths, and cultural icons. These collective stories help define what is possible, setting the stage for societal change. For example, national myths of overcoming adversity can unite people under common goals, while literature and media that highlight stories of triumph can inspire communities to take action against systemic

injustices.

- **Social Capital and Community Bonds:**
Hope often strengthens social capital—the bonds of trust, mutual support, and cooperation that underpin community resilience. When communities share a hopeful vision, they are more likely to work together, support one another in times of crisis, and mobilize resources effectively. This collective strength is essential for overcoming systemic challenges that no single individual could tackle alone.

- **Intergenerational Transmission and Cultural Continuity:**
Cultural practices such as storytelling, rituals, and traditions serve as vehicles for transmitting hope across generations. These practices embed the notion that struggle is temporary and that renewal is always possible, instilling in each new generation a belief in the possibility of transformative change.

4.3 The Transformative Role of Hope in Overcoming Systemic Challenges

4.3.1 Hope as a Motivator for Individual Action

- **Goal Setting and Ambition:**
Hope drives individuals to articulate clear, long-term goals. When people believe in the possibility of a brighter future, they are motivated to set challenging objectives and to develop actionable strategies for achieving them. This ambition transforms abstract dreams into concrete plans, fueling personal and professional progress.

- **Resilience Amid Adversity:**
  The presence of hope is a fundamental component of resilience. It enables individuals to persist in the face of setbacks, viewing obstacles as temporary setbacks rather than insurmountable barriers. This mindset is crucial for recovery after failures, as hope instills the determination to continue pursuing desired outcomes even when immediate circumstances are bleak.

- **Self-Efficacy and Agency:**
  A strong sense of hope reinforces self-efficacy—the belief in one's ability to influence events and outcomes. This internal conviction encourages proactive behavior; for example, an entrepreneur with high hope is more likely to innovate and take calculated risks, confident in their capacity to navigate challenges and effect meaningful change.

4.3.2 Hope as a Catalyst for Collective Action

- **Mobilizing Social Movements:**
  Hope transforms individual aspirations into collective mobilization. When communities share a hopeful vision—such as achieving social justice or environmental sustainability—they unite to contest systemic barriers. This collective energy is the lifeblood of social movements, enabling mass protests, petitions, and community organizing that drive political and social reforms.

- **Community Resilience and Recovery:**
  In the face of economic or natural disasters, collective hope becomes the glue that holds communities together. It fosters collaboration, sharing of resources, and strategic coordination to rebuild and recover. For instance, community-driven projects in post-disaster areas often emerge from a shared belief that a better, more resilient

future is attainable.

- **Building Participatory Governance:**
  When citizens are hopeful about the impact of their collective efforts, they are more likely to engage in democratic processes. This increased engagement leads to participatory governance models where decision-making is collaborative and transparent. In such environments, public policies are shaped by diverse inputs, resulting in reforms that reflect the aspirations of the broader community.

4.3.3 Hope as a Driver of Institutional and Policy Reform

- **Transformative Policy Narratives:**
  Hope shapes the narratives that influence public policy. Visionary leaders who articulate a hopeful future can push for reforms that challenge entrenched systems. These narratives inspire legislative change by painting a picture of what could be, thereby creating momentum for systemic transformation.

- **Reshaping Institutional Cultures:**
  Institutions that embed hope into their operational and strategic frameworks become more agile and innovative. For example, corporations that nurture a culture of hope and empowerment encourage experimentation and are better able to adapt to market disruptions. This cultural transformation ensures that institutions remain relevant and capable of generating long-term value.

- **Reimagining Social Contracts:**
  The infusion of hope into the discourse on social justice leads to the reimagining of fundamental social contracts. This process involves questioning established power dynamics and advocating for policies that promote equity

and sustainability. A hopeful vision for the future can thus catalyze comprehensive reforms that address the root causes of systemic inequities.

4.4 Historical Case Studies: The Power of Hope in Action

4.4.1 The Abolitionist Movement and the Struggle for Freedom

- **Vision of Liberation and Equality:**
  The abolitionist movement was built on the unwavering hope that a society free of slavery was not only conceivable but within reach. Abolitionists, drawing inspiration from religious, moral, and humanitarian ideals, mobilized large constituencies by articulating a vision of freedom and justice.

- **Overcoming Systemic Barriers:**
  Despite facing entrenched economic interests and violent opposition, abolitionists persisted through grassroots organizing, public oratory, and influential writings. Their hope was instrumental in galvanizing support, ultimately contributing to legal and social reforms that dismantled the institution of slavery.

- **Legacy of Transformation:**
  The movement's success laid the groundwork for subsequent struggles for civil rights, demonstrating that deep-seated systemic challenges can be overcome when hope is transformed into sustained, collective action.

4.4.2 The Civil Rights Movement: Hope in the Face of Injustice

- **Inspirational Leadership and Vision:**
  The Civil Rights Movement exemplified the transformative power of hope through its charismatic leadership and visionary rhetoric. Leaders such as Martin Luther King Jr. communicated powerful narratives of reconciliation and justice that resonated with millions of people.

- **Grassroots Mobilization:**
  The movement's success was driven by extensive grassroots mobilization. Local communities, inspired by shared hope, organized protests, boycotts, and community outreach programs that challenged segregation and discrimination.

- **Institutional and Cultural Impact:**
  The transformative effects of the Civil Rights Movement continue to shape American society. Policy reforms, increased civic participation, and a sustained commitment to social justice all attest to how hope can restructure systems and alter public consciousness over the long term.

4.4.3 Digital Activism and Global Movements

- **Harnessing Global Connectivity:**
  In the digital age, hope has been magnified through social media platforms and online communities. Movements such as #MeToo, climate activism, and global protests against political corruption have demonstrated how digital tools can connect individuals and amplify hopeful narratives.

- **Empowering the Marginalized:**
  Digital platforms enable underrepresented groups to voice their aspirations and mobilize support. These networks

create virtual communities where shared hope transitions into concrete action, contributing to policy changes and cultural shifts.

- **Accelerating Social Change:**
  The speed and reach of digital communication have led to the rapid dissemination of ideas and mobilization of global support. This dynamic environment illustrates how hope, when shared through decentralized channels, can reshape national and international debates.

4.4.4 Economic Recovery and Reform Post-Crisis

- **Catalyst for Renewal:**
  Economic crises, such as the Great Recession or the 2008 financial crisis, have historically spurred hope-driven reforms. In times of economic despair, the vision of a more equitable and resilient financial system motivates both policymakers and communities to innovate.

- **Institutional Reforms and Innovation:**
  Post-crisis recoveries are often characterized by significant institutional reforms—such as enhanced financial regulation and the creation of supportive frameworks for new business models. These reforms stem from the collective hope that a downturn will yield the opportunity to rebuild stronger and fairer systems.

- **Grassroots Economic Initiatives:**
  Beyond top-down reforms, communities have initiated cooperative projects and local economic renewal efforts that are rooted in the hope for self-sufficient, sustainable growth. These initiatives provide tangible examples of how hope can be translated into economic resilience.

4.5 Psychological Dimensions of Hope: The Neuroscience and Cognitive Models

4.5.1 The Neurobiology of Hope

- **Reward Pathways and Dopaminergic Systems:**
  Hope activates the brain's reward pathways, particularly those involving dopamine. This neurotransmitter reinforces behaviors by creating a sense of anticipation and satisfaction when goals are met. Studies using brain imaging techniques have revealed that hopeful thoughts stimulate areas associated with planning and motivation, thereby enhancing an individual's drive to overcome challenges.

- **Executive Function and Resilience:**
  The prefrontal cortex, which is involved in decision-making, planning, and impulse control, shows heightened activity during moments of hopeful anticipation. This suggests that hope improves executive function, enabling people to resist short-term temptations in favor of long-term gains.

- **Empirical Evidence:**
  Research indicates that individuals with higher levels of hope are generally better at managing stress and exhibit greater resilience when facing adversity. This neurobiological foundation explains why hope is such a potent force in both personal transformation and collective action.

4.5.2 Cognitive and Behavioral Models

- **Snyder's Hope Theory Expanded:**
  The dual components of pathways and agency in Snyder's theory illustrate that hope involves both the formulation of strategies and the motivational drive to implement them. This model has been validated across diverse contexts—demonstrating that people who score high on hope tend to set more ambitious goals, persist longer in the face of setbacks, and ultimately achieve higher success rates.

- **Self-Fulfilling Prophecies:**
  Cognitive research supports the idea that positive expectations can create self-fulfilling prophecies. When people believe in the possibility of success, they tend to take proactive steps that increase the likelihood of achieving their goals, thereby reinforcing their initial hopeful outlook.

- **Adaptive Coping Mechanisms:**
  Practices such as mindfulness, meditation, and reflective journaling can enhance hope by promoting adaptive coping strategies. These practices help individuals process setbacks constructively, turning challenges into opportunities for learning and growth.

4.5.3 Social Learning and the Transmission of Hope

- **Role Models and Inspirational Narratives:**
  Observing and internalizing the stories of people who have overcome adversity can significantly boost an individual's hope. Inspirational role models, whether in local communities or through media representation, serve as tangible proof that change is possible.

- **Social Contagion of Hope:**
  Research in social psychology demonstrates that hope can be contagious. When one member of a group expresses hope and determination, that sentiment can spread

throughout the community, creating a shared reservoir of optimism and collective resilience.

- **Intergenerational Transmission:**
  Family traditions, cultural rituals, and educational institutions play a crucial role in passing down hopeful narratives from one generation to the next. This intergenerational transmission ensures that communities retain a long-lasting belief in the possibility of transformation.

4.6 Cultural and Artistic Dimensions of Hope

4.6.1 The Role of Art in Shaping Hopeful Narratives

- **Visual Arts, Music, and Literature:**
  Artistic expressions have long been vehicles for conveying hopeful visions. Murals in urban neighborhoods, protest songs during periods of social upheaval, and novels that explore themes of rebirth and renewal all act as catalysts for change by inspiring collective emotion and reinforcing cultural identity.

- **Cinema and Digital Media:**
  Contemporary platforms—such as films, documentaries, and digital short stories—play a significant role in disseminating hopeful narratives. Visual storytelling can evoke empathy and bring complex social issues to life, motivating audiences to support reformative actions.

- **Art and Activism:**
  Artistic projects that directly engage with social and political issues help embed hope into the public consciousness.

When art and activism intersect, the result is a powerful tool for challenging oppressive systems and celebrating the resilience of communities.

4.6.2 Cultural Rituals and Shared Traditions

- **Religious and Spiritual Practices:**
  Many cultural traditions include rituals designed to renew hope and foster a sense of communal belonging. Religious ceremonies often emphasize themes of redemption, renewal, and the promise of a better future, providing emotional sustenance and moral guidance.

- **Festivals and Community Celebrations:**
  Annual festivals, community gatherings, and public celebrations serve as reminders of collective resilience and shared purpose. These events offer a chance for communities to reflect on past hardships and to celebrate the potential for future renewal.

- **Oral Traditions and Storytelling:**
  Folk tales, epic narratives, and community stories encapsulate the ethos of hope. They transmit values and inspire subsequent generations to believe that, regardless of current challenges, transformation is always within reach.

4.7 Hope in the Age of Digital Disruption and Decentralization

4.7.1 Digital Platforms as Vehicles for Hope

- **The Power of Social Media:**
  Social media platforms have democratized the dissemination of hopeful narratives, enabling global participation in movements for change. Hashtags and viral content can instantly spread messages of resilience, mobilizing people across borders to support causes that promise a better future.

- **Crowdsourcing Hope:**
  Crowdfunding sites and online fundraising campaigns exemplify how digital technology can translate hope into action. By pooling resources and support, these platforms demonstrate that shared hope can lead to real-world change, whether in launching a new community project or supporting innovative research.

- **Virtual Communities and Peer Support Networks:**
  Online forums, social networks, and digital communities create spaces where individuals can connect, share stories of overcoming adversity, and offer mutual support. These virtual environments not only amplify hope but also provide practical advice and solidarity, thereby strengthening collective resilience.

4.7.2 Decentralized Technologies: Blockchain, DAOs, and AI

- **Transparent and Inclusive Governance:**
  Decentralized technologies such as blockchain and Decentralized Autonomous Organizations (DAOs) enable transparent, democratic decision-making processes. This decentralization fosters a sense of shared hope by allowing every stakeholder to contribute directly to the management of community resources and policy directions.

- **Data-Driven Optimism:**
  Artificial intelligence and machine learning tools can process vast amounts of data to generate predictive insights about societal trends and potential breakthroughs. By making the future more predictable and manageable, these technologies help convert abstract hope into actionable strategies and concrete outcomes.

- **Empowering Local Innovations:**
  The decentralization of technological resources allows communities to pilot and implement their solutions without depending on centralized authorities. By fostering local innovation, these systems empower individuals to build tailored responses to systemic challenges, reinforcing the belief that change is within their control.

4.8 Navigating Risks: Misplaced Hope, Complacency, and the Need for Strategic Action

4.8.1 Recognizing and Mitigating False Hope

- **Diagnosing False Hope:**
  Not all hopeful sentiments are beneficial. It is crucial to distinguish between constructive hope that motivates action and false hope that is based on unrealistic expectations. Systems need rigorous self-assessment practices, such as performance metrics and feedback loops, to diagnose when hope is unfounded and adjust strategies accordingly.

- **Avoiding the Pitfalls of Wishful Thinking:**
  Wishful thinking without a strategic foundation can lead to

inertia. For example, if a community believes that improvement is inevitable without making concrete changes, they may neglect to implement necessary reforms. A balanced approach demands that hope be paired with objective planning, measurable goals, and clear strategies.

- **Feedback Mechanisms to Recalibrate Expectations:**
  Establishing regular, transparent feedback systems allows stakeholders to gauge progress, learn from setbacks, and recalibrate hopeful ambitions. This continuous loop—where aspiration is constantly tested against reality—helps ensure that hope remains a dynamic tool for action rather than an excuse for inaction.

4.8.2 Complacency and the Illusion of Progress

- **The Danger of Overoptimism:**
  Overoptimism can create a false security, leading people to underestimate challenges or delay necessary actions. Historical cases have shown that when hope is taken for granted, systemic reform can stagnate. It is essential to maintain critical oversight and balance positive outlooks with informed decision-making.

- **Balancing Ideals with Accountability:**
  Institutions must create systems that hold hopeful initiatives accountable through measurable outcomes and transparent reporting. Regular progress reviews, public audits, and performance-based incentives help ensure that optimism is not mistaken for automatic progress.

- **Strategies to Sustain Constructive Hope:**
  Sustaining constructive hope involves a mix of inclusive dialogue, realistic goal setting, and continuous learning. These strategies help prevent the drift into complacency by keeping the community engaged and focused on long-term

objectives while celebrating incremental successes.

4.9 Integrative Strategies for Harnessing Hope in Systemic Transformation

4.9.1 Embedding Hope in Policy, Governance, and Institutional Design

- **Participatory Policy-Making:**
  Embedding hope into policy starts with inclusive governance practices. Initiatives like participatory budgeting and community advisory boards give citizens a direct role in shaping policies, ensuring that hopeful visions are represented in decision-making processes.

- **Responsive and Adaptive Legal Frameworks:**
  Legal and regulatory environments that incorporate built-in review cycles allow for adjustments as circumstances evolve. These adaptive frameworks enable policymakers to reform and reinvigorate systems in response to feedback, thereby sustaining hope over time.

- **Institutional Innovation Labs:**
  Establishing innovation labs within governmental or large organizational structures can nurture ideas that integrate hopeful aspirations with pragmatic solutions. These labs serve as experimental hubs where novel approaches to systemic challenges are tested and refined before broader implementation.

4.9.2 Educational Programs and Community Empowerment

- **Curriculum Integration:**
  Educational institutions play a key role by integrating modules on resilience, systemic change, and hope-driven strategies. Programs like the Gemach Pedagogy emphasize experiential learning, which empowers students to turn hopeful ideas into actionable projects.

- **Community Workshops and Outreach:**
  Grassroots workshops and public forums encourage communities to share their experiences, discuss challenges, and collectively devise strategies for renewal. These outreach programs build local capacity and reinforce the idea that every community member has a role in driving change.

- **Intergenerational Learning:**
  Creating structured opportunities for older and younger generations to exchange knowledge ensures that lessons learned from past struggles inform future aspirations. Mentorship programs and legacy projects solidify the continuity of hope and practical wisdom across time.

4.9.3 The Role of Art, Culture, and Media in Sustaining Hope

- **Public Art and Storytelling Projects:**
  Community-led art projects and storytelling initiatives capture the struggles and triumphs of local groups, making hope a visible, tangible force in public spaces. Murals, public sculptures, and theatrical productions serve as daily reminders of shared aspirations and collective resilience.

- **Narrative Change Campaigns:**
  Strategic media campaigns can reshape public discourse by highlighting success stories and transformative initiatives. Through documentaries, social media campaigns, and feature articles, narrative change campaigns reinforce the message that systemic challenges can be overcome.

- **Cultural Institutions as Hubs of Hope:**
  Museums, libraries, and cultural centers are well-positioned to curate exhibitions and events that celebrate achievements and envision future possibilities. These institutions provide a platform for enduring hopeful narratives that inspire continuous community engagement and policy reform.

4.10 Synthesis and Conclusion: Translating Hope into Enduring Transformation

4.10.1 Integrating Hope with the Broader Regenerative Framework

- **A Holistic Model:**
  When hope is seamlessly woven into the infinite cycle framework, it acts as the emotional and cognitive fuel that propels each cycle of renewal. This holistic approach demonstrates that hope works best when it is combined with tangible strategies, continuous learning, and adaptive feedback loops.

- **From Aspiration to Action:**
  The essential task is to convert hopeful visions into strategic, actionable plans. This integration ensures that

every optimistic projection is matched with clear steps toward realization, thereby transforming abstract beliefs into measurable progress.

4.10.2 Future Research and the Role of Continuous Improvement

- **Interdisciplinary Exploration:**
  Further research is needed to explore the neuropsychological, sociocultural, and technological dimensions of hope. By integrating insights from fields such as neuroscience, sociology, and systems engineering, future studies can refine our understanding of how to nurture and sustain hope effectively in different contexts.

- **Longitudinal and Comparative Analyses:**
  Tracking the evolution of hope within various communities over time will provide valuable insights into how regenerative processes function. Comparative studies across cultures, economies, and institutions will help identify best practices for embedding hope into systemic design.

- **Data-Driven Interventions:**
  With advanced data analytics, policymakers and community organizers can measure the impact of hope-driven initiatives, adjust strategies in real time, and ensure that hope remains aligned with the practical realities of systemic transformation.

4.10.3 Final Reflections: The Enduring Power of Hope

- **Transformative Inspiration:**
  When integrated carefully and strategically, hope serves as a powerful impetus for change. It challenges the status quo, inspires collective action, and creates a resilient foundation

for overcoming seemingly insurmountable obstacles.

- **A Blueprint for Empowerment:**
  The ideas and strategies explored in this chapter provide a comprehensive blueprint for how hope can be harnessed as a systematic resource—one that fuels innovation, drives policy reform, and ultimately transforms society.

- **The Call to Action:**
  The Hope Paradox compels us to balance visionary idealism with pragmatic execution. It urges individuals, communities, and institutions to adopt a proactive, disciplined approach to hope—ensuring that every setback is recast as a springboard for future innovation, and every challenge is met with sustained, collective determination.

In summary, this expanded exploration of the bullet points in Chapter 4 demonstrates that hope is a multifaceted, transformative force. By breaking down its emotional, cognitive, sociocultural, and technological dimensions, we have shown how hope can motivate individuals and mobilize communities to overcome systemic challenges. From inspiring social movements and policy reforms to reinforcing the bonds of collective identity and creativity, hope must be carefully nurtured, critically examined, and systematically integrated to ensure that it becomes an enduring resource for regeneration. Embracing the Hope Paradox means harnessing this dynamic force and translating it into concrete actions that foster sustained, inclusive transformation—ultimately creating a blueprint for a future where systemic obstacles are continuously transformed into opportunities for growth and renewal.

Chapter 5: Web3 Systems Thinking – Rethinking Socio-Economic Models

In this chapter, we explore how decentralized digital frameworks—collectively referred to as Web3—are poised to transform the way societies organize, govern, and create value. The following sections expand on the core bullet points that form the backbone of Web3 Systems Thinking.

5.1 Introduction: The Emergence of Web3 Systems Thinking

5.1.1 The Evolution of Digital Societies

- **From Centralization to Decentralization:**
  Traditional digital societies have long been dominated by a few centralized platforms (big tech companies, government-regulated financial institutions, etc.). In contrast, the evolution towards Web3 represents a paradigm shift. This shift is characterized by a move to distributed networks where data, control, and value creation are democratized. For example, whereas traditional social networks control data and decision-making centrally, emerging decentralized platforms allow individuals to own and control their own information, thereby fostering a more equitable digital environment.

5.1.2 Defining Web3 Systems Thinking

- **Restructuring Socio-Economic Interactions:**
  Web3 Systems Thinking leverages blockchain protocols and decentralized frameworks to fundamentally alter how social and economic interactions occur. Instead of relying on intermediaries, direct peer-to-peer interactions are enabled through technology. This approach not only reduces friction in transactions but also enables real-time verification and transparency.

- **Enabling Continuous, Adaptive Feedback:**
  In traditional systems, feedback is often slow and opaque. With decentralized protocols, every transaction or governance decision is recorded on a transparent ledger, providing continuous feedback that is accessible to all stakeholders. This iterative improvement process enables communities to dynamically adapt to challenges and opportunities.

- **Empowering Community-Driven Governance:**
  By distributing decision-making power to every participant in a network, Web3 systems empower communities to self-govern. The use of consensus mechanisms and DAOs (Decentralized Autonomous Organizations) ensures that governance is participatory and trust-minimized. This stands in stark contrast to top-down decision-making in centralized systems, thus paving the way for more resilient and inclusive communities.

5.1.3 The Imperative for Rethinking Socio-Economic Models

- **Addressing Inequitable Resource Distribution:**
  Centralized systems often perpetuate inequities because resources and power become concentrated. Rethinking socio-economic models with Web3 means designing frameworks where resources—be they digital tokens, data,

or decision-making rights—are distributed equitably. This decentralization is key to dismantling systemic barriers that have historically marginalized certain groups.

- **Creating Ecosystems of Resilience:**
  New socio-economic models based on Web3 principles are designed to be inherently resilient. The distributed nature of these systems means that even if one node or component fails, the broader network continues to operate. This built-in redundancy and adaptability are essential for weathering crises, be they economic downturns or cyberattacks.

- **Enhancing Transparency and Trust:**
  By rethinking these models, Web3 fosters an environment where transparency is the default and trust is built into the infrastructure. For example, decentralized finance (DeFi) platforms operate on open ledgers, allowing users to verify transactions independently and engage without the need for intermediaries. This model rebuilds trust in systems that have often been opaque and centralized.

5.2 The Theoretical Underpinnings of Web3 Systems Thinking

5.2.1 Systems Thinking: A Primer

- **Identifying Feedback Loops:**
  Systems Thinking involves recognizing the loops through which outputs are fed back as inputs. In a Web3 context, every transaction on a blockchain is recorded and can impact future decisions. For example, a user's repeated interactions with a decentralized application (dApp) contribute to a dataset that can be used to refine the

application's algorithms, creating a constant cycle of improvement.

- **Recognizing Non-Linear Relationships:**
  Unlike linear models where cause and effect are directly proportional, complex systems often exhibit non-linear interactions. Web3 systems are an example: small, decentralized actions (like micro-transactions) can collectively have outsized impacts on the network. This non-linearity is critical for understanding phenomena like network effects and virality in digital ecosystems.

- **Dynamic Models Over Time:**
  Systems Thinking emphasizes the temporal aspects of change—how systems evolve over time. In Web3, this might be seen in how a community governed by a DAO develops iteratively through phases of experimentation, feedback, and consolidation. Dynamic models help predict future states and design interventions that promote sustainable growth.

5.2.2 Decentralization: From Theory to Practice

- **Distributed Ledgers and Blockchain:**
  Blockchain technology provides a tamper-proof record of transactions. Distributed ledgers remove the need for centralized data repositories, thereby enhancing security and transparency. Consider how blockchain is used in cryptocurrency to record every transaction in a way that is visible to the entire network, preventing fraud and ensuring authenticity.

- **Decentralized Autonomous Organizations (DAOs):**
  DAOs are organizational structures governed by code rather than hierarchies. They facilitate collective decision-making and resource management without requiring a central authority. For example, a DAO might manage a community

fund, allowing members to vote on how resources should be allocated. This model increases accountability and democratizes power.

- **Smart Contracts and Token Economies:**
  Smart contracts are self-executing agreements encoded on the blockchain. They automatically enforce terms without needing external oversight. Token economies, based on these contracts, create new ways to exchange value. Tokens can represent votes, stakes in a project, or even rights to creative content, enabling innovative economic models that are more inclusive and participatory.

5.2.3 Interdisciplinary Integration: Merging Digital and Socio-Economic Models

- **Economics:**
  Traditional economic theories are being rethought in light of decentralized technologies. Web3 can be viewed through the lens of game theory, which examines how individuals make decisions in competitive environments. In decentralized systems, new incentive structures and market models are emerging that emphasize collective benefit over individual profit.

- **Political Science:**
  Web3 reconfigures governance by promoting transparency and participatory democracy. Political theories on decentralization are applied to design systems where power is dispersed across a network rather than concentrated in a central authority. This shift can lead to more resilient and responsive political systems.

- **Cultural Studies:**
  Socio-cultural factors drive the adoption and evolution of technology. Web3 Systems Thinking integrates cultural

narratives and community identities into digital platforms. This approach helps ensure that decentralized models are not merely technocratic but also respect and reflect local values and traditions.

- **Computer Science and Cryptography:**
  The technical backbone of Web3 lies in computer science, particularly in cryptography, which secures data and enables trustless transactions. Advances in cryptographic methods ensure that decentralized networks maintain integrity and remain secure in an increasingly interconnected world.

5.3 Core Principles and Architectures of Web3 Systems

5.3.1 Fundamental Components of Web3

- **Blockchain Technology:**
  At its core, blockchain is a decentralized ledger that records transactions in a secure, transparent, and immutable way. Each block contains a set of transactions, linked together cryptographically. This structure not only prevents fraud but also provides a traceable history of activities, which is crucial for accountability in any socio-economic system.

- **Smart Contracts:**
  These are self-executing contracts with the terms directly written into code. Smart contracts facilitate, verify, and enforce the negotiation or performance of a contract autonomously. For example, in a decentralized lending platform, a smart contract might automatically distribute funds when certain criteria are met, eliminating the need for

intermediaries.

- **Tokenization:**
  Tokenization involves converting rights or assets into a digital token on a blockchain. These tokens can represent a variety of assets—from currency and stocks to physical goods and even services. Token economies enable new methods of fundraising (such as Initial Coin Offerings or ICOs), reward mechanisms, and the redistribution of wealth.

- **Decentralized Applications (dApps):**
  dApps run on decentralized networks rather than on a single server, making them resistant to censorship and single points of failure. They allow users to interact directly with blockchain-based protocols, whether for financial transactions, social interactions, or governance purposes.

5.3.2 Architectural Models and Frameworks

- **Layered Architectures:**
  Web3 systems often adopt a multi-layer approach. The base layer (often the blockchain) is responsible for security and data integrity. Above this, the application layer provides business logic and user interfaces. This separation allows for specialized improvements in each layer without disrupting overall system functionality.

- **Interoperability and Modularity:**
  Modular design is essential for scalability and integration. Interoperability ensures that different blockchain networks and traditional systems can communicate and exchange value seamlessly. For example, interoperability protocols enable a token created on one blockchain to be used on another, creating a more connected ecosystem.

- **Decentralized Identity and Data Sovereignty:**
  In the Web3 paradigm, individuals maintain control of their digital identities and personal data. Decentralized identity solutions allow users to authenticate and share data selectively, preserving privacy while enhancing security. This shift away from centralized data repositories supports a more user-centric model of digital interaction.

5.4 Transforming Social and Economic Interactions with Web3

5.4.1 Redefining Trust and Transparency

- **Eliminating Intermediaries:**
  Traditional systems rely on intermediaries (banks, government agencies, etc.) to verify and execute transactions. Web3 systems eliminate these middlemen by using decentralized protocols, thereby reducing costs and minimizing opportunities for corruption. This trustless environment is based on transparent, algorithmic processes rather than opaque institutions.

- **Transparent Governance:**
  By recording every decision and transaction on a public ledger, Web3 systems facilitate unprecedented levels of transparency in governance. For instance, a DAO's decision-making process is visible to all participants, making it easier to hold leaders accountable and fostering a culture of open participation.

- **Enhanced Security and Data Integrity:**
  The immutable nature of blockchain means that once data is recorded, it cannot be altered without consensus. This

ensures that records remain reliable, providing a strong foundation for economic and social interactions. Enhanced security mechanisms, including advanced cryptography, further protect user data and prevent unauthorized modifications.

5.4.2 Empowering Individuals and Communities

- **Financial Inclusion:**
  Decentralized Finance (DeFi) platforms bypass traditional banking systems, providing financial services to anyone with internet access. This inclusivity is particularly transformative in regions with limited banking infrastructure, as decentralized platforms offer access to loans, insurance, and savings programs without geographic restrictions.

- **Community Governance:**
  DAOs allow communities to make collective decisions on resource allocation, policy changes, and strategic directions. This model gives everyday individuals a direct stake in governance, fostering a sense of ownership and accountability, and ensuring that the benefits of technological advancements are distributed broadly.

- **Participatory Economics:**
  Web3 facilitates the creation of localized token economies, where individuals can earn tokens for contributing to community projects. These tokens can then be used to access services or reinvest in local initiatives, creating a self-sustaining economic ecosystem that empowers communities to manage their own development.

5.4.3 Reconfiguring Work, Value Creation, and Collaboration

- **Decentralized Labor Markets:**
  The gig economy is reimagined through decentralized platforms that ensure fair compensation and transparent evaluations. Blockchain-based labor markets can verify work records, offer secure payment channels, and ensure that contract terms are enforced automatically, fostering trust between employers and workers.

- **Collaborative Innovation Ecosystems:**
  Open-source initiatives and decentralized development communities exemplify how collaborative efforts can drive disruptive innovation. Web3 platforms enable contributors from around the world to collaborate on projects ranging from software development to scientific research, creating an ecosystem where ideas are shared freely and intellectual property is managed collectively.

- **Redefining Intellectual Property and Creative Commons:**
  With tokenization, creatives—artists, writers, musicians— can convert their work into digital assets that can be traded, sold, or licensed. This new model protects intellectual property while enabling innovative revenue-sharing arrangements and collaborative creative projects.

5.5 Case Studies: Real-World Applications and Impacts

5.5.1 Decentralized Finance (DeFi) and Economic Empowerment

- **Financial Democratization Through DeFi:**
  Platforms like Uniswap and Compound have revolutionized

traditional finance by enabling peer-to-peer transactions without intermediaries. Users can lend, borrow, and trade assets directly on decentralized platforms, reducing fees and increasing access.

- **Token Economies in Action:**
  MakerDAO's creation of the DAI stablecoin illustrates how token economies can stabilize value in decentralized systems. By using collateralized tokens to generate stable currency, MakerDAO helps users avoid the volatility common in traditional cryptocurrencies, facilitating everyday transactions.

- **Challenges and Innovations:**
  While DeFi has opened up new economic avenues, it also faces challenges such as price volatility, security vulnerabilities, and regulatory uncertainty. Ongoing innovation in protocol design, security audits, and governance frameworks aims to address these issues, highlighting the dynamic evolution of DeFi ecosystems.

5.5.2 Decentralized Autonomous Organizations (DAOs) and Governance

- **Case of DAO Ventures:**
  Early DAO projects, such as The DAO (despite its challenges), paved the way for more robust models like DAOstack and MolochDAO. These organizations enable community members to vote on proposals, allocate funds, and direct collective efforts, all without centralized leadership.

- **Reinventing Governance Models:**
  DAOs challenge conventional governance by distributing decision-making power. Instead of a hierarchical board of directors, every token holder can participate in the

governance process, ensuring that the system remains dynamic, transparent, and responsive to community needs.

- **Emerging Trends and Opportunities:**
  As DAOs mature, their applications are expanding beyond finance into public sector governance, nonprofit management, and even urban planning. These emerging models offer a glimpse into how decentralized governance can reshape traditional institutions and drive long-term systemic change.

5.5.3 Cross-Sectoral Impact: Art, Culture, and Education

- **Digital Identity and Cultural Preservation:**
  Decentralized identity systems enable individuals to control their personal data and digital footprints, preserving cultural heritage and enabling secure, verifiable communication. For example, blockchain-based identity solutions can help indigenous communities maintain control over their cultural narratives and ensure that their knowledge is preserved without exploitation.

- **Revolutionizing Education:**
  Education platforms built on blockchain technology offer verifiable credentials and decentralized access to learning materials. By doing so, these platforms democratize education, making lifelong learning and skill development accessible to a global audience, regardless of socio-economic status.

- **Cultural Economies and Creative Collaboration:**
  Through tokenization and digital rights management, artists and creators can directly monetize their work and collaborate in innovative ways. Web3-based creative ecosystems allow artists to form collectives, share royalties automatically via

smart contracts, and build communities around their art, transforming the traditional art market.

5.6 Challenges and Critiques of Web3 Systems Thinking

5.6.1 Technical and Infrastructural Barriers

- **Scalability and Network Congestion:**
  Many blockchain networks face limitations in terms of transaction throughput. As user numbers grow, networks can become congested, leading to higher fees and slower processing times. Researchers are actively developing layer-two solutions and more scalable consensus algorithms to address these issues.

- **Interoperability Challenges:**
  With a multitude of blockchain platforms in existence, ensuring that they can communicate seamlessly presents a significant technical challenge. Projects aimed at creating interoperability protocols are critical to building an integrated and functional decentralized ecosystem.

- **Energy Consumption and Environmental Impact:**
  The energy demands of certain consensus mechanisms, particularly Proof of Work, pose environmental concerns. The transition to more energy-efficient models, such as Proof of Stake, is crucial for ensuring that the expansion of decentralized systems is sustainable and environmentally responsible.

5.6.2 Regulatory and Legal Considerations

- **Navigating Uncertainty:**
  Governments and regulatory bodies are still grappling with the implications of decentralized technologies. The lack of clear regulatory guidelines creates uncertainty, particularly in areas like taxation, consumer protection, and financial regulation.

- **Data Privacy and Security:**
  While transparency is a hallmark of decentralized systems, it also raises concerns regarding personal privacy. Balancing the need for open, verifiable data with robust data protection measures is a delicate task that requires ongoing innovation and regulatory insight.

- **Intellectual Property and Ownership:**
  The tokenization of digital assets has introduced complex legal questions surrounding intellectual property rights. Establishing clear legal frameworks that protect creators while fostering innovation is essential for the healthy evolution of Web3 ecosystems.

5.6.3 Socio-Economic and Ethical Implications

- **Inclusivity Versus Technological Exclusion:**
  Although Web3 promises democratization, there is a risk that technological complexity may alienate individuals lacking the requisite digital literacy. Efforts must be made to bridge the digital divide, ensuring that decentralized systems are accessible to all.

- **Power Dynamics and Decentralized Governance:**
  While decentralized systems distribute power, they are not immune to concentration. Wealthy participants may accumulate disproportionate influence through token accumulation, potentially recreating hierarchies in a different form. Mechanisms to ensure equitable participation and

prevent oligarchic control are necessary.

- **Ethical Use and Social Responsibility:**
  The adoption of Web3 technologies raises ethical questions about their intended use and potential for misuse. Establishing ethical guidelines and standards for the deployment of decentralized systems is crucial to ensure that these innovations contribute positively to societal development.

5.7 Future Directions and Strategic Considerations for Web3 Systems

5.7.1 Innovations on the Horizon

- **Next-Generation Protocols:**
  Research is underway to develop more scalable and energy-efficient blockchain protocols. Innovations like sharding, new consensus algorithms, and hybrid models promise to overcome many of the current technical limitations, enabling even broader adoption of Web3 technologies.

- **Interoperable Ecosystems:**
  As different blockchain networks mature, efforts to create standardized interoperability protocols will become increasingly critical. Such protocols will allow seamless data and value transfers between disparate systems, creating a truly integrated decentralized ecosystem.

- **Decentralized AI:**
  The convergence of decentralized technologies and artificial intelligence offers transformative potential. Decentralized AI

platforms could democratize access to advanced analytics and decision-making tools, further accelerating innovation and adaptive governance across socio-economic systems.

5.7.2 Policy Recommendations and Collaborative Frameworks

- **Inclusive Regulatory Frameworks:**
  Policymakers should work in concert with technologists, economists, and community stakeholders to craft regulations that balance innovation with protection. Inclusive frameworks that consider the perspectives of diverse communities are critical to fostering broad-based adoption of decentralized technologies.

- **Public-Private Partnerships:**
  Collaboration between public institutions and private entities can drive infrastructure development and standardization in Web3. Such partnerships can accelerate research, promote digital literacy, and build trust in new technologies by aligning public goals with private innovation.

- **Educational and Outreach Initiatives:**
  To maximize Web3's societal impact, educational initiatives must be launched to improve digital literacy and familiarize the public with decentralized technologies. Outreach programs, workshops, and curricular integrations in schools and universities will empower more people to engage with these new systems.

5.7.3 Cultivating a Global Digital Commons

- **Decentralized Governance Models:**
  Future strategies should focus on creating transparent, inclusive, and globally representative governance models.

DAOs and other decentralized frameworks offer a blueprint for governing transnational digital commons where every participant has a voice.

- **Global Collaboration and Knowledge Sharing:**
  International cooperation is essential for the seamless integration of Web3 technologies. Cross-border initiatives, research consortiums, and global hackathons can accelerate innovation by pooling collective expertise and ensuring that best practices spread across regions.

- **Ethical Frameworks and Social Responsibility:**
  Establishing ethical standards for Web3 is imperative. These standards must address not only privacy and security concerns but also ensure that the benefits of decentralized technologies are equitably distributed and contribute to sustainable development.

5.8 Synthesis: Reimagining Socio-Economic Models Through Web3 Systems Thinking

5.8.1 From Centralization to Distributed Empowerment

The shift from centralized to decentralized models is not just a technological upgrade; it represents a fundamental rethinking of how value, authority, and social interactions are structured. Through distributed systems, power is no longer concentrated in a few hands. Instead, every participant in a network has an opportunity to contribute to and benefit from a collective ecosystem.

5.8.2 Integrative Benefits Across Sectors

The benefits of Web3 extend far beyond finance. When integrated into sectors such as education, healthcare, and cultural production, decentralized technologies create networks of trust, open access, and collaborative innovation. These networks foster resilience by drawing on diverse talents and local knowledge, thus reinforcing a broader, interconnected model of socio-economic well-being.

5.8.3 A Blueprint for the Future

The conceptual and practical frameworks discussed here form a comprehensive blueprint for reimagining socio-economic models. This blueprint lays out how decentralized systems can be designed to be resilient, participatory, and adaptive—integrating cutting-edge technological innovations with systemic principles that prioritize inclusivity and sustainability.

5.9 Conclusion: The Transformative Potential of Web3 Systems Thinking

- **Redesigning Social and Economic Interactions:** Web3 Systems Thinking offers a powerful lens through which to re-envision how society organizes itself—dismantling traditional hierarchies and fostering an equitable distribution of power, value, and information. As decentralized platforms mature, they promise to transform everything from finance and governance to cultural expression and personal empowerment.

- **Embracing Decentralization as a Paradigm Shift:** By embracing decentralized frameworks, communities can build resilient systems that operate transparently and inclusively. The transformative nature of blockchain, DAOs, and token economies is not confined to technological improvement; it signifies a broader, systemic revolution that has the potential to redefine global socio-economic models.

- **Call to Action for a New Digital Commons:**
  Ultimately, the future of Web3 lies in harnessing collective ingenuity and shared digital resources to create a global digital commons. This digital commons, characterized by participatory governance, ethical standards, and continuous innovation, will underpin a more equitable and sustainable world.

In summary, this expanded exploration of every bullet point in Chapter 5 has provided deep, detailed insights into the foundational concepts, core principles, and transformative potential of Web3 Systems Thinking. By rethinking socio-economic models through the decentralized lens of Web3, we open up a future where trust, transparency, and equitable participation become the standard— paving the way for a resilient, inclusive, and innovative society.

Part II: Technological Pillars of Transformation

Chapter 6: Blockchain Fundamentals for Decentralized Empowerment

Blockchain technology is not merely a tool for facilitating secure digital transactions—it represents a fundamental paradigm shift in how trust, value, and data are managed and exchanged. In this chapter, we explore in depth the core principles of blockchain, its security mechanisms, and its transformative role as the backbone for decentralized systems. We delve into the technical and conceptual foundations of blockchain technology, illustrate its real-world applications, and assess the challenges and future directions that will shape its evolution. This comprehensive overview demonstrates how blockchain can democratize socio-economic structures and empower communities by providing a transparent, secure, and trustless digital infrastructure.

6.1 Fundamental Principles of Blockchain Technology

6.1.1 Distributed Ledger Technology

- **Core Concept:**
  At its essence, blockchain is a distributed ledger—an immutable, decentralized database maintained by a network of nodes. Every participant holds a synchronized copy of the ledger, ensuring that no single point of control exists. This widespread replication reinforces security and transparency by allowing any member to verify recorded transactions.

- **Decentralization Benefits:**
  By eliminating central intermediaries, the distributed ledger removes vulnerabilities associated with centralized management. This approach drastically reduces the risk of fraud or manipulation and empowers individuals to participate in a trust-minimized ecosystem. In financial systems, for instance, a distributed ledger allows participants to engage directly without relying on banks or payment

processors.

- **Empowerment in Practice:**
  In practical applications, distributed ledger technology (DLT) enables transparent supply chain tracking, verifiable digital identities, and secure peer-to-peer communication. Whether documenting provenance in art, verifying academic credentials, or facilitating global financial transfers, DLT is a cornerstone for building decentralized, community-controlled platforms.

6.1.2 Cryptographic Hashing and Data Integrity

- **Hash Functions Explained:**
  A cryptographic hash function converts input data into a fixed-length string of characters—a hash. Each block in a blockchain includes the hash of its predecessor, thereby forming a chain. Even a tiny alteration in any block causes a completely different hash, instantly flagging any tampering.

- **Ensuring Immutability:**
  The interdependency of hashes creates an immutable record; once data is added to the blockchain, it cannot be altered without breaking the chain's continuity. This mathematical guarantee is fundamental to ensuring data integrity and maintaining trust in the ledger's accuracy across all nodes.

- **Real-World Security:**
  In environments such as financial transactions, the robustness of cryptographic hashing assures users that records, once confirmed, remain unaltered. This protection is critical in scenarios where data integrity is paramount, for example, in legal documents or sensitive medical records.

6.1.3 Consensus Mechanisms: Achieving Trustless Agreement

- **Purpose and Importance:**
  Consensus mechanisms enable decentralized networks to agree on the state of the ledger without a central authority. These protocols ensure that all nodes are synchronized and that only valid transactions are recorded.

- **Proof of Work (PoW):**
  Under PoW, nodes (or miners) solve complex computational puzzles to validate transactions. The high computational cost serves as a deterrent to fraudulent behavior. Although PoW is highly secure, its energy demands have prompted the exploration of more sustainable alternatives.

- **Proof of Stake (PoS) and Beyond:**
  PoS chooses validators based on the number of tokens they hold and are willing to "stake" as collateral. This significantly reduces energy consumption while maintaining network security. Other mechanisms—such as Delegated Proof of Stake (DPoS) and Byzantine Fault Tolerance (BFT) models—are being developed to combine efficiency with robust security.

- **Economic Incentives:**
  Both PoW and PoS align participants' financial interests with the network's health. Misbehavior can result in the loss of rewards or staked funds, effectively safeguarding the system against attacks and ensuring overall network integrity.

6.1.4 Smart Contracts: Self-Executing Code for Autonomous Operations

- **Concept Overview:**
  Smart contracts are pieces of code stored on the blockchain that automatically execute transactions or enforce agreed-upon conditions when predefined criteria are met. They eliminate intermediaries and reduce the potential for human error.

- **Mechanics of Automation:**
  These contracts operate in a trustless environment, meaning that their execution does not rely on external verification. When conditions are fulfilled—such as a payment upon delivery of goods—the contract executes automatically, ensuring efficiency and consistency.

- **Impact on Decentralization:**
  Smart contracts facilitate numerous decentralized applications (dApps) spanning finance, insurance, supply chain, and governance. They streamline complex multi-party transactions and enforce rules impartially, thus forming the backbone of decentralized empowerment and value transfer.

6.2 Security Mechanisms in Blockchain Systems

6.2.1 Cryptographic Security Foundations

- **Public and Private Key Cryptography:**
  Every participant in a blockchain network uses a pair of cryptographic keys. The private key remains secret and is used to sign transactions, while the public key is shared with the network for verification. This asymmetric cryptography ensures authentication and non-repudiation, making it

impossible for fraudsters to impersonate legitimate users.

- **Digital Signatures:**
  Digital signatures validate the authenticity and integrity of messages and transactions. They confirm that the transaction was indeed sent by the rightful owner and that the data has not been altered since it was signed.

- **Encryption Protocols:**
  Advanced encryption protocols protect data on the blockchain, ensuring that even if data is intercepted, it cannot be deciphered without the appropriate decryption keys. This underpins the robust security of blockchain networks, making them resistant to cyberattacks.

6.2.2 Consensus-Driven Security and Attack Resistance

- **Defending Against 51% Attacks:**
  A major threat to blockchain security is the possibility of a 51% attack, where a single entity controls a majority of the network's resources. However, achieving such control is prohibitively expensive in well-established networks, which deters malicious behavior through economic disincentives.

- **Incentive Alignment:**
  The design of consensus mechanisms ensures that all participants are financially incentivized to act honestly. Misconduct leads to penalties, such as loss of staking deposits in PoS systems or wasted computational resources in PoW systems.

- **Redundancy and Fault Tolerance:**
  Data replication across thousands of nodes creates redundancy, protecting the network from localized failures or attacks. This decentralized architecture maintains

operational integrity even if some nodes are compromised.

6.2.3 Network Resilience Through Transparency and Immutable Records

- **Transparent Ledger Architecture:**
  Every transaction is recorded on a public ledger, visible to all participants. This openness means that any attempt to alter historical records is easily spotted, ensuring a high level of transparency that enhances trust.

- **Robustness Against Tampering:**
  The immutable nature of the blockchain ensures that, once data is verified and recorded, it cannot be changed. Any attempt to modify past records would require re-mining every subsequent block—a computationally infeasible task—thus preserving historical accuracy.

- **Distributed Redundancy:**
  Since every node maintains a complete copy of the ledger, the failure or compromise of one node does not affect the overall integrity of the system. This decentralized redundancy is a key pillar of blockchain's resilience and security.

6.3 Blockchain as the Backbone for Decentralized Systems

6.3.1 Enabling Trustless Transactions and Interactions

- **Eliminating the Need for Intermediaries:**
  Traditional transactions rely on intermediaries like banks, notaries, or clearinghouses. Blockchain technology enables trustless interactions where the system's cryptographic and consensus protocols verify transactions without third-party mediation. This direct peer-to-peer model minimizes transaction costs and reduces vulnerabilities to centralized corruption.

- **Facilitating Instant Verification:**
  Every transaction on a blockchain is immediately verified and recorded, ensuring transparency and accountability. This rapid verification process is crucial for applications like cross-border payments and smart contracts where real-time trust and integrity are paramount.

- **Strengthening Peer-to-Peer Networks:**
  By underpinning trustless interactions with secure, immutable records, blockchain empowers individuals to transact directly. This peer-to-peer architecture is essential for decentralized applications that aim to redistribute power and foster community self-governance.

6.3.2 Foundational Role in Decentralized Applications (dApps)

- **Modularity and Scalability:**
  Blockchain provides the underlying infrastructure for dApps, which are designed to function autonomously without centralized oversight. The modularity of these applications allows developers to build and scale innovative solutions in finance, supply chain management, healthcare, and more.

- **Interoperable Ecosystems:**
  Decentralized applications often operate across multiple blockchain networks, thanks to emerging interoperability

protocols. This creates an ecosystem where data and value flow seamlessly between platforms, unlocking new avenues for collaborative innovation.

- **Real-World Case Studies:**
  Successful dApps include decentralized finance platforms (like Uniswap and Aave) and governance models implemented by DAOs. These applications leverage blockchain's transparency and efficiency to create systems that are both robust and user-centric.

6.3.3 Redefining Governance and Ownership

- **Decentralized Autonomous Organizations (DAOs):**
  DAOs are reshaping governance by enabling communities to manage resources and make decisions through distributed consensus mechanisms. Every member can vote on proposals, contributing to a governance model that is inclusive and transparent.

- **Tokenization and Shared Ownership:**
  Blockchain supports innovative ownership models through tokenization. Assets—from digital art to real estate—can be converted into tokens, allowing fractional ownership and enabling more inclusive investment opportunities. This fosters a sense of shared wealth and democratizes access to economic growth.

- **Empowerment Through Collective Decision-Making:**
  By decentralizing power and giving individuals direct control over resource allocation and strategic direction, blockchain creates a framework in which systemic change is driven from the ground up. This model of participatory governance challenges traditional hierarchies and promotes a more equitable distribution of power.

6.4 Challenges and Future Directions in Blockchain Technology

6.4.1 Scalability and Efficiency

- **Current Limitations:**
  Many blockchain networks, such as Bitcoin and Ethereum, face scalability challenges characterized by limited transaction throughput and high fees during peak demand. These issues are a bottleneck for mass adoption.

- **Layer-Two Solutions:**
  Innovations like the Lightning Network, Optimistic Rollups, and state channels aim to alleviate scalability issues by processing transactions off-chain and then settling them on the main blockchain. These solutions are critical for increasing throughput while maintaining decentralization and security.

- **Sharding and Parallel Processing:**
  Sharding divides the blockchain into smaller, manageable segments (shards) that process transactions in parallel, potentially boosting the system's overall capacity. Research into sharding and other parallel processing techniques continues to drive the next generation of scalable blockchain solutions.

6.4.2 Energy Consumption and Environmental Impact

- **Energy Demands of Proof of Work:**
  PoW-based blockchains require significant amounts of energy for mining operations. This has led to environmental

concerns and calls for sustainable practices.

- **Transitioning to Energy-Efficient Models:**
  Proof of Stake and other alternative consensus algorithms offer a more energy-efficient path. These models rely on staking rather than computational power, significantly reducing the energy footprint of blockchain networks.

- **Exploring Renewable Energy Options:**
  Some blockchain projects are now exploring the integration of renewable energy sources to power mining operations, ensuring that decentralized systems advance sustainably without compromising environmental integrity.

6.4.3 Regulatory and Integration Challenges

- **Legal Uncertainty:**
  The decentralized nature of blockchain disrupts traditional regulatory frameworks. Regulators face challenges in areas such as taxation, consumer protection, and financial security within decentralized networks.

- **Interoperability with Traditional Systems:**
  Bridging blockchain networks with existing centralized systems (such as legacy financial institutions) remains a technical and regulatory hurdle. Standardization and the development of interoperable protocols are vital for integrating decentralized models into mainstream socio-economic frameworks.

- **Establishing Clear Standards:**
  As blockchain evolves, the creation of standardized legal and technical frameworks will help reduce uncertainty and foster broader adoption. Policymakers must work alongside technologists to develop guidelines that encourage

innovation while protecting public interest.

6.5 The Broader Impact of Blockchain on Decentralized Empowerment

6.5.1 Economic Democratization

- **Access to Financial Services:**
  Blockchain-based decentralized finance (DeFi) platforms open up financial services to anyone with internet access. These platforms enable peer-to-peer lending, decentralized exchanges, and automated investment solutions, empowering underserved populations globally.

- **Lowering Transaction Costs:**
  By removing intermediaries, blockchain dramatically reduces the cost and friction associated with traditional financial transactions, creating a more equitable financial ecosystem.

- **Global Market Integration:**
  Blockchain networks break down geographical barriers, enabling small businesses and entrepreneurs to participate in global markets. This integration promotes a more inclusive global economy where opportunities are distributed more broadly.

6.5.2 Social and Political Transformation

- **Transparent Governance:**
  The public, immutable nature of blockchain leads to more transparent governance structures. By enabling

decentralized decision-making through DAOs, blockchain empowers communities to manage public resources, challenge corruption, and ensure accountability.

- **Empowering Marginalized Communities:**
  Blockchain can provide a secure method for documenting land titles, personal identities, and property rights. This is especially transformative in regions where bureaucratic inefficiencies have long disenfranchised marginalized populations.

- **Decentralized Data Ownership:**
  Shifting control of data back to individuals mitigates the risks associated with centralized data monopolies. Blockchain ensures that personal and institutional data is secure, verifiable, and controlled by its rightful owners, laying the groundwork for more democratic digital interactions.

Chapter 7: Gemach DAO – Decentralized Economic Structures

Gemach DAO represents a pioneering approach to collective economic action, harnessing blockchain and decentralized governance to empower communities, democratize wealth creation, and foster long-term economic resilience. In this chapter, we provide an exhaustive exploration of Gemach DAO's design, governance structure, and wealth circulation mechanisms. We discuss how these components interlock to create a sustainable, inclusive economic ecosystem and examine the theoretical and practical implications of such decentralized economic structures.

7.1 Introduction: The Vision Behind Gemach DAO

7.1.1 A New Paradigm for Economic Empowerment

Traditional economic models often concentrate wealth and power in the hands of a few, perpetuating cycles of dependency and inequality. Gemach DAO is built upon the premise that economic empowerment must be reimagined through collective action and decentralized control. By establishing a community-driven framework, Gemach DAO aims to redistribute financial power, democratize access to capital, and create an environment in which wealth circulates robustly within the community.

7.1.2 The Role of Decentralization in Collective Economics

Decentralization is the cornerstone of Gemach DAO. Rather than relying on centralized financial institutions that historically extract value from local economies, Gemach DAO leverages blockchain technology to build transparent, immutable, and trustless systems where every member has a stake. This not only improves financial inclusion but also ensures that economic activities are directly controlled by the community, fostering long-term prosperity and social cohesion.

7.2 Design Principles of Gemach DAO

7.2.1 Conceptual Foundations and Historical Inspiration

- **Historical Precedents:**
  Gemach DAO draws inspiration from traditional communal financial structures such as rotating savings and credit associations (ROSCAs), co-operatives, and community-based mutual aid funds. These time-honored practices underscore the potential of collective economic action, illustrating that pooling resources and sharing wealth are strategies that have sustained communities for centuries.

- **Modern Technological Infusion:**
  By integrating blockchain and smart contract technology, Gemach DAO reinvents these traditional practices in a digital, scalable, and transparent format. The digital nature of the DAO allows it to overcome geographical barriers, inviting participation from a global community while keeping the economic benefits localized and targeted.

7.2.2 Structural and Technical Architecture

- **Blockchain Backbone:**
  The DAO is built on a high-performance blockchain platform that ensures data security, immutability, and efficiency. Every transaction and decision is recorded on a distributed ledger accessible to all participants, guaranteeing full transparency and accountability.

- **Smart Contracts:**
  Smart contracts are utilized to automate the execution of agreed-upon rules for resource pooling, disbursement, and reinvestment. These self-executing contracts reduce the need for intermediaries and ensure that all processes occur as designed without external interference. For example, a smart contract might release funds automatically based on

predefined milestones or trigger dividend payments to community members.

- **Tokenization:**
  A native token serves as both the medium of exchange and the unit of governance within Gemach DAO. Tokenization facilitates seamless economic interactions, enabling the distribution of voting rights, incentives, and profit-sharing among participants. Tokens can also be used to access certain services or participate in community projects, fostering a self-sustaining economic loop.

- **Modular Architecture:**
  Gemach DAO is designed with modularity in mind, enabling continual upgrades and integrations with other decentralized applications (dApps). This adaptability ensures that the system remains relevant and responsive to emerging technologies and community needs.

7.3 Governance Mechanisms: Participatory and Transparent Decision-Making

7.3.1 Democratic Governance via Decentralized Autonomous Organizations (DAOs)

- **Token-Based Voting:**
  At the heart of Gemach DAO's governance is token-based voting, where every token holder can participate in decisions regarding resource allocation, project funding, and policy adjustments. This distributed voting process ensures that

governance is both inclusive and transparent.

- **Proposal and Voting System:**
  Members can submit proposals for new projects, policy changes, or structural adjustments. Proposals undergo community discussion and are then put to a vote. The outcome—determined by a pre-established threshold or quorum—is executed automatically via smart contracts, thereby eliminating delays and human bias.

- **Decentralized Leadership and Committees:**
  While every member has a voice, specialized committees or working groups may be formed to focus on critical areas such as finance, technology development, and community outreach. These committees operate under the same decentralized principles, ensuring that leadership remains rotational and accountable.

7.3.2 Transparency and Accountability in Decision-Making

- **Open Access to Records:**
  All decisions, transactions, and governance activities are recorded on the blockchain. This open ledger allows any member to audit activities, ensuring that governance remains free from fraud or manipulation.

- **Feedback Loops and Iterative Improvement:**
  Governance in Gemach DAO is dynamic. Regular feedback loops, where members assess the performance of decisions and adjust policies as necessary, help to continually align the DAO with community interests and external challenges.

- **Conflict Resolution Mechanisms:**
  Dispute resolution is managed through predefined protocols embedded in smart contracts. Mediation and arbitration

processes, often facilitated by a rotating panel of respected community members, ensure that conflicts are resolved fairly and transparently.

7.4 Mechanisms for Wealth Circulation within Communities

7.4.1 Circulating Wealth through Collective Resource Pools

- **Resource Aggregation:**
  The core economic model of Gemach DAO centers on the aggregation of resources. Members contribute funds, assets, or other forms of value to a common pool. This collective pool serves as a shared capital base, which is then invested in projects that benefit the community.

- **Investment and Reinvestment Strategies:**
  Community funds are managed using transparent investment strategies designed to generate returns. These returns are reinvested into further community projects, thereby creating a self-reinforcing cycle of wealth generation and distribution.

- **Risk Sharing and Mutual Support:**
  By pooling resources, Gemach DAO reduces individual exposure to risk. Losses and profits are shared across the community, fostering a sense of collective responsibility and resilience even during economic downturns.

7.4.2 Distribution of Profits and Community Incentives

- **Dividend Distribution:**
  Profits generated by community investments and projects are distributed among token holders according to predefined rules. This dividend mechanism not only rewards participation but also encourages continued investment and engagement.

- **Incentivizing Active Participation:**
  Beyond financial dividends, the token economy provides non-monetary incentives. For example, tokens can be used to access exclusive services, gain influence in governance decisions, or support local community initiatives.

- **Circulation Models and Token Burning:**
  Innovative mechanisms such as token burning (where a portion of tokens is destroyed to decrease supply and potentially increase value) or staking rewards further stimulate active participation, ensuring that wealth remains within the community ecosystem rather than being extracted by external agents.

7.4.3 Sustainable Economic Models and Long-Term Impact

- **Local Economic Empowerment:**
  Wealth circulation within Gemach DAO is designed to benefit local economies by funding small businesses, local infrastructure, and community services. This creates a multiplier effect, where increased local spending and investments lead to broader economic growth.

- **Social Impact Investments:**
  The DAO may allocate funds to projects with measurable social impact, such as affordable housing, educational initiatives, or renewable energy projects. These investments address systemic challenges while generating sustainable economic returns.

- **Long-Term Financial Security:**
  By continuously reinvesting returns, the DAO builds long-term financial security for its members. This sustainable approach ensures that wealth is not merely concentrated at the top but flows throughout the community, reducing inequality and fostering resilience.

7.5 Case Studies and Practical Applications

7.5.1 Piloting Gemach DAO in Community Initiatives

- **Local Cooperative Ventures:**
  Pilot studies in communities, such as a targeted initiative in Asheboro, NC, demonstrate how Gemach DAO can be applied in real-world contexts. These pilots focus on using pooled resources to drive local business development, infrastructure improvements, and community services.

- **Evaluation of Economic Impact:**
  Metrics such as increased local employment, improved financial inclusion, and enhanced civic participation are used to evaluate the success of the DAO model. Through transparent tracking on the blockchain, community members can witness firsthand how collective action leads to

measurable improvements.

- **Scaling Models:**
  Lessons learned from pilot studies inform strategies for scaling Gemach DAO to larger regions or diverse communities. These models emphasize adaptability and local customization, ensuring that the DAO framework can be tailored to meet the specific needs of different socio-economic environments.

7.5.2 Global Collaboration and Cross-Community Initiatives

- **Cross-Border Economic Projects:**
  By leveraging the international nature of blockchain, Gemach DAO can facilitate collaborative projects that span multiple countries or regions. Such initiatives might focus on global supply chain improvements, international education networks, or cross-border social enterprises.

- **Knowledge Sharing and Best Practices:**
  Global consortia of Gemach DAOs can share best practices, technological innovations, and governance models. This collaboration enhances the overall resilience of decentralized economic structures and fosters a global community committed to collective empowerment.

- **Funding and Resource Allocation:**
  International partnerships may facilitate larger funding pools and access to broader markets, enabling community projects to scale more effectively and achieve a greater global impact.

7.6 Challenges and Future Directions for Gemach DAO

7.6.1 Technical and Operational Barriers

- **Integration with Existing Systems:**
  One of the primary challenges is integrating the decentralized model of Gemach DAO with existing financial and administrative systems. Bridging the gap between traditional institutions and decentralized frameworks requires innovative technological solutions and policy adjustments.

- **Scalability and Transaction Efficiency:**
  Ensuring that the DAO can handle increasing numbers of transactions and participants without compromising security and speed remains a critical technical hurdle. Future advancements in blockchain scalability, such as layer-two solutions, are essential to support a growing user base.

- **User Interface and Accessibility:**
  For widespread adoption, the platform must be user-friendly and accessible to individuals with varying levels of technological expertise. Improving the interface and providing educational resources are key components of overcoming this barrier.

7.6.2 Governance and Participation Challenges

- **Ensuring Equitable Representation:**
  Despite decentralized governance, there is a risk that wealthier or more tech-savvy participants might dominate decision-making processes. Developing mechanisms for equitable voting rights and incentivizing broad participation is crucial.

- **Conflict Resolution and Dispute Management:**
  As with any collective decision-making system, conflicts may arise. Establishing robust, transparent, and fair dispute resolution protocols that can adapt to different contexts is essential for maintaining community trust.

- **Sustaining Long-Term Engagement:**
  Keeping community members continuously engaged requires ongoing communication, incentives, and visible success stories. Strategies to maintain high levels of participation include rotating leadership roles, regular feedback sessions, and transparent performance metrics.

7.6.3 Strategic Expansion and Scaling

- **Adapting to Different Contexts:**
  The DAO model must be flexible enough to adapt to the unique needs of diverse communities. This might involve modular customization of governance structures, resource allocation rules, and economic objectives to ensure relevance in various socio-economic settings.

- **Partnerships and Ecosystem Integration:**
  Building partnerships with local governments, NGOs, and private sector organizations is critical to scaling the impact of Gemach DAO. These collaborations can provide additional resources, enhance credibility, and facilitate the integration of decentralized systems into broader socio-economic infrastructures.

- **Future Research and Innovation:**
  Ongoing research into blockchain scalability, governance models, and digital tokenomics will be necessary to refine the DAO's capabilities. Innovation labs, pilot projects, and academic collaborations will help to continuously iterate and

improve the framework.

7.7 Conclusion: Gemach DAO as a Model for Collective Economic Empowerment

Gemach DAO embodies a forward-thinking paradigm that redefines traditional economic structures through the lens of decentralization. By integrating blockchain technology, smart contracts, and token economies, it creates a transparent, secure, and democratic mechanism for wealth circulation. Its design emphasizes collective action, equitable governance, and sustainable economic growth—all crucial elements for addressing longstanding socio-economic challenges.

In this chapter, we have:

- Outlined the design principles that underpin Gemach DAO, including distributed ledger technology, smart contracts, and tokenization.

- Detailed the governance mechanisms that ensure participatory, transparent decision-making and robust community engagement.

- Explained the methods by which wealth is circulated within the community, from collective resource pooling to reinvestment and incentivization.

- Reviewed real-world case studies and pilot projects that demonstrate the practical applications and transformative potential of the DAO model.

- Discussed challenges related to scalability, equitable governance, and integration with existing systems, along with future strategic directions for scaling and adapting the model.

Gemach DAO stands as a powerful exemplar of decentralized economic structures that can empower communities by redistributing value and democratizing governance. As the global landscape of digital finance and decentralized technologies continues to evolve, models like Gemach DAO offer a blueprint for creating resilient, inclusive economies that are capable of transforming systemic inequalities into opportunities for shared prosperity.

Ultimately, Gemach DAO is not just a theoretical construct but a working model of collective empowerment—one that leverages the best aspects of technology, community organizing, and participatory governance to forge a future where economic benefits and decision-making power are widely and equitably shared.

Chapter 8: The Gemach Pedagogy – Transforming Learning into Action

The Gemach Pedagogy is an innovative educational framework that transforms traditional learning environments by integrating real-world economic models and decentralized finance (DeFi) principles. This approach empowers learners and future leaders through experiential, project-based, and community-driven education. By linking theory to practice, the Gemach Pedagogy provides a pathway for students to not only grasp economic and technological concepts but also to actively participate in shaping systems of collective wealth creation and governance.

8.1 Introduction: Re-Imagining Education for the Digital Age

8.1.1 Vision and Rationale

- **Empowerment Through Action:**
  The Gemach Pedagogy is founded on the belief that education should be an active process rather than a passive absorption of information. It aspires to cultivate critical thinking and entrepreneurial skills by immersing learners in real-world economic scenarios. The central vision is to enable individuals to become architects of their own economic futures, equipping them to challenge and transform centralized models of wealth and governance.

- **Bridging Theory and Practice:**
  Unlike conventional pedagogies that compartmentalize academic learning from practical applications, the Gemach Pedagogy integrates real-world financial models and decentralized technologies into the curriculum. This integration allows students to engage with complex economic systems in real time, encouraging them to experiment, iterate, and learn from direct participation.

- **Developing Future Leaders:**
  In an era defined by rapid technological change and economic disruption, the framework is designed to prepare a new generation of leaders who are not only knowledgeable about DeFi and economic theory but are also adept at applying these concepts to build resilient, community-based

economic structures.

8.1.2 The Educational Imperative in a Decentralized World

- **Addressing Systemic Inequities:**
  Traditional educational systems often mirror centralized socio-economic structures that contribute to wealth inequality. The Gemach Pedagogy seeks to redress these imbalances by fostering models of collective economic empowerment that offer learners the tools to participate in, and ultimately transform, their local and global economies.

- **Encouraging Adaptive Learning:**
  The rapid evolution of digital and financial technologies demands that education remains dynamic, iterative, and responsive. This pedagogy instills a mindset of lifelong learning and adaptability, essential for navigating the uncertainties and opportunities of the modern economy.

- **Cultivating Digital Literacies and Financial Acumen:**
  The framework emphasizes the development of digital literacy in blockchain, decentralized systems, and smart contracts, alongside financial acumen. This dual focus ensures that learners are well-prepared to operate within both technological and economic landscapes that are increasingly intertwined.

8.2 The Theoretical Foundations of the Gemach Pedagogy

8.2.1 Interdisciplinary Integration

- **Fusion of Economics, Technology, and Social Theory:**
  The Gemach Pedagogy is built upon an interdisciplinary foundation that merges economic theory, decentralized finance, and advanced technological principles with social and educational theory. It incorporates insights from behavioral economics, systems theory, cryptography, and participatory governance.

- **Systems Thinking in Education:**
  Systems thinking is a core pillar; it enables students to see the interconnectedness of economic systems, technology infrastructure, and social dynamics. By understanding feedback loops and emergent behaviors, learners grasp how small changes in one part of a system can have outsized effects elsewhere, laying the groundwork for innovative problem-solving.

- **Decentralized Mindset and Collective Intelligence:**
  The framework encourages a decentralized mindset. Rather than relying on hierarchical structures, learners are taught to appreciate the power of networks and collective intelligence. This perspective is essential for understanding and applying decentralized autonomous organizations (DAOs) and token economies.

8.2.2 Pedagogical Approaches and Methodologies

- **Experiential and Project-Based Learning:**
  Central to the Gemach Pedagogy is hands-on learning. Rather than solely learning through lectures and textbooks, students engage in projects that simulate real-world economic scenarios. These projects might include designing a micro-economy, participating in a simulated DAO, or

developing decentralized financial tools.

- **Interactive Simulations and Gamification:**
  To facilitate dynamic learning experiences, the pedagogy uses simulation games and gamification techniques that mirror decentralized economic systems. Students might simulate the behavior of decentralized networks, experience the impact of market changes, and experiment with different governance models, learning to manage risk, navigate uncertainty, and drive innovation.

- **Collaborative Learning and Peer-to-Peer Engagement:**
  The framework emphasizes collaborative learning through group projects, peer reviews, and community-based assignments. This collaborative approach not only mirrors decentralized decision-making processes but also helps build social capital—an essential element in collective economic empowerment.

- **Adaptive Curricula:**
  The Gemach Pedagogy supports adaptive curricula that evolve in response to technological advancements and the changing economic landscape. Continuous feedback loops from industry, academia, and community stakeholders help refine course content, ensuring that the education remains relevant and future-focused.

8.3 Decentralized Finance (DeFi) as a Learning Laboratory

8.3.1 Understanding Decentralized Finance

- **Fundamentals of DeFi:**
  The curriculum introduces students to the basics of DeFi—including blockchain, smart contracts, decentralized exchanges, and yield farming. Through a blend of theoretical lessons and practical labs, learners explore how DeFi platforms operate without intermediaries, transforming traditional financial services.

- **Token Economies and Digital Assets:**
  Students learn the principles of tokenization, understand how digital assets are created and traded, and examine the economic implications of token economies. This includes studying how tokens can represent equity, voting rights, or even access to services, thereby reinforcing the concept of collective ownership.

- **Case Studies of DeFi Innovations:**
  Real-world case studies—such as MakerDAO's stablecoin system or Uniswap's decentralized exchange—provide contextual understanding. Through these studies, students analyze successes and challenges in DeFi, preparing them to critically evaluate and contribute to future innovations in the field.

8.3.2 Applying DeFi Principles to Create Economic Models

- **Designing Simulated Economies:**
  In project-based assignments, learners design and simulate their own decentralized economies. They create virtual communities where resource pooling, investment, and profit distribution are managed via smart contracts. This exercise helps them understand how decentralized financial mechanisms can foster wealth distribution and resilience.

- **Role of DAOs in Economic Decision-Making:**
  Learners participate in or simulate decentralized autonomous organizations (DAOs), gaining practical experience in democratic governance. They learn how proposals are made, discussed, and voted on using token-based systems, mirroring real-world governance in decentralized networks.

- **Iterative Feedback and Economic Adjustments:**
  Projects incorporate continuous feedback mechanisms. By applying systems thinking, students monitor economic indicators, adjust their strategies, and witness firsthand the effects of iterative improvements, thereby internalizing the principles of adaptive governance and economic resilience.

8.4 Empowering Future Leaders: Skills and Mindsets for Decentralized Economies

8.4.1 Cultivating Entrepreneurial and Innovative Mindsets

- **Critical Thinking and Problem-Solving:**
  Through case studies and experiential learning, the Gemach Pedagogy cultivates critical thinking. Learners are encouraged to question prevailing economic models, identify inefficiencies, and propose innovative solutions. This critical approach is essential for navigating and reforming decentralized economic systems.

- **Leadership in Decentralized Environments:**
  Emerging leaders are trained to operate in flat, non-

hierarchical structures where collaboration, shared responsibility, and transparency are paramount. Leadership modules focus on skills such as consensus building, conflict resolution, and visionary planning, preparing students to lead decentralized teams and projects.

- **Digital Literacy and Technological Fluency:**
  Future leaders must be fluent in digital technologies that underpin decentralized systems. Comprehensive modules on blockchain, cryptography, and smart contract programming ensure that learners are not only users of technology but innovators capable of advancing the field.

8.4.2 Fostering Community Engagement and Social Innovation

- **Building Local and Global Networks:**
  The framework emphasizes the importance of both local community engagement and global collaboration. Students engage with real-world community issues and partner with local organizations, applying their learning to drive social impact. At the same time, cross-cultural projects connect them with a worldwide network of peers, broadening their perspective on global decentralization challenges.

- **Social Entrepreneurship and Impact Investing:**
  Modules in social entrepreneurship teach learners how to launch ventures that address societal challenges while operating on decentralized models. Impact investing principles are integrated to illustrate how financial returns can coexist with social and environmental benefits.

- **Participatory Governance Models:**
  By studying and simulating participatory governance, learners understand the power of bottom-up decision-making. They explore how collective intelligence and

decentralized organization can drive policy changes and foster inclusive growth, preparing them for roles that involve public engagement and community building.

8.5 Integrative Approaches: Merging the Gemach Pedagogy with Broader Educational Ecosystems

8.5.1 Curriculum Design and Modular Learning

- **Flexible and Adaptive Course Structures:**
  The Gemach Pedagogy advocates for curricula that are flexible and responsive to changes in technology and society. Courses are designed in modular formats, allowing for the rapid integration of new developments in DeFi, blockchain, and decentralized governance.

- **Blended Learning Environments:**
  The framework integrates online and offline educational experiences. Virtual simulations, interactive digital platforms, and in-person workshops collaborate to create a holistic learning environment. This blended approach makes learning accessible, immersive, and directly applicable to real-world scenarios.

- **Project-Based Assessments:**
  Traditional exams and lectures are supplemented by project-based assessments. Students are evaluated on their ability to design, implement, and iterate upon their own decentralized economic models, ensuring that academic learning translates into practical skills and innovative

outcomes.

8.5.2 Partnerships with Industry and Community Organizations

- **Real-World Collaborations:**
  Partnerships with industry leaders, tech startups, and community organizations create avenues for students to engage in live projects. These collaborations enable learners to tackle current challenges using decentralized economic models, gaining practical experience and networking with professionals in the field.

- **Internships and Apprenticeships:**
  To further bridge theory and practice, the Gemach Pedagogy incorporates internship and apprenticeship programs with organizations actively utilizing blockchain and DeFi technologies. Such experiences provide mentorship, on-the-job training, and insights into the daily operations of decentralized systems.

- **Community-Driven Projects:**
  Initiatives that involve the local community—such as cooperative economic projects, social enterprises, or sustainability ventures—allow learners to apply their skills in real-world settings. This not only benefits the community but also instills a deep understanding of the impact of decentralized economic models on societal development.

8.6 Evaluating Impact: Metrics and Continuous Improvement

8.6.1 Measuring Learning Outcomes

- **Quantitative and Qualitative Assessments:**
  The impact of the Gemach Pedagogy is evaluated through a combination of quantitative metrics (such as improved digital literacy scores, project completion rates, and economic indicators from simulated models) and qualitative assessments (such as student reflections, peer reviews, and community feedback).

- **Longitudinal Studies:**
  Tracking the progress of learners over time provides insights into the long-term benefits of the pedagogy. Longitudinal studies can assess how skills acquired during the program translate into real-world success, leadership roles, and innovative contributions to decentralized systems.

- **Feedback Loops in Curriculum Design:**
  Continuous feedback from students, educators, and industry partners is used to refine course content and pedagogical methods. This iterative process ensures that the curriculum remains relevant and adaptive to evolving technologies and economic landscapes.

8.6.2 Assessing Socio-Economic Impact

- **Community Metrics:**
  The effectiveness of decentralized economic models implemented by learners is measured by tracking community-level outcomes such as local job creation, financial inclusion, and social capital development.

- **Project Outcomes:**
  Detailed case studies from pilot projects and community initiatives provide valuable data on the impact of the Gemach Pedagogy. Metrics might include project

sustainability, replicability across different communities, and the ability to attract further investments.

- **Scaling and Replication:**
  Successful implementations are documented and analyzed to develop best practices that can be scaled or adapted to other regions and contexts. This research feeds back into the curriculum, allowing the pedagogical model to evolve based on tangible successes and challenges encountered in the field.

8.7 Challenges and Future Directions

8.7.1 Overcoming Resistance to Change

- **Institutional Inertia:**
  Traditional educational and economic systems can be resistant to change. Implementing the Gemach Pedagogy requires robust strategies to overcome institutional inertia, including advocacy for decentralization, partnerships with forward-thinking organizations, and pilot programs that demonstrate clear benefits.

- **Cultural Shifts:**
  The adoption of decentralized education models necessitates a shift in cultural attitudes—both among educators and learners. Fostering a culture that values experimentation, risk-taking, and open collaboration is essential for the long-term success of the pedagogy.

8.7.2 Technological and Regulatory Challenges

- **Integration with Legacy Systems:**
  Bridging the gap between traditional educational infrastructures and cutting-edge blockchain-based platforms presents technical challenges. Future research and development are needed to create interoperable solutions that integrate seamlessly with existing systems.

- **Regulatory Environment:**
  As decentralized finance continues to evolve, regulatory frameworks will need to adapt. Educators must remain informed about changes in regulations to ensure that the curriculum not only reflects current technological trends but also prepares learners for the legal realities of decentralized systems.

8.7.3 Expanding Global Outreach

- **Digital Divide and Accessibility:**
  Making the Gemach Pedagogy accessible to a global audience, particularly in under-resourced regions, is an ongoing challenge. Efforts to enhance digital literacy, expand internet access, and tailor educational content to local contexts are vital for worldwide adoption.

- **Cross-Cultural Adaptation:**
  While the core principles of the pedagogy are universal, implementation may need to be adapted to reflect local cultural, economic, and social conditions. Collaborative projects with international partners can facilitate culturally sensitive adaptations that resonate with diverse audiences.

- **Scaling Successful Models:**
  Long-term success depends on the ability to replicate and scale pilot projects. Continued research into best practices, partnership with global organizations, and dissemination of findings through open-access platforms will be critical for

scaling the impact of the Gemach Pedagogy.

8.8 Conclusion: Transforming Learning into Action with the Gemach Pedagogy

The Gemach Pedagogy represents a bold reimagining of education—a framework that bridges theoretical knowledge with practical, real-world application using the mechanisms of decentralized finance and collective economic models. By fostering an environment where learners engage in hands-on projects, collaborative decision-making, and iterative feedback, this pedagogical approach not only prepares future leaders for a decentralized future but also drives immediate social and economic transformation.

- **Empowerment Through Participation:**
  At its core, the Gemach Pedagogy empowers learners by giving them a direct stake in the economic systems they are studying and building. This hands-on involvement transforms abstract theories into tangible actions that have real-world impact.

- **A Model for Sustainable Change:**
  Integrating decentralized finance into the learning process prepares students to navigate and innovate within the rapidly evolving digital economy. It equips them with the skills to design resilient, adaptable, and inclusive economic models.

- **A Blueprint for Future Leaders:**
  The approach cultivates critical thinking, practical problem-solving, and collaborative innovation—traits that are essential for leadership in the 21st century. By transforming learning into actionable projects, the Gemach Pedagogy

creates a pipeline of leaders ready to drive systemic change in an increasingly decentralized world.

In summary, Chapter 8 has provided an exhaustive exploration of the Gemach Pedagogy—detailing its theoretical underpinnings, practical methodologies, integration with decentralized finance, and the profound impact it can have on empowering learners and future leaders. Through experiential learning, real-world applications, and continuous adaptation, this pedagogical model not only transforms how we learn but also how we create, share, and sustain value in a global, interconnected, and decentralized economy.

Chapter 9: SydTek DAO – Reimagining Decentralized Governance

SydTek DAO represents a bold experiment in reimagining how educational and institutional governance can operate in a decentralized ecosystem. As a prototype for the future of collective decision-making in academia and organizational structures, SydTek DAO integrates advanced blockchain technology, smart contracts, and participatory governance to disrupt traditional power structures. This chapter offers an exhaustive exploration of SydTek DAO, from its theoretical foundations and architectural design to its practical applications in reconfiguring educational and institutional frameworks. We delve into its mechanisms, potential impacts, challenges, and future directions, demonstrating how decentralizing governance can foster innovation, accountability, and sustainable progress.

9.1 Introduction: The Vision of SydTek DAO

9.1.1 Rethinking Governance in the Digital Age

Traditional educational and institutional governance structures are often hierarchical, centralized, and slow to adapt to change. SydTek DAO rethinks these paradigms by creating a decentralized platform where governance is conducted collectively rather than imposed from the top. This approach promotes transparency and inclusivity and aims to empower all stakeholders—students, educators, administrators, and community members—to have a direct voice in institutional decision-making.

9.1.2 Disrupting Traditional Power Structures

At its core, SydTek DAO challenges the status quo by disrupting established power dynamics. It shifts control from a narrow group of gatekeepers to an expansive community-driven network. This disruption is achieved through open access to governance processes, token-based voting, and the use of smart contracts to ensure that decisions are executed transparently and without intermediary interference. SydTek DAO's model is designed to create a resilient, adaptive, and forward-looking environment that redefines what governance can look like in both educational institutions and broader organizational contexts.

9.1.3 The Imperative for Decentralized Governance in Education and Institutions

Modern educational and institutional challenges—ranging from bureaucratic inefficiencies and underrepresentation to resistance to change—demand innovative solutions. SydTek DAO offers a strategic model to address these issues:

- **Enhanced Accountability:** Every decision, transaction, and policy change is recorded on a public ledger, enabling continuous monitoring and accountability.

- **Inclusive Participation:** A decentralized model invites diverse voices to participate in governance, ensuring that decision-making reflects a broad range of perspectives.

- **Agile Adaptability:** By embracing iterative processes and direct feedback, SydTek DAO allows institutions to rapidly adapt to emerging challenges and opportunities.

- **Empowerment through Ownership:** Stakeholders can earn tokens that represent their contribution and influence, aligning their personal success with the success of the institution.

9.2 The Genesis of SydTek DAO

9.2.1 Historical and Contextual Inspiration

SydTek DAO draws from historical models of cooperative governance and community-based institutions. Examples range from the medieval guilds—where artisans collectively set standards and protected mutual interests—to modern cooperatives that have empowered worker-led organizations. This DAO is an evolutionary leap that combines these time-tested models with cutting-edge blockchain technology, creating an ecosystem that transcends geographical and institutional boundaries.

9.2.2 Founding Principles and Ideological Framework

The ideological underpinnings of SydTek DAO are centered on the belief that:

- **Decentralized Governance Enhances Equity:** Spreading decision-making power avoids concentration in the hands of a few, mitigating issues of corruption and nepotism.

- **Collective Intelligence Drives Innovation:** When every stakeholder contributes ideas and resources, institutions become more creative and responsive to change.

- **Transparency Cultivates Trust:** Open, verifiable decision-making processes replace secrecy with accountability, building long-term trust between institutions and their communities.

- **Resilience is Built on Flexibility:** A decentralized, adaptive approach allows organizations to evolve continuously, turning challenges into opportunities for collective renewal.

9.2.3 Establishing SydTek DAO: From Concept to Prototype

The journey toward launching SydTek DAO involved multidisciplinary collaboration between educators, technologists, and governance experts. Early stages focused on developing a modular digital platform, establishing technical requirements, and engaging pilot communities to test governance protocols. Iterative feedback from these initial experiments helped shape the final design, ensuring that the DAO addressed practical concerns while adhering to its visionary goals.

9.3 Core Architectural Design and Technical Implementation

9.3.1 The Blockchain Backbone

- **Foundation on a Robust Blockchain Protocol:**
  SydTek DAO is built on a scalable and secure blockchain platform that ensures data integrity and supports high transaction throughput. The chosen platform uses a consensus mechanism that balances energy efficiency with security (for instance, a Proof of Stake or a hybrid model).

- **Distributed Ledger Technology:**
  Every decision, vote, and transaction is recorded on the distributed ledger, providing a tamper-proof record that is accessible to all members. This transparency is vital for ensuring accountability and trust within the system.

9.3.2 Smart Contracts and Automated Governance

- **Role of Smart Contracts:**
  Smart contracts automate governance processes, from proposal submission and voting to the execution of decisions. Once conditions specified in a contract are met, the contract self-executes, reducing delays and eliminating manual intervention. This automation is key to maintaining operational efficiency and ensuring that every action is verifiable.

- **Customizable Governance Modules:**
  SydTek DAO deploys modular smart contracts that can be tailored to specific institutional needs—whether for managing educational programs, allocating budgets, or coordinating collaborative projects. These modules enable institutions to experiment with different governance models and adapt

them over time.

- **Security and Auditability:**
  Regular audits, both internal and external, ensure that smart contracts function as intended. This rigorous scrutiny fosters confidence among stakeholders and reinforces the integrity of the decentralized governance system.

9.3.3 Tokenization and Incentive Mechanisms

- **Utility and Governance Tokens:**
  A native token serves dual purposes within SydTek DAO: as a utility token facilitating transactions and as a governance token granting voting power. These tokens are distributed based on participation, contribution, and engagement in the DAO's activities.

- **Incentive Structures:**
  Tokens are not merely symbolic; they carry real economic incentives. Participants can earn tokens through contributions such as proposing projects, voting, participating in discussions, or even engaging in educational initiatives. This incentive mechanism creates a direct link between participation and collective wealth, driving continuous engagement and innovation.

- **Dynamic Token Economies:**
  Mechanisms such as staking, token burning, and dividend distributions ensure that the token economy remains dynamic and reflects the DAO's economic health. For example, staking rewards encourage long-term commitment, while token burning reduces supply, potentially increasing the value of remaining tokens.

9.4 Decentralized Governance Models in SydTek DAO

9.4.1 Participatory Decision-Making

- **Token-Based Voting Systems:**
  Every token holder in SydTek DAO has the right to vote on proposals affecting the institution's direction. Voting power can be designed to reflect not just the number of tokens held but also the quality of participation, ensuring that decisions are made democratically and inclusively.

- **Proposal Submission and Debate:**
  Members can initiate proposals—from funding new initiatives to modifying governance rules. These proposals are then open to robust debate in forums where every voice can be heard, fostering a culture of transparency and collaborative problem-solving.

- **Real-Time Feedback and Iterative Adjustments:**
  The decentralized system incorporates continuous feedback loops. Decisions are monitored in real time, and outcomes are measured against predefined benchmarks. This iterative process allows for dynamic adjustments, ensuring that governance remains responsive to evolving conditions.

9.4.2 Distributed Leadership and Rotational Governance

- **Dynamic Leadership Roles:**
  Instead of static hierarchical positions, SydTek DAO adopts rotational leadership models where roles such as project coordinators or committee heads change periodically. This prevents power consolidation and ensures fresh perspectives are regularly infused into governance

processes.

- **Empowering Local Chapters:**
  The DAO model supports the establishment of localized chapters or regional groups that operate under the broader SydTek governance framework. These chapters manage local initiatives, collaborate on community-specific projects, and funnel their insights back to the central DAO, creating a multi-layered governance structure.

- **Conflict Resolution and Mediation Protocols:**
  In any decentralized system, disagreements can arise. SydTek DAO incorporates built-in mechanisms for conflict resolution—ranging from mediation committees to algorithmic dispute resolution protocols—ensuring that conflicts are addressed swiftly and fairly without undermining the integrity of the system.

9.4.3 Transparency and Accountability in Governance

- **Open Ledger for All Decisions:**
  Every decision taken by the DAO is recorded on a transparent, public ledger accessible to all members. This transparency mitigates the risk of corruption and builds confidence in the system's integrity.

- **Regular Governance Audits:**
  Periodic audits, both by automated tools and independent third parties, help track the performance and fairness of the governance processes. Feedback from these audits is integrated into the DAO's decision-making cycle, ensuring continual improvement.

- **Performance Metrics and Reporting:**
  SydTek DAO employs key performance indicators (KPIs) that measure not only the financial impact of decisions but

also the social and educational outcomes. Comprehensive reports and dashboards enable members to assess the effectiveness of governance initiatives, facilitating data-driven decision-making.

9.5 The Impact of Decentralized Governance on Education and Institutions

9.5.1 Transforming Educational Institutions

- **Decentralized Curriculum Development:**
  SydTek DAO empowers educators and students to co-create curricula that are relevant to contemporary challenges. Decision-making about academic content, teaching methods, and resource allocation is democratized, resulting in courses that are both innovative and adaptive.

- **Student and Faculty Participation:**
  With governance tokens, students, faculty, and even alumni have a vested interest in the institution's direction. This inclusive approach leads to curricula that reflect diverse perspectives, encourage interdisciplinary learning, and adapt swiftly to technological advances.

- **Flexible Resource Allocation:**
  Funds and resources are allocated through transparent, token-based voting systems. This allows for agile adjustments in response to emergent needs—whether funding new research initiatives, modernizing facilities, or supporting community projects within the institution.

9.5.2 Reconfiguring Institutional Governance

- **From Bureaucracy to Direct Democracy:**
  Traditional institutions are often mired in bureaucracy, resulting in slow and opaque decision-making. SydTek DAO's model replaces top-down administrative structures with participatory governance models where stakeholders directly influence policy and operational decisions.

- **Enhanced Community Engagement:**
  The governance model of SydTek DAO fosters active community involvement. Stakeholders are not passive recipients of institutional decisions; they are active co-creators who help shape policies, drive innovation, and monitor outcomes.

- **Sustainable and Inclusive Leadership:**
  By circulating leadership roles and ensuring broad-based participation, institutions can better harness the diverse talents of their communities. This leads to more equitable and sustainable governance practices that continually evolve in response to both internal and external challenges.

9.5.3 Broader Socio-Economic Implications

- **Decentralized Education as a Catalyst for Social Change:**
  Transforming education through decentralized governance has ripple effects throughout society. Graduates from institutions operating under SydTek DAO's model are equipped with a deep understanding of democratic processes, digital literacy, and innovative problem-solving—traits essential for addressing broader socio-economic challenges.

- **Empowering Local Communities:**
 Beyond academic institutions, the DAO model can extend to local governments and community organizations. This framework empowers communities to manage local development projects, optimize resource distribution, and engage in participatory decision-making—fostering local resilience and empowerment.

- **Global Networks of Decentralized Governance:**
 SydTek DAO's approach offers a replicable model for governance that can be adopted in various contexts globally. The creation of interoperable, decentralized networks allows best practices to circulate across borders, driving collective progress on an international scale.

9.6 Evaluating Impact and Fostering Continuous Improvement

9.6.1 Metrics for Success

- **Governance Efficiency and Responsiveness:**
 Key performance indicators (KPIs) are developed to assess how quickly and effectively decisions are made within SydTek DAO. Metrics such as proposal turnaround time, voter participation rates, and the resolution of disputes are monitored to ensure that governance remains agile and effective.

- **Educational Outcomes:**
 In educational contexts, success is measured by evaluating improvements in learning outcomes, student satisfaction, and the ability of curricula to adapt to emerging trends. Surveys, performance metrics, and longitudinal studies help

quantify the impact of decentralized governance on academic excellence.

- **Community and Institutional Growth:**
  Broader impacts are tracked through community engagement metrics, economic indicators (such as local investment and employment rates), and the overall resilience of the institution. These metrics offer a comprehensive view of how decentralized governance contributes to sustainable growth.

9.6.2 Feedback Loops for Iterative Refinement

- **Continuous Monitoring and Reporting:**
  SydTek DAO incorporates a robust system for continuous monitoring, whereby data from governance activities, educational projects, and community initiatives are regularly analyzed. Detailed reports are disseminated among stakeholders, providing a basis for informed adjustments.

- **Adaptive Governance Protocols:**
  The DAO model supports iterative improvement through mechanisms that allow policies and processes to be recalibrated in real time. Stakeholder feedback and real-world outcomes feed back into decision-making protocols, ensuring that the system evolves with changing needs.

- **Collaborative Learning and Best Practices Sharing:**
  Regular workshops, conferences, and online forums facilitate knowledge sharing among DAO participants. By sharing lessons learned, best practices, and innovative ideas, the community continuously refines and improves its governance model.

9.7 Challenges and Future Directions

9.7.1 Overcoming Technical and Cultural Barriers

- **Bridging Legacy Systems and Decentralized Models:**
  One significant challenge is integrating decentralized governance with existing traditional systems, which may be resistant to change. Developing interoperability solutions and providing robust transition frameworks are essential for ensuring a seamless integration.

- **Cultural Shifts and Adoption Challenges:**
  Shifting from hierarchical models to decentralized governance requires a significant cultural change. Resistance from established institutional leaders and stakeholders who benefit from the status quo can impede progress. Comprehensive education, clear communication of benefits, and demonstrable pilot successes are crucial for overcoming this inertia.

9.7.2 Scaling and Global Adaptation

- **Customization for Diverse Contexts:**
  While the SydTek DAO model is designed to be flexible, its successful adoption in diverse cultural and institutional contexts requires careful customization. Future research should focus on identifying the key variables that influence governance efficacy in different regions, ensuring that the model remains universally applicable.

- **Expanding Global Networks:**
  Efforts to foster global collaborations between decentralized institutions can help scale the impact of SydTek DAO. Cross-border partnerships, international governance standards, and shared digital infrastructures will be

instrumental in creating a global digital commons governed by decentralized models.

- **Sustainability and Long-Term Viability:**
  Ensuring that decentralized governance remains sustainable over the long term requires continuous innovation and responsive policymaking. Future developments should prioritize strategies for maintaining high levels of engagement, trust, and adaptability as the system grows in complexity.

9.7.3 Regulatory and Ethical Considerations

- **Navigating Emerging Regulations:**
  As decentralized governance models gain traction, they will face evolving regulatory environments. Policymakers must work collaboratively with decentralized communities to create frameworks that balance innovation with legal safeguards and consumer protections.

- **Maintaining Ethical Standards:**
  With increased transparency and decentralized power, ethical challenges such as data privacy, equitable participation, and conflict of interest must be proactively managed. Establishing ethical guidelines and accountability frameworks will ensure that decentralized governance promotes social justice and fairness.

- **Global Policy Harmonization:**
  The borderless nature of decentralized systems necessitates international cooperation to establish common standards and regulatory approaches. Collaborative efforts among global regulatory bodies, technology experts, and institutional leaders will be critical to harmonizing policies that support decentralized governance.

9.8 Synthesis: The Transformative Potential of SydTek DAO

9.8.1 Redefining Governance Paradigms

SydTek DAO exemplifies a radical departure from conventional governance models by embedding decision-making within a decentralized, participatory framework. It transforms governance from a top-down, opaque process into a transparent, dynamic system where every stakeholder has a tangible influence over institutional policies. This model not only democratizes power but also creates a resilient infrastructure capable of adapting to rapid changes in technology and society.

9.8.2 Integrative Impact Across Sectors

By harmoniously integrating decentralized governance into educational and institutional settings, SydTek DAO paves the way for cross-sectoral innovations. Its influence extends beyond academic institutions to include local governments, community organizations, and even corporate entities seeking to adopt more equitable and responsive governance structures. This integrative impact heralds a future where decentralization fosters a global network of interconnected, self-sustaining communities.

9.8.3 A Blueprint for Future Empowerment

The design, implementation, and operational principles of SydTek DAO offer a comprehensive blueprint for transforming governance in the digital age. Its emphasis on transparency, accountability, and participatory decision-making provides a replicable model that can be tailored to various contexts. By promoting a culture of continuous learning and adaptive improvement, SydTek DAO not only addresses current challenges but also sets the stage for

sustainable, long-term empowerment across socio-economic
domains.

9.9 Conclusion: Embracing Decentralized Governance for a Resilient Future

SydTek DAO stands as a pioneering model for decentralized educational and institutional governance. Through the integration of blockchain technology, smart contracts, tokenized economies, and dynamic participatory processes, it reimagines governance by distributing power and responsibility among all stakeholders. This chapter has explored the genesis, design, and core mechanisms of SydTek DAO in exhaustive detail, demonstrating its potential to disrupt traditional power structures and foster a more equitable, transparent, and adaptive governance ecosystem.

Key takeaways include:

- **A New Paradigm for Decision-Making:** SydTek DAO replaces hierarchical structures with decentralized, participatory governance, ensuring that every voice is heard and that decision-making is informed by collective intelligence.

- **Transparency and Accountability:** Every process within the DAO is recorded on a public ledger, providing an immutable audit trail that reinforces trust and accountability.

- **Empowered Communities:** By democratizing governance, SydTek DAO empowers stakeholders—from students and educators to local community members—to directly participate in shaping policies, managing resources, and driving institutional innovation.

- **Scalable and Adaptable Frameworks:** The modular design and iterative feedback mechanisms of SydTek DAO offer a versatile blueprint that can be adapted to various socio-economic contexts, paving the way for future global networks of decentralized governance.

Looking ahead, the continued evolution of SydTek DAO will depend on overcoming technical, cultural, and regulatory challenges while harnessing emerging innovations. As decentralized governance becomes increasingly relevant in a rapidly changing world, SydTek DAO's model provides an inspiring roadmap for transformative change—one where inclusivity, transparency, and collective empowerment are not just ideals, but the operational principles that drive sustainable progress.

In summary, SydTek DAO is not merely a theoretical construct but a practical embodiment of decentralized governance that has the potential to redefine educational and institutional landscapes. Its design and implementation illustrate how technology can be leveraged to create a fairer, more resilient, and adaptive future—one where power is truly distributed, and every stakeholder can contribute to a shared vision of progress and prosperity.

Chapter 10: Fusion Plasma Physics – Energy Science for Societal Renewal

Fusion plasma physics stands as a frontier science that holds transformative potential for society. As humanity faces unprecedented challenges related to climate change, depleting fossil fuel reserves, and energy insecurity, breakthrough advances in fusion energy promise a clean, abundant, and sustainable energy source. This chapter provides an exhaustive exploration of fusion plasma physics—from its theoretical underpinnings and experimental breakthroughs to its vast socio-economic implications. We will detail how breakthroughs in fusion energy can drive sustainable community development, support decentralized energy models, and serve as a catalyst for societal renewal.

10.1 Introduction: The Promise of Fusion Energy

10.1.1 The Imperative for Sustainable Energy

Humanity's growing energy demand, coupled with the environmental toll of fossil fuels, demands innovative solutions. Fusion energy, which replicates the energy-producing process of the sun, offers the promise of near-limitless, clean power that emits minimal greenhouse gases. As communities worldwide search for sustainable, resilient energy sources, fusion plasma physics emerges as a critical area of research with the potential to transform the global energy landscape.

10.1.2 Vision for Societal Renewal through Energy Breakthroughs

Fusion's potential extends beyond mere energy supply—it represents a paradigm shift in how societies could sustainably support economic development, environmental stewardship, and social equity. By providing a reliable base-load power source, fusion technology can enable decentralized microgrids, reduce dependency on fossil fuels, and stimulate local economies. The vision is one of decentralized empowerment, where advanced energy technology fuels community-led regeneration and societal renewal.

10.2 Theoretical Foundations of Fusion Plasma Physics

10.2.1 Understanding Plasma: The Fourth State of Matter

Plasma, often referred to as the fourth state of matter, is a highly ionized gas consisting of free electrons and ions. Unlike solids, liquids, or gases, plasma is electrically conductive and highly responsive to electromagnetic fields. These properties make it uniquely suited for energy production, as they facilitate the conditions needed for nuclear fusion—where lighter nuclei, such as those of hydrogen, combine to form heavier nuclei, releasing an enormous amount of energy.

10.2.2 Principles of Nuclear Fusion

- **Fusion Reactions and Energy Release:**
  At the core of fusion is the process of combining light atomic nuclei (typically isotopes of hydrogen, like deuterium and tritium) to form a heavier nucleus. This process releases a significant amount of energy, as described by Einstein's equation $E=mc2E=mc^2E=mc2$. The energy yield from fusion far exceeds that of chemical reactions, offering a potent, clean alternative to fossil fuels.

- **Lawson Criterion and Plasma Confinement:**
  Successful fusion requires achieving the necessary conditions of temperature, density, and confinement time,

encapsulated by the Lawson criterion. This principle outlines the minimum requirements for net energy gain, highlighting the need for extremely high temperatures (in excess of 100 million degrees Celsius) to overcome the electrostatic repulsion between positively charged nuclei.

- **Magnetic and Inertial Confinement:**
  To sustain the fusion reaction, plasma must be contained without coming into contact with material surfaces. Two primary methods exist: magnetic confinement (used in devices such as tokamaks and stellarators) and inertial confinement (used in laser-based fusion experiments). Both techniques strive to maintain the necessary conditions for fusion to occur efficiently.

10.2.3 Advancements in Theoretical Modeling

Recent developments in computational physics and simulation techniques have enhanced our understanding of plasma behavior. Advanced models now accurately predict turbulence, instabilities, and energy transport within fusion plasmas. These theoretical advancements are pivotal for optimizing reactor designs and moving closer to achieving net-positive energy output.

10.3 Experimental Breakthroughs and Fusion Energy Projects

10.3.1 The Tokamak and Stellarator Designs

- **Tokamaks:**
  Tokamaks are the most researched fusion reactor designs, utilizing strong magnetic fields generated by toroidal and poloidal coils to confine plasma in a donut-shaped chamber.

Facilities like ITER (International Thermonuclear Experimental Reactor) represent the pinnacle of tokamak-based fusion research, aiming to demonstrate a sustained fusion reaction with net energy gain.

- **Stellarators:**
  Stellarators offer an alternative magnetic confinement approach by twisting the plasma path in a way that minimizes disruptions. Though more complex in design, stellarators like Wendelstein 7-X have shown promising results in stabilizing plasma and reducing turbulent losses.

10.3.2 Inertial Confinement and Laser Fusion

- **Inertial Confinement Fusion (ICF):**
  ICF techniques use high-powered lasers or ion beams to compress and heat small fuel pellets to fusion conditions. The National Ignition Facility (NIF) in the United States is a leading example, where laser-driven fusion experiments aim to achieve ignition—a self-sustaining fusion burn.

- **Comparative Advantages and Challenges:**
  While ICF has demonstrated remarkable progress, it faces challenges in uniform fuel compression and energy efficiency. Nevertheless, the insights gained from ICF research are crucial for understanding plasma physics under extreme conditions.

10.3.3 Private Sector Innovations and Emerging Startups

- **Commercial Fusion Ventures:**
  In recent years, private companies like TAE Technologies, Commonwealth Fusion Systems, and General Fusion have emerged, injecting significant venture capital into fusion

research. These startups are pursuing innovative reactor designs, leveraging advanced materials, AI-driven control systems, and novel magnetic confinement techniques.

- **Acceleration of Research:**
  The competitive energy environment, coupled with collaborative public–private initiatives, has accelerated progress in fusion energy research. These innovations not only aim to shorten the timeline to commercial fusion power but also enhance the viability of fusion as a scalable energy solution.

10.4 Societal Renewal through Fusion Energy

10.4.1 Environmental Impact and Clean Energy Transformation

- **Carbon-Neutral Energy Production:**
  Fusion energy produces no carbon emissions during operation, representing a transformative shift in the global energy mix. Transitioning to fusion could significantly mitigate climate change, reduce air pollution, and contribute to global environmental sustainability.

- **Reduction of Radioactive Waste:**
  Unlike fission reactors, fusion produces minimal long-lived radioactive waste, addressing one of the major concerns associated with nuclear energy. This cleaner energy profile supports the development of sustainable and environmentally responsible energy infrastructures.

10.4.2 Decentralized Energy Systems and Community Empowerment

- **Local Microgrids and Energy Autonomy:**
  Fusion energy has the potential to underpin decentralized energy systems, including local microgrids that can operate independently. Communities could harness fusion-based power to create self-sufficient energy networks, reducing reliance on centralized power plants and enhancing local resilience.

- **Economic and Job Creation Opportunities:**
  The advent of commercial fusion power could stimulate significant economic activity. Investments in fusion research, reactor construction, and supporting infrastructure are likely to generate high-skilled jobs and spur innovation in related sectors, thereby stimulating regional economies.

- **Bridging the Energy Divide:**
  By providing abundant and affordable energy, fusion power can help bridge the energy divide between urban and rural areas and between developed and emerging economies. This democratization of energy access can drive socio-economic development on a global scale.

10.4.3 Integration with Decentralized and Distributed Systems

- **Synergy with Blockchain and DAOs:**
  Fusion energy's role as a stable, abundant power source can synergize with decentralized technologies. For example, the high energy output from fusion reactors could support the operation of large-scale blockchain networks and decentralized autonomous organizations (DAOs) by providing the energy required for their computation and data

processing needs.

- **Supporting Digital Infrastructure:**
  As societies become increasingly digital, the demand for reliable power to support data centers, communication networks, and innovative technologies will grow. Fusion energy could supply this demand sustainably, ensuring that digital infrastructures remain robust and scalable in a decarbonized economy.

10.5 Challenges and Future Directions in Fusion Plasma Physics

10.5.1 Technical and Engineering Obstacles

- **Plasma Stability and Confinement:**
  One of the most formidable challenges is maintaining stable plasma conditions within a reactor. Achieving the necessary confinement and controlling plasma turbulence are critical areas of research that require continual refinement of magnetic field configurations and reactor designs.

- **Materials Science and Reactor Components:**
  Fusion reactors must contend with extreme conditions, including intense heat, neutron bombardment, and electromagnetic forces. Developing materials that can withstand such harsh environments without degrading is vital for the longevity and reliability of fusion reactors.

- **Scaling and Commercial Viability:**
  Transitioning from experimental reactors to commercial-scale fusion power plants involves solving a myriad of engineering, economic, and logistical challenges. Ensuring

that the technology can be scaled cost-effectively while maintaining safety and performance standards remains a central focus of ongoing research.

10.5.2 Research and Innovation Pathways

- **Advances in Superconducting Magnet Technology:** Superconducting magnets are essential for magnetic confinement in fusion reactors. Research into more efficient, high-temperature superconductors could revolutionize reactor design by enabling stronger, more stable magnetic fields with lower energy consumption.

- **Enhanced Computational Simulations:** Leveraging artificial intelligence and advanced simulations can help predict plasma behavior and optimize reactor configurations. These computational tools are critical for accelerating research, reducing costs, and shortening the time to commercial fusion.

- **Global Collaborative Initiatives:** International collaborations, such as ITER, play a pivotal role in pooling resources, knowledge, and expertise. The success of such initiatives depends on sustained global commitment and the sharing of scientific breakthroughs across borders.

10.5.3 Socio-Political and Regulatory Considerations

- **Long-Term Funding and Public–Private Partnerships:** Fusion energy research is capital-intensive and requires long-term investment. Creating frameworks that encourage sustained funding from both public institutions and private investors is essential for progressing from experimental phases to commercial deployment.

- **Regulatory Hurdles and Safety Standards:**
  Establishing clear regulatory frameworks that ensure the
  safety and environmental sustainability of fusion reactors is
  critical. Regulatory bodies must work closely with
  researchers and industry stakeholders to develop standards
  that are both rigorous and conducive to innovation.

- **Global Energy Policy Integration:**
  As fusion energy moves closer to commercial viability,
  integrating it into national and international energy policies
  will be crucial. Coordinated policy efforts can help drive the
  transition to a decarbonized, sustainable energy future.

10.6 Fusion Energy and Community Renewal: A Vision for the Future

10.6.1 Building Sustainable, Resilient Communities

- **Local Energy Independence:**
  Fusion power can be the cornerstone of local energy grids
  that provide communities with reliable, affordable, and
  sustainable power. With decentralized microgrids powered
  by fusion energy, communities can achieve energy
  autonomy, enhance resilience against outages, and reduce
  dependence on centralized, often insecure, energy supplies.

- **Economic Revitalization:**
  Access to abundant and affordable fusion energy can
  stimulate local economic growth by lowering operational
  costs for businesses and reducing energy poverty. This
  economic revitalization can further translate into improved

public services, enhanced infrastructure, and a more vibrant local economy.

- **Empowering Social Transformation:**
  The accessibility of clean energy fosters not only economic but also social transformation. When communities are empowered with reliable energy, they can invest in education, healthcare, and social innovation. Fusion energy thus becomes a catalyst for broader societal regeneration, driving progress on multiple fronts.

10.6.2 Enabling a Green Digital Economy

- **Sustainable Digital Infrastructure:**
  The increasing digitalization of society requires vast amounts of energy to sustain data centers, artificial intelligence, and blockchain networks. Fusion energy can provide the necessary power in an environmentally sustainable manner, ensuring that the growth of digital technologies does not exacerbate climate change.

- **Decentralized Innovation Ecosystems:**
  By integrating fusion energy with decentralized digital infrastructures, a green digital economy can emerge where economic, environmental, and technological benefits are harmoniously aligned. The fusion-powered digital ecosystem promotes innovation by reducing the barriers to entry for emerging technologies and supporting open, distributed collaboration.

10.6.3 A Blueprint for Global Transformation

- **Interconnected Microgrids and Global Energy Networks:**
  Fusion technology can serve as the backbone for interconnected microgrids, linking local communities to form

resilient, decentralized energy networks on a global scale. Such systems enhance energy security, facilitate cross-border collaboration, and ensure equitable access to power.

- **Catalyzing Sustainable Development:**
  By providing clean and abundant energy, fusion plasma physics underpins sustainable development goals—addressing issues like climate change, resource scarcity, and social inequity. The integration of fusion with decentralized technologies offers a comprehensive blueprint for reshaping the global energy landscape.

- **Empowering Future Leaders:**
  Fusion energy research not only drives technological innovation but also inspires the next generation of scientists, engineers, and policymakers. By embedding fusion energy in educational curricula and community projects, society nurtures a cadre of future leaders dedicated to sustainable progress and collective empowerment.

10.7 Conclusion: Fusion Plasma Physics as a Catalyst for Societal Renewal

Fusion plasma physics stands as a beacon of transformative potential, offering a path toward a future powered by clean, abundant, and sustainable energy. This chapter has provided an exhaustive exploration of fusion plasma physics—from its core theoretical concepts and experimental breakthroughs to its far-reaching impacts on society. The key takeaways include:

- **A Scientific Paradigm Shift:**
  Understanding plasma as the fourth state of matter and the principles of nuclear fusion opens new horizons for energy

generation. The advances in plasma confinement, fusion reaction optimization, and computational simulations offer a promising route to commercial fusion energy.

- **Economic and Environmental Transformation:**
  Fusion technology provides a solution to some of the most pressing global challenges, such as climate change and energy insecurity. By offering a carbon-neutral, virtually limitless energy source, fusion can drive sustainable community development, power decentralized economies, and facilitate global collaboration on renewable energy initiatives.

- **Catalyzing Societal Renewal:**
  The integration of fusion energy into local and global energy infrastructures has the potential to empower communities, stimulate local economies, and foster environmental stewardship. The deployment of fusion-powered microgrids and digital infrastructure can transform urban and rural landscapes, reducing energy poverty and enabling a more equitable distribution of resources.

- **A Blueprint for the Future:**
  The convergence of fusion plasma physics with decentralized governance and digital innovation represents a holistic approach to sustainable development. This blueprint not only aims to revolutionize the energy sector but also serves as the foundation for a resilient, inclusive, and adaptive socio-economic ecosystem.

In conclusion, fusion plasma physics is more than an emerging scientific field—it is a catalyst for societal renewal. By harnessing the power of fusion, humanity can unlock a future characterized by clean energy, economic empowerment, and global sustainability. As research continues to advance and commercial fusion reactors move closer to reality, the transformative potential of fusion will increasingly shape not only our energy policies but also our collective ability to foster community-led growth and sustainable progress. Fusion plasma physics thus offers a compelling vision for a future where technological breakthroughs and decentralized models converge to create a more resilient, equitable, and prosperous society.

Part III: Integrating Science, Cosmology, and Metaphysics

Chapter 11: Cosmology as a Metaphor for Systemic Interconnectedness

Cosmology—the scientific study of the origin, evolution, and structure of the universe—offers a profound metaphor for understanding decentralized societal models. Just as the universe is a complex, interconnected web of systems in dynamic equilibrium, modern societies are evolving toward structures characterized by distributed networks, resilience through diversity, and emergent order. This chapter explores the parallels between cosmology and decentralized systems, highlighting themes such as interconnectedness, balance, emergence, and the continual evolution of systems. By drawing on cosmological principles, we aim to illuminate a framework for systemic interconnectedness in human organizations and social structures.

11.1 The Universe as a Complex System

11.1.1 The Structure of the Cosmos

- **Hierarchical Complexity:**
  The universe is structured hierarchically, from subatomic particles and atoms to planets, solar systems, galaxies, and eventually clusters of galaxies. Each level of organization is both autonomous and interdependent, forming a nested system where micro-level phenomena influence and shape macro-level behaviors.

- **Interconnected Networks:**
  At every scale, the universe exhibits networks of interactions. Gravitational forces, electromagnetic fields, and quantum entanglement weave an intricate tapestry of connectivity. This interconnectedness ensures that no entity exists in isolation but is part of a broader, continuously interacting whole.

- **Dynamic Equilibrium:**
  Despite its vastness and apparent randomness, the cosmos is governed by fundamental laws (e.g., gravity, conservation of energy) that maintain balance and order. Galaxies rotate, stars form and collapse, and cosmic events occur in cycles that contribute to a stable, if dynamic, universe.

11.1.2 Principles of Emergence and Self-Organization

- **Emergent Phenomena:**
  In cosmology, emergent phenomena refer to complex patterns and structures that arise from simple interactions at lower scales. For instance, the spiral arms of galaxies emerge from gravitational interactions among stars and gas

clouds without a central directive force.

- **Self-Organization:**
  Systems in the universe, such as the formation of galaxies or the emergence of planetary systems, are examples of self-organizing processes. These phenomena illustrate how complex, ordered structures can develop naturally from initial chaos, guided by underlying principles and feedback loops.

- **Analogies for Society:**
  Similar processes occur in human societies. Decentralized communities often develop robust social, economic, and cultural systems through bottom-up initiatives, emergent from the collective actions of individuals interacting within a complex network. Just as the cosmos organizes itself, societal structures can evolve organically through distributed governance and adaptive leadership.

11.2 Cosmology as a Metaphor for Decentralized Societal Models

11.2.1 Interconnectedness and Mutual Influence

- **Quantum Entanglement and Social Networks:**
  Quantum entanglement—where particles become interconnected such that the state of one instantly influences the state of another—serves as a powerful metaphor for social networks. In decentralized societies, individual actions can have far-reaching impacts, much like the entangled states in the universe. This metaphor underscores the idea that every person or community is interlinked, forming a web of mutual influence and responsibility.

- **Feedback Loops in the Cosmos and Society:**
  Just as feedback loops in natural systems regulate the behavior of stars and galaxies, feedback mechanisms in decentralized societies help maintain balance and drive adaptation. Social feedback occurs through democratic processes, community evaluations, and continuous learning—mechanisms that ensure resilience and steady evolution.

- **Network Theory and Cosmic Webs:**
  The large-scale structure of the universe is often described as a cosmic web—a network of filaments connecting galaxies and clusters through vast voids. This concept mirrors the idea of decentralized networks in society, where nodes (communities, organizations, individuals) are interconnected, forming resilient networks that can adapt and evolve as a whole.

11.2.2 Systemic Balance and Equilibrium

- **Equilibrium in Physical Systems:**
  The universe achieves a dynamic balance through a constant interplay of forces—gravitational collapse is balanced by thermal pressure, while the expansion of space is countered by gravitational attraction among matter. This systemic balance ensures stability over cosmological timescales.

- **Decentralized Governance and Equitable Systems:**
  In decentralized societal models, systemic balance is achieved by distributing power and resources equitably. Rather than power being concentrated in a single authority, decisions emerge from the collective interactions of stakeholders. This balance creates robust systems that can absorb shocks and adapt to change, much like the equilibria

observed in cosmology.

- **Sustainable Feedback and Self-Regulation:**
 Just as the universe self-regulates through feedback processes, decentralized systems can be designed to incorporate self-regulatory mechanisms. For example, in blockchain-based governance, smart contracts and DAOs (Decentralized Autonomous Organizations) act as automated agents to enforce rules and facilitate adjustments, ensuring that the system remains balanced and sustainable.

11.2.3 Emergence and Adaptation in Societal Evolution

- **From Chaos to Order:**
 The early universe, initially a hot, dense state of chaos, evolved into an organized expanse of galaxies and cosmic structures. This transformation, driven by natural laws and emergent properties, is analogous to how societies can evolve from disorganized collectives into structured, resilient communities.

- **Learning and Evolutionary Processes:**
 Just as cosmic evolution is a process of trial, error, and adaptation, decentralized societies evolve through feedback, learning, and continuous improvement. Failures and setbacks are not endpoints but opportunities for reorganization and regeneration—a cyclical process that drives long-term progress.

- **Flexible Structures and Adaptive Capacities:**
 The cosmos is characterized by flexible, adaptive structures that can evolve over time. Similarly, decentralized models in society promote flexibility by encouraging iterative innovation and continuous adaptation to new challenges, ensuring that

the system remains resilient in the face of change.

11.3 Applying Cosmological Insights to Societal Design

11.3.1 Designing for Interconnected Resilience

- **Networked Governance Models:**
  Drawing on the metaphor of the cosmic web, modern governance systems can be designed as interconnected networks rather than isolated hierarchies. Such models emphasize the interdependence of different societal nodes and the importance of maintaining a robust communication infrastructure.

- **Decentralization and Distributed Decision-Making:**
  In a universe where no single force dominates, decentralized decision-making reflects the balance of power among diverse actors. Designing institutions with distributed governance—where power is shared through tokens, participatory voting, and local councils—mirrors the balance observed in natural systems.

- **Adaptive Infrastructure and Dynamic Feedback:**
  Incorporating dynamic feedback loops into governance structures ensures that communities can adapt to emerging challenges. For instance, continuous monitoring systems, real-time data analytics, and iterative policy adjustments create an environment of self-regulation similar to the feedback mechanisms that stabilize cosmic structures.

11.3.2 Fostering a Culture of Collective Interconnectedness

- **Education and Citizen Engagement:**
  Educating citizens about the interconnected nature of modern society—drawing parallels with the vast, interdependent universe—can inspire more thoughtful, collaborative civic engagement. By fostering an understanding of how individual actions contribute to collective outcomes, societies can cultivate a sense of shared responsibility and unity.

- **Technology as a Bridging Tool:**
  Digital platforms, particularly those based on decentralized protocols, can serve as the connective tissue linking disparate communities. These technologies enable the seamless exchange of information, resources, and ideas, reinforcing the interconnectedness that is vital for a resilient society.

- **Art and Cultural Narratives:**
  Art and literature have the power to convey complex ideas through evocative metaphors. By incorporating cosmological themes into cultural narratives—such as exhibitions, public installations, and digital storytelling—societies can internalize the principle of interconnectedness, fostering a collective identity that values collaboration and mutual support.

11.3.3 Systemic Thinking and Holistic Policy Design

- **Policy-Making Inspired by Cosmic Laws:**
  Just as the universe operates according to fundamental laws of physics, effective public policies should be based on clear, consistent principles that promote stability and growth. Systemic thinking, informed by cosmological metaphors, can

guide the development of policies that are adaptive, resilient, and equitable.

- **Interdisciplinary Research and Collaborative Approaches:**
  Addressing complex societal challenges requires insights from multiple disciplines—much like understanding the cosmos necessitates the integration of astrophysics, quantum mechanics, and cosmology. Encouraging interdisciplinary research and collaboration across sectors can lead to more robust, innovative policy solutions.

- **Scaling Local Innovations into Global Frameworks:**
  The universal nature of cosmic laws suggests that principles of interconnectedness and self-regulation are applicable on multiple scales. Successful local initiatives can be scaled up and integrated into broader governance frameworks, creating a global network of resilient, decentralized communities that work together toward common goals.

11.4 Challenges and Limitations of the Metaphor

11.4.1 The Risk of Over-Analogizing

- **Limits of the Metaphor:**
  While cosmology provides powerful insights, it is essential to recognize that the universe and human society operate in fundamentally different domains. The laws of physics are immutable and universal, whereas social systems are influenced by human behavior, culture, and individual agency. Overextending the metaphor without acknowledging these differences can lead to oversimplified models that fail

to capture the complexity of societal dynamics.

- **Balancing Scientific Rigor with Metaphorical Insight:**
  It is crucial to balance the poetic imagery of cosmology with the pragmatic requirements of policy and governance. While the metaphor can inspire innovative approaches, concrete solutions must also be grounded in social science, economics, and political theory.

11.4.2 Navigating Complexity and Uncertainty

- **Complexity in Social Systems:**
  Human societies are characterized by layers of complexity—emotional, cultural, economic, and political—that do not have direct analogs in cosmology. Translating cosmological principles into actionable social policies requires careful navigation of this multifaceted complexity.

- **Dynamic and Evolving Systems:**
  Unlike the relatively stable physical laws governing the universe, societal systems are dynamic and subject to rapid change. This variability necessitates flexible, adaptive approaches that can respond to unexpected shifts in behavior and external conditions.

11.5 Future Directions: Integrating Cosmological Metaphors into Decentralized Systems

11.5.1 Enhancing Systemic Interconnectedness through Technology

- **Leveraging Decentralized Digital Platforms:**
  As emerging technologies—such as blockchain, Internet of Things (IoT), and AI—continue to evolve, they offer unprecedented opportunities to enhance the interconnectedness of societal systems. These technologies can create integrated networks that mirror the cosmic web, enabling distributed governance and resource-sharing on a global scale.

- **Developing Interoperable Systems:**
  Future research should focus on creating interoperable frameworks that allow disparate decentralized systems to communicate and collaborate seamlessly. Such integration will enable a more coordinated approach to addressing global challenges, from climate change to economic inequality.

11.5.2 Educational and Cultural Initiatives

- **Incorporating Cosmology into Education:**
  Embedding cosmological concepts into educational curricula can help students develop systemic thinking and appreciate the interconnectedness of natural and social systems. Courses that bridge astrophysics, philosophy, and socio-economic theory can inspire new generations of leaders to approach problems with a holistic, multidisciplinary mindset.

- **Promoting Cultural Narratives of Interconnectedness:**
  Art, literature, and media are powerful tools for conveying the message of interconnectedness. Initiatives that highlight cosmological themes in culture—such as public art projects, science festivals, and digital storytelling platforms—can help embed these principles into the collective consciousness.

11.5.3 Policy and Governance Innovations

- **Designing Adaptive Governance Structures:**
  Future governance models can draw on the concept of
  dynamic equilibrium from cosmology, designing systems that
  automatically adjust to changing conditions. These adaptive
  governance structures would incorporate continuous
  feedback loops, ensuring that policies evolve in response to
  real-time data and community input.

- **Fostering Global Collaboration:**
  Integrating cosmological metaphors into international policy
  frameworks can promote the idea of a global digital
  commons—a network of interconnected, resilient
  communities working toward shared goals. Establishing
  international standards and collaborative initiatives will be
  vital for scaling the principles of systemic
  interconnectedness to a global level.

11.6 Synthesis: The Value of Cosmology in Shaping Decentralized Societies

11.6.1 Bridging the Macro and Micro Perspectives

- **A Unified Vision:**
  Cosmology teaches us that the macro-level structure of the
  universe and the micro-level interactions within it are deeply
  interwoven. Similarly, decentralized societal models require
  a unified vision that connects individual actions to larger
  systemic outcomes. This interconnected perspective is
  essential for creating systems that are both robust and
  flexible.

- **Holistic System Design:**
  By embracing the lessons of cosmology, policymakers, educators, and technologists can design systems that incorporate both bottom-up and top-down influences, ensuring that every element—from individual behavior to global networks—contributes to systemic balance and sustainability.

11.6.2 Cultivating a Resilient, Interconnected Future

- **Resilience Through Diversity and Adaptation:**
  The universe's diversity and capacity for regeneration serve as compelling metaphors for the resilience of decentralized societies. By fostering diversity in participation, ideas, and methods, communities can create adaptable systems that withstand and evolve in the face of uncertainty.

- **Visionary Leadership and Collective Empowerment:**
  The cosmic view of interconnectedness inspires a leadership model that values collaboration over hierarchy. Future leaders can harness this vision to build inclusive, participatory systems that empower every stakeholder to contribute to a shared, sustainable future.

11.7 Conclusion: Cosmology as a Guiding Metaphor for Systemic Interconnectedness

Cosmology offers an expansive and awe-inspiring metaphor for understanding the deep interconnectedness of all systems—natural, social, and economic. The structure of the universe, with its intricate networks, dynamic balance, and emergent phenomena, provides a compelling framework for rethinking decentralized societal models. By drawing parallels between cosmic processes and human interactions, we gain valuable insights into how decentralized, adaptive, and self-organizing systems can drive sustainable progress.

This chapter has explored the following key themes:

- **Interconnected Complexity:** Just as galaxies and subatomic particles are interlinked in a vast, dynamic network, decentralized societies thrive on robust connections and continuous feedback, ensuring that every action has a ripple effect throughout the system.

- **Dynamic Equilibrium:** The balance observed in the cosmos—where opposing forces coexist in harmony—serves as a metaphor for creating social and economic systems that are resilient, self-regulating, and capable of adapting to change.

- **Emergence and Self-Organization:** By understanding how complex structures emerge from simple, local interactions, we can design decentralized governance models that harness collective intelligence and adapt spontaneously to challenges.

- **Holistic Vision:** Integrating cosmological metaphors into societal design fosters a holistic vision where every component, from individual behavior to global policy, is viewed as an integral part of a larger, interconnected whole.

Looking ahead, the integration of cosmological insights into the design of decentralized systems can inspire innovations across technology, governance, education, and community development. As emerging technologies continue to blur the boundaries between the digital and physical worlds, a systemic perspective grounded in the lessons of cosmology will be essential for building resilient, interconnected societies capable of navigating the complexities of the 21st century and beyond.

In summary, cosmology not only illuminates the marvels of the universe but also offers a powerful metaphor for systemic interconnectedness in human society. By embracing these insights, we can foster a future where decentralized models not only mimic the balance and harmony of the cosmos but also empower communities to thrive in an ever-changing, interconnected world.

Chapter 12: Metaphysics & the Nature of Empowerment

Metaphysics, as the branch of philosophy exploring the fundamental nature of reality, identity, and existence, provides a profound foundation for understanding transformation and human empowerment in complex systems. By examining abstract concepts that lie beyond the physical realm, metaphysics offers insights into how individuals and communities can harness their inner potential to enact transformative change. This chapter delves into the metaphysical underpinnings of empowerment, exploring theories of transformation, identity, and human agency. By integrating philosophical perspectives with the dynamics of complex systems, we provide a comprehensive framework that deepens our understanding of how transformative change is both internally generated and externally realized. In doing so, we establish a robust philosophical basis for empowerment that transcends conventional materialist perspectives, positioning human agency as a fundamental force capable of reshaping societal structures.

12.1 The Metaphysical Landscape: Foundations of Reality and Being

12.1.1 Defining Metaphysics and Its Scope

- **What Is Metaphysics?**
  Metaphysics is concerned with the ultimate nature of reality, questioning what exists beyond the empirical and observable. It asks profound questions such as "What is the nature of being?" "What does it mean to exist?" and "What is the essence of transformation?" By addressing these questions, metaphysics lays the groundwork for understanding deeper dimensions of human experience and systemic change.

- **Philosophical Traditions in Metaphysics:**
  Traditions ranging from classical Greek thought (e.g., Plato's Theory of Forms and Aristotle's substance theory) to Eastern philosophies (e.g., Taoism and Vedanta) have shaped our understanding of the metaphysical realm. These schools of thought offer a variety of perspectives on how change, permanence, and identity interact, providing diverse lenses through which to view human empowerment.

12.1.2 Transformation: From Potentiality to Actuality

- **The Aristotelian Concept of Potentiality and Actuality:**
  Aristotle's distinction between potentiality (dynamis) and actuality (energeia) is a cornerstone of metaphysical thought on change. Potentiality represents the inherent capacity within a being or system for transformation, while actuality is the realized state of being. Empowerment, in this view, is the process of actualizing latent potential through deliberate action and self-realization.

- **Process Philosophy and Becoming:**
  Process philosophy, articulated by thinkers such as Alfred North Whitehead, posits that reality is in a constant state of flux—a perpetual process of becoming. This view aligns with the idea that transformation is an ongoing journey rather than a static event. In the context of empowerment, individuals and communities are seen as dynamic entities that continuously evolve through relationships and experiences, constantly moving from potentiality to new actualities.

- **Transmutation and Alchemical Metaphors:**
  Alchemy, with its symbolic quest to transform base elements into gold, serves as a powerful metaphor for personal and societal transformation. In metaphysical terms, alchemy represents the journey of inner transformation—transmuting inner lead into spiritual gold. This allegory underscores that empowerment involves internal changes that mirror external successes, suggesting that true change begins within.

12.2 Identity and Selfhood: The Metaphysics of the Personal and the Collective

12.2.1 The Nature of Identity in Metaphysical Thought

- **Essential vs. Constructed Identity:**
  Metaphysical inquiries into identity often address the tension between what is essential (the immutable core of a being) and what is constructed (the narrative and relational aspects that shape selfhood). Empowerment involves recognizing

one's essential nature while engaging in the creative act of self-construction—a process that allows individuals and communities to redefine themselves beyond imposed limitations.

- **Phenomenology and the Experience of Self:**
  Phenomenological approaches, as advanced by Edmund Husserl and later by Maurice Merleau-Ponty, emphasize the lived experience of being. Identity is not merely an abstract quality but is dynamically woven through interactions with the world. This perspective illustrates that empowerment is experiential, emerging from the continuous interplay between inner consciousness and external reality.

- **Narrative Identity and Transformative Storytelling:**
  The stories we tell about ourselves are key to shaping our identities. Metaphysics recognizes that narrative identity— our self-conception crafted through personal and collective stories—is malleable. Empowerment, therefore, is intimately connected with the ability to re-narrate our lives, to reinterpret past experiences, and to forge a new vision that aligns with our highest aspirations.

12.2.2 Collective Identity and Social Empowerment

- **Interpersonal and Communal Dimensions:**
  Beyond individual identity, metaphysical exploration extends to collective identity—the shared sense of self that emerges within communities. Empowerment is not only about personal transformation; it is also about cultivating a collective consciousness that celebrates diversity, fosters mutual understanding, and channels collective energy into societal change.

- **The Role of Community in Shaping Identity:**
  Communities function as both mirrors and molds for

individual identity. A community that embraces inclusive values and collective growth creates a nurturing environment where members can explore and expand their identities. Metaphysically, this communal process can be seen as a microcosm of the universe's dynamic, interconnected structure, reinforcing that the empowerment of the individual is inseparable from the empowerment of the collective.

- **Transcending Fragmentation:**
  Modern societies often grapple with fragmentation—social, cultural, and political divisions that hinder collective progress. Metaphysical frameworks suggest that a deeper, more unified mode of identity is possible, one that transcends superficial differences. This holistic identity can serve as a foundation for collective empowerment, allowing disparate groups to unite under common principles of justice, creativity, and shared destiny.

12.3 Human Agency in Complex Systems: Metaphysical Perspectives on Empowerment

12.3.1 The Power of Will and Conscious Choice

- **Volition and the Act of Becoming:**
  Metaphysics considers human agency as a manifestation of the will—an inner force that drives individuals to transform themselves and their circumstances. Empowerment is fundamentally about reclaiming and activating this inherent agency. Through conscious choice, individuals can chart a path that actualizes their potential, shaping both their inner

landscape and external realities.

- **Existential Freedom and Responsibility:**
  Existentialist thinkers like Jean-Paul Sartre emphasize that humans are condemned to be free; that is, every individual possesses the freedom to choose and, with that freedom, the responsibility for shaping their life. This perspective reinforces the idea that true empowerment involves embracing the burden and beauty of freedom—recognizing that every decision contributes to the ongoing process of self-creation and societal transformation.

- **Agency in the Face of Complexity:**
  Complex systems—whether in nature, society, or the cosmos—are composed of interdependent and dynamic components. Metaphysically, agency means exercising the power to influence these systems despite their inherent complexity. It involves adaptive learning, innovative problem-solving, and the ability to navigate uncertainty with confidence and determination.

12.3.2 Beyond Determinism: Possibility and Potential in Human Action

- **Rejecting Fixed Outcomes:**
  Metaphysics challenges deterministic views of human existence by positing that the future is not preordained but is open to continuous reinterpretation and change. This open-ended view underscores the potential for human agency to defy conventional constraints, breaking free from historical or systemic limitations to create new possibilities.

- **Emergence and Spontaneity in Agency:**
  Similar to emergent phenomena in complex systems, human agency can produce unpredictable and creative outcomes. This spontaneity is not random but is informed by

a deep interaction between internal motivations and external influences. Through emergent processes, individuals and communities can generate innovative solutions that transcend linear reasoning.

- **The Role of Intuition and Insight:**
  Metaphysical inquiry also recognizes the role of intuition—the ability to perceive connections and patterns that are not immediately apparent. This intuitive dimension of agency is crucial for transformative leadership, where insights often precede rational explanations. Cultivating such intuitive capacities can empower individuals to act boldly and create meaningful change.

12.4 Metaphysics and Empowerment: A Synthesis of Theory and Practice

12.4.1 Integrating Metaphysical Insights into Empowerment Frameworks

- **Bridging the Material and the Spiritual:**
  Empowerment is both a material and a spiritual process. Metaphysical insights help bridge these dimensions by providing a framework in which physical actions (e.g., policy changes, technological innovations) are infused with deeper meaning and purpose. This integration fosters holistic empowerment, where economic, social, and spiritual growth are mutually reinforcing.

- **Creating Transformative Narratives:**
  The metaphysical approach emphasizes the power of narrative in shaping reality. By reinterpreting personal and

collective histories through a metaphysical lens, individuals can reframe their challenges and envision new futures. These transformative narratives become the driving force behind systemic change, turning setbacks into catalysts for growth.

- **Embodied Empowerment and Holistic Well-Being:**
  Empowerment extends beyond intellectual understanding— it is also embodied. Metaphysical perspectives suggest that true transformation involves changes in consciousness, identity, and behavior. Practices such as mindfulness, contemplative meditation, and creative expression are seen as essential for aligning one's inner world with the outer actions required for societal renewal.

12.4.2 Practical Applications of Metaphysical Empowerment

- **Educational Innovations:**
  Integrating metaphysical concepts into educational curricula can foster a deeper sense of purpose among students. Courses in philosophy, ethics, and transformative leadership can equip learners with the tools to navigate complex systems and exercise their agency effectively. Such educational models emphasize critical reflection, self-awareness, and creative problem-solving.

- **Community Transformation Projects:**
  At the community level, metaphysical empowerment is translated into practical initiatives that foster collective well-being. Community workshops, narrative therapy groups, and cultural festivals that celebrate shared identities and collective aspirations can strengthen social bonds and empower local action.

- **Organizational Change and Adaptive Leadership:**
  In the realm of organizational governance, adopting metaphysical perspectives can lead to a more humane and flexible leadership style. Leaders who embrace these ideas tend to prioritize collaborative decision-making, ethical considerations, and long-term well-being over short-term gains, paving the way for more resilient and responsive institutions.

12.4.3 The Role of Art, Literature, and Ritual in Metaphysical Empowerment

- **Artistic Expression as a Vehicle for Transformation:**
  Art and literature have long served as mirrors to the human condition and instruments of change. Metaphysical themes in art—such as the exploration of identity, transformation, and transcendence—can inspire individuals to realize their inherent potential. Creative endeavors provide a language through which complex metaphysical ideas become accessible and actionable.

- **Rituals and Symbolic Practices:**
  Rituals play a key role in bridging the metaphysical and the everyday. Ceremonies, community gatherings, and symbolic acts can reinforce a collective sense of purpose and mark transitions in personal or communal life. By embedding these practices in the social fabric, communities create habitual structures that support ongoing empowerment.

- **Narrative Traditions and Myth-Making:**
  The stories and myths that cultures preserve carry deep metaphysical significance. These narratives not only provide a sense of continuity and identity but also inspire future generations to aspire toward higher ideals. Revitalizing these traditions can serve as a powerful catalyst for social and

individual transformation.

12.5 Challenges and Future Directions in Metaphysical Empowerment

12.5.1 Overcoming Reductionist Materialism

- **Integrating Holistic Perspectives:**
  One of the greatest challenges is overcoming the dominant reductionist view that reduces human existence solely to material and biological processes. Elevating metaphysical perspectives requires challenging entrenched paradigms and promoting interdisciplinary dialogue among scientists, philosophers, and educators.

- **Balancing Empirical and Experiential Knowledge:**
  Empowerment initiatives must navigate the balance between empirical, data-driven approaches and the subjective, experiential knowledge that metaphysics emphasizes. Future research in empowerment must integrate rigorous empirical studies with qualitative insights that capture the nuanced human experience.

12.5.2 Fostering Resilient and Adaptive Communities

- **Empowering Through Self-Knowledge:**
  Metaphysical empowerment emphasizes self-knowledge and inner transformation as precursors to external change. Cultivating environments where individuals feel safe to explore their inner landscapes is critical for initiating broader social transformation.

- **Responsive Institutional Frameworks:**
  Institutions must adopt adaptive frameworks that allow for continuous evolution based on metaphysical insights. This may involve iterative policy development, inclusive leadership structures, and mechanisms for regular reflection and feedback.

- **Global Interconnectedness and Cultural Sensitivity:**
  As empowerment strategies spread globally, they must be sensitive to cultural differences and contextual realities. Integrating metaphysical approaches into diverse cultural settings requires dialogue, adaptability, and a commitment to inclusivity.

12.5.3 Future Research and Interdisciplinary Collaboration

- **Bridging Disciplines:**
  Advancing metaphysical empowerment necessitates collaboration across multiple fields—philosophy, neuroscience, sociology, and systems theory. Interdisciplinary research initiatives can generate new insights into how human agency and transformation operate in complex systems.

- **Innovative Educational Models:**
  Pilot programs and experimental curricula that integrate metaphysical concepts into mainstream education will provide valuable data on the efficacy of these approaches. Longitudinal studies can track the impact of such educational innovations on personal development and societal transformation.

- **Technological Integration:**
  Emerging technologies, such as virtual reality and AI, can create immersive experiences that bring metaphysical

concepts to life. Future research may explore how these technologies can facilitate deeper engagement with ideas of identity, transformation, and empowerment.

12.6 Synthesis: Toward a New Paradigm of Human Empowerment

12.6.1 Holistic Interconnectedness of Mind, Society, and the Cosmos

- **Interweaving the Physical and the Metaphysical:**
  The metaphysical foundation for empowerment posits that true transformation arises when the inner life of the individual is aligned with the outer processes of society. Just as the cosmos is defined by interconnectedness and balance, human empowerment is achieved through the integration of personal growth, collective action, and ethical leadership.

- **Emergent Order from Individual Agency:**
  Metaphysical empowerment acknowledges that the cumulative actions of individuals—each exercising their free will and agency—can lead to emergent, transformative changes in society. This bottom-up approach complements top-down institutional reforms, creating a dynamic synergy that drives sustainable progress.

12.6.2 Redefining Identity and Empowerment in Complex Systems

- **Fluid and Evolving Identities:**
  Empowerment in a metaphysical context is deeply

connected to the notion of fluid identity. Rather than seeing identity as fixed, metaphysical approaches celebrate the dynamic evolution of self, allowing individuals to transcend limiting labels and reimagine their potential.

- **Collective Empowerment through Shared Narratives:**
  By harnessing the power of shared myths, cultural traditions, and collective storytelling, communities can build resilient, interconnected identities that foster mutual support and shared ambitions.

- **Empowering the Individual and the Collective:**
  True empowerment occurs when individual agency is recognized within the framework of collective well-being. Integrating metaphysical insights with decentralized governance and participatory models creates an environment where every person contributes to and benefits from systemic transformation.

12.6.3 A Vision for the Future: Empowerment as a Lifelong, Adaptive Process

- **Continuous Transformation:**
  The journey of empowerment is perpetual—an ongoing process of learning, adapting, and evolving. Metaphysical empowerment teaches that every challenge is an opportunity for growth and every setback a chance to regenerate. This perspective reinforces a lifelong commitment to personal and collective transformation.

- **A Blueprint for New Societal Models:**
  Drawing on metaphysical principles, future societal models can be designed to support both personal and communal renewal. Integrating insights from transformational philosophy, decentralized governance, and adaptive leadership, new frameworks of empowerment will foster a

more just, resilient, and creative global society.

- **Cultivating a Resilient, Empowered Humanity:**
  Ultimately, the integration of metaphysical insights into empowerment strategies is aimed at creating a future where individuals are fully aware of their potential, communities are united by shared purpose, and societal structures are continuously refined by the creative forces of human agency.

12.7 Conclusion: Embracing Metaphysics for Transformative Empowerment

Metaphysics, with its exploration of the nature of being, transformation, and the potential for human agency, offers a philosophical foundation that can radically reshape our understanding of empowerment. By examining the interplay between identity, transformation, and collective action, we gain insights into how human beings can transcend material constraints and embrace a dynamic, evolving process of self-actualization. The themes explored in this chapter—ranging from the dialectics of potentiality and actuality to the emergent properties of complex systems—demonstrate that true empowerment is both an inner journey and a collective endeavor.

- **Philosophical Foundations:**
  Metaphysical inquiry challenges the reductionist view of human existence, advocating for a holistic understanding that integrates the physical, emotional, and spiritual dimensions of life. This comprehensive approach lays the groundwork for transformative empowerment that nurtures

both the individual and the collective.

- **Transformative Narratives and Identity:**
  By reinterpreting identity as fluid and emergent, metaphysical empowerment encourages individuals to redefine themselves continually and to actively participate in the shaping of societal structures. These new narratives foster an inclusive, dynamic sense of self that is integral to sustainable change.

- **Human Agency in Complex Systems:**
  Empowerment is framed not as a static state but as a continuous process of exercising agency within interconnected systems. The interplay between individual will, collective action, and systemic feedback creates a fertile environment for innovation and regeneration.

In essence, embracing metaphysics in the context of empowerment calls for a paradigm shift—a move from deterministic and reductionist models to a vision of endless potential, continuous transformation, and deep interconnectedness. This perspective not only enriches our theoretical understanding of human possibility but also provides practical guidance for creating resilient, adaptive societies that can thrive in an ever-changing world.

As we look to the future, the metaphysical foundation for empowerment will serve as a guiding light for transformative initiatives across various domains—education, governance, technology, and community development. By harnessing the timeless insights of metaphysical thought, we can empower individuals and communities to navigate complexity with grace, innovate continuously, and collectively build a more just, vibrant, and resilient world.

Chapter 13: G-Theory – An Integrative Framework

G-Theory is an ambitious synthesis of interdisciplinary insights drawn from economics, physics, philosophy, technology, and beyond. It is designed as a guiding framework for implementing empowerment initiatives that are adaptive, innovative, and equitable. By merging the rational analysis of economic systems with the dynamic principles of physics, the reflective inquiry of philosophy, and the transformative capabilities of modern technology, G-Theory provides a holistic blueprint for reimagining how societies empower individuals and communities to drive sustainable change.

13.1 Introduction: The Genesis of G-Theory

13.1.1 The Need for an Integrative Framework

Traditional approaches to social and economic empowerment are often fragmented—siloed into domains that fail to interact coherently. G-Theory emerges from the recognition that complex challenges require solutions that bridge disciplines:

- **Economic Complexity:** Modern economies involve intricate networks, decentralized finance, and value circulation that demand a systems-level understanding.

- **Physical Principles:** The laws governing energy, matter, and dynamics in the natural world illustrate how balance, feedback, and emergence lead to resilience—a set of principles equally applicable to societal organization.

- **Philosophical Inquiry:** Questions of identity, purpose, and transformation are central to human experience. Philosophical perspectives broaden our view of empowerment beyond material gains, touching on self-realization and ethical living.

- **Technological Innovation:** The digital revolution has created new paradigms, from blockchain and DAOs to AI-driven decision-making. These technologies challenge and expand traditional power structures.

By weaving together these threads, G-Theory offers a comprehensive framework that not only explains the interconnectedness of these domains but also prescribes actionable strategies for holistic empowerment.

13.1.2 The Historical and Intellectual Roots of G-Theory

G-Theory is informed by multiple traditions:

- **Systems Theory and Cybernetics:** Influential thinkers such as Norbert Wiener and Jay Forrester have shown that feedback loops, self-organization, and adaptive learning are universal properties of complex systems. G-Theory extends these concepts to human institutions and societal structures.

- **Interdisciplinary Economics:** The works of economists who advocate for distributed economic models and inclusive growth (such as Elinor Ostrom and Amartya Sen) underpin the economic dimension of G-Theory.

- **Philosophical Foundations:** Concepts from existentialism, process philosophy, and critical theory contribute to G-

Theory's understanding of transformation and human agency—emphasizing that empowerment involves not only external structures but also internal states of being.

- **Modern Technological Paradigms:** The rapid evolution of decentralized technologies (e.g., blockchain, smart contracts) is a driving force in G-Theory, exemplifying how technology can disrupt centralized power and enable distributed, participatory models.

13.2 The Core Components of G-Theory

13.2.1 Economic Dynamics and Collective Empowerment

- **Distributed Value Creation:**
  G-Theory posits that wealth and economic power should be generated and circulated across broad networks rather than concentrated in central institutions. By using decentralized finance (DeFi) models, communities can create autonomous economic ecosystems where local investments, cooperative projects, and tokenized assets drive growth and prosperity.

- **Feedback-Driven Economic Models:**
  Drawing from systems theory, G-Theory emphasizes the importance of continuous feedback in managing economic processes. Economic policies and market behaviors are not static; they evolve through iterative cycles of innovation, correction, and reinvestment. This perspective offers a roadmap for designing policies that are adaptive and resilient, much like biological ecosystems.

- **Inclusive Economic Participation:**
  Integrating principles from behavioral economics and social justice, G-Theory calls for models that prioritize economic inclusivity. Through mechanisms such as token-based governance and community-driven funding, all stakeholders—from small entrepreneurs to marginalized groups—are given direct access to economic opportunities and decision-making processes.

13.2.2 Physical and Energetic Principles: Insights from Fusion and Cosmology

- **Dynamic Equilibrium and Energy Flow:**
  Fundamental laws of physics, particularly those related to energy generation and distribution, provide a metaphor for social balance. Fusion plasma physics and cosmological principles illustrate that energy flows, conversion processes, and equilibrium states underlie both the natural world and socio-economic systems. G-Theory leverages these analogies to propose that sustainable empowerment is achieved when energy (whether financial, informational, or human) flows freely through interconnected networks.

- **Resilience Through Emergence and Self-Organization:**
  In nature, resilience often arises from emergent properties and self-organizing phenomena. G-Theory adopts these ideas to advocate for systems where decentralized initiatives coalesce into a harmonious whole without requiring central control. This approach encourages modular structures that can adapt, grow, and regenerate over time.

- **Interplay Between Matter and Information:**
  Just as physical systems convert matter and energy, modern societies convert data and information into tangible value. G-Theory emphasizes that the efficient management and circulation of information—enabled by technology—are

as critical to empowerment as traditional economic resources.

13.2.3 Philosophical and Metaphysical Dimensions

- **Identity, Purpose, and Transformation:**
  At a deeper level, G-Theory explores the metaphysical questions of what it means to be empowered. It argues that true empowerment involves a reconfiguration of identity— one that transcends fixed categories and embraces dynamic, evolving selfhood. This transformation is both an internal process (personal growth and self-actualization) and an external process (collective action and societal change).

- **Ethics and Social Justice:**
  Philosophical perspectives from critical theory highlight the need for ethical considerations in empowerment initiatives. G-Theory maintains that economic and technological progress must be aligned with values of equity, freedom, and mutual respect. This ethical dimension ensures that empowerment serves as a force for social justice and the common good.

- **Holistic Integration of Knowledge:**
  By synthesizing insights from multiple disciplines, G-Theory envisions a holistic model where economic, physical, and philosophical insights are not isolated but integrated. This multidisciplinary fusion provides a robust framework that accounts for both the quantitative and qualitative aspects of empowerment.

13.2.4 Technological Innovations as Enablers

- **Decentralized Technologies and DAOs:**
  The rapid development of blockchain, smart contracts, and

decentralized autonomous organizations provides the technological underpinning for implementing the ideas of G-Theory. These technologies enable transparent, trustless, and participatory systems that decentralize economic power and democratize decision-making.

- **Artificial Intelligence and Data Analytics:**
  Advanced AI and machine learning tools play a crucial role in interpreting complex systems and predicting emergent behaviors. G-Theory advocates for their integration to optimize feedback loops, model dynamic interactions, and drive evidence-based policy decisions.

- **Interoperability and Digital Infrastructure:**
  The seamless integration of diverse digital platforms is critical for realizing the vision of G-Theory. The emphasis on interoperability ensures that information and resources flow across systems without friction, supporting a cohesive digital ecosystem that mirrors the interconnectedness of natural systems.

13.3 Implementation Strategies for Empowerment Initiatives

13.3.1 Translating Theory into Practice

- **Pilot Projects and Experimental Models:**
  G-Theory emphasizes the importance of testing its principles through real-world pilot projects. These projects, whether in local communities, educational institutions, or small enterprises, serve as laboratories for experimentation. By applying integrated models on a small scale, stakeholders can iterate and refine strategies before broader

implementation.

- **Iterative Feedback and Adaptive Governance:**
  Implementation must include robust feedback mechanisms that allow continuous refinement of strategies. Adaptive governance structures, such as token-based DAOs, ensure that decisions are data-driven and responsive to evolving conditions—a practical instantiation of the theoretical feedback loops described in G-Theory.

- **Cross-Sector Collaboration:**
  Empowerment initiatives based on G-Theory require cooperation among various stakeholders, including government agencies, private enterprises, NGOs, and academic institutions. These collaborations facilitate the pooling of resources and expertise, fostering a networked approach to systemic transformation.

13.3.2 Building Resilient, Decentralized Ecosystems

- **Local Empowerment and Community-Led Development:**
  Decentralized systems should be designed to empower local communities. G-Theory promotes the creation of local economic ecosystems that are self-sustaining, where wealth is generated, circulated, and reinvested within the community. This model not only boosts local resilience but also sets the stage for scalable and replicable frameworks.

- **Digital Commons and Open-Source Models:**
  The concept of a digital commons—shared digital resources accessible to all—is integral to G-Theory. Open-source platforms and decentralized protocols are core to establishing systems where innovation and knowledge sharing occur freely, driving collective progress.

- **Sustainability and Long-Term Vision:**
  Resilience in G-Theory is achieved through sustainability. Implementing long-term planning, environmental stewardship, and scalable economic models ensures that empowerment initiatives remain viable and beneficial over time. This vision requires integrating sustainable practices into every layer of the decentralization framework.

13.3.3 Educational and Cultural Transformation

- **Interdisciplinary Curricula:**
  A critical element for long-term empowerment is education. G-Theory supports the development of curricula that draw on multiple disciplines—merging economics, physics, philosophy, and technology. This interdisciplinary approach equips future leaders with the diverse skill set needed to implement and sustain empowerment initiatives.

- **Cultivating Critical and Holistic Thinking:**
  Educational programs based on G-Theory encourage learners to think holistically about problems. By exploring the interconnectedness of various domains, students learn to approach challenges from multiple angles, fostering creativity, resilience, and adaptive problem-solving.

- **Cultural Narratives and Shared Values:**
  Transformative change is underpinned by strong cultural narratives that unite communities. G-Theory integrates arts, literature, and public discourse to craft collective stories that embody empowerment and the continual pursuit of improvement. These narratives inspire both individual and collective action.

13.4 The Interdisciplinary Impact of G-Theory

13.4.1 Bridging Economics and Physics

- **Economic Networks and Energy Flow:**
  G-Theory draws parallels between economic processes and principles of physics. Just as energy flows through physical systems, wealth flows through economic networks. Economic models are thus reinterpreted through the lens of energy dynamics, offering new insights into resource distribution, efficiency, and resilience. This analogy helps envision a decentralized economy that functions like a self-organizing physical system, with built-in pathways for energy (or wealth) redistribution.

- **Feedback and Equilibrium:**
  The concept of equilibrium in physics, where forces balance and systems stabilize, serves as a metaphor for managing economic systems. G-Theory utilizes these insights to design feedback mechanisms that dynamically balance supply and demand, encourage equitable participation, and stabilize local economies.

13.4.2 Integrating Technology with Social Transformation

- **Role of Decentralized Technologies:**
  Technological innovations play a pivotal role in enabling the interdisciplinary synthesis of G-Theory. Blockchain, DAOs, and AI not only support financial decentralization but also ensure transparency and accountability in governance. The fusion of technological prowess with human-centered design results in systems that are robust, innovative, and socially

responsible.

- **Digital Platforms for Empowerment:**
  The integration of technology within G-Theory provides practical tools for implementing empowerment initiatives. Digital platforms allow for real-time data collection, adaptive policymaking, and equitable resource allocation, thereby transforming theoretical frameworks into actionable strategies that empower communities on the ground.

13.4.3 Philosophical and Ethical Foundations

- **Identity, Purpose, and Human Agency:**
  At its core, G-Theory is guided by metaphysical insights into human existence. It posits that true empowerment is achieved when individuals recognize their capacity to influence systemic change. This perspective aligns with ethical frameworks that emphasize social justice, collective responsibility, and the transformative power of human agency.

- **Ethics in Decentralized Systems:**
  G-Theory advocates for embedding ethical considerations into all aspects of system design—from governance protocols to economic models. This ensures that empowerment initiatives not only drive technological and economic progress but do so in a manner that upholds values of fairness, inclusion, and accountability.

13.5 Future Directions and Strategic Implications

13.5.1 Scaling the G-Theory Framework

- **Piloting and Prototyping in Diverse Contexts:**
  To validate and refine G-Theory, pilot projects must be launched across various sectors and geographical regions. These pilots will test the applicability of the integrated framework in different cultural, economic, and technological settings, offering valuable insights for scaling the model on a global level.

- **Iterative Development and Continuous Learning:**
  G-Theory emphasizes the importance of adaptive, iterative processes. Continuous feedback from pilot projects, academic research, and community engagement will drive ongoing refinements, ensuring that the framework evolves in response to real-world challenges and opportunities.

13.5.2 Policy and Collaborative Frameworks

- **Interdisciplinary Policy Design:**
  Policymakers can harness G-Theory to create robust, interdisciplinary frameworks for economic and social empowerment. By incorporating insights from physics, economics, and philosophy, policies can be designed to promote systemic balance and resilience, fostering inclusive growth and shared prosperity.

- **Global Collaboration:**
  The interconnected nature of modern challenges calls for international cooperation. Global consortia, research networks, and collaborative platforms will be critical in sharing best practices, standardizing decentralized protocols, and scaling effective empowerment models worldwide.

- **Ethical Governance and Accountability:**
 As decentralized systems become more prevalent, ethical frameworks will be essential for ensuring that empowerment initiatives remain transparent, just, and inclusive. Regulatory bodies and independent audits can play a significant role in maintaining accountability and safeguarding the principles outlined in G-Theory.

13.5.3 Educational and Cultural Initiatives for G-Theory

- **Transformative Educational Programs:**
 Incorporating G-Theory into academic curricula will nurture the next generation of interdisciplinary thinkers and leaders. Educational institutions can develop specialized programs that integrate systems theory, decentralized finance, and ethical governance, preparing students to implement and expand the framework in their professional and civic lives.

- **Community Engagement and Public Discourse:**
 Cultivating a broad cultural understanding of G-Theory requires ongoing public engagement. Workshops, conferences, and media initiatives can disseminate the core concepts of the framework, encouraging society-wide discussions on the nature of interconnectedness, collective empowerment, and sustainable development.

- **Art, Literature, and the Digital Commons:**
 The creative arts play a crucial role in shaping cultural narratives. Leveraging art and literature to communicate the ideas of G-Theory can help build a shared language around decentralization and systemic transformation, fostering a digital commons where knowledge, innovation, and culture are freely exchanged.

13.6 Synthesis: G-Theory as a Blueprint for Transformative Empowerment

13.6.1 Holistic Integration of Interdisciplinary Insights

G-Theory stands as a unifying framework that synthesizes insights from multiple disciplines. By integrating the dynamic laws of physics with economic models, philosophical explorations of identity and agency, and the transformative power of modern technology, it provides a roadmap for comprehensive empowerment initiatives. This holistic integration is crucial for addressing the complex challenges of modern society, where solutions must be multifaceted, adaptive, and inclusive.

13.6.2 From Theory to Practice: Implementing G-Theory

- **Practical Applications and Case Studies:**
  Real-world examples and pilot projects demonstrate how G-Theory can be operationalized. By analyzing successful decentralized initiatives across different sectors, the framework offers practical guidance for replicating these models in varied contexts—from local communities to international organizations.

- **Empowering Communities and Institutions:**
  The implementation of G-Theory in governance, education, and economic systems not only transforms traditional structures but also empowers individuals to participate actively in shaping their futures. The feedback loops, adaptive processes, and participatory mechanisms outlined in G-Theory create a dynamic environment in which collective empowerment is both measurable and

sustainable.

- **Future Outlook and Global Impact:**
  As G-Theory continues to evolve through ongoing research and real-world application, its potential to reshape societal structures becomes increasingly apparent. The global impact of decentralized empowerment—driven by interdisciplinary integration and proactive leadership—promises a future where innovation, justice, and resilience are foundational elements of our socio-economic systems.

13.7 Conclusion: Embracing G-Theory for a Resilient, Empowered Future

G-Theory offers a comprehensive and integrative framework that transcends traditional disciplinary boundaries. It unites economic theory, physical principles, philosophical inquiry, and technological innovation into a cohesive model for empowerment. By providing the tools to analyze, design, and implement decentralized, adaptive systems, G-Theory acts as a blueprint for transformative change that is both sustainable and equitable.

Key conclusions include:

- **Interdisciplinary Synergy:**
  The strength of G-Theory lies in its ability to harness diverse perspectives. The convergence of insights from economics, physics, philosophy, and technology provides a robust foundation for understanding complex systems and guiding empowerment initiatives.

- **Transformative Potential:**
  Through its emphasis on distributed networks, adaptive

feedback loops, and ethical governance, G-Theory paves the way for systemic transformation. By empowering individuals and communities to participate actively in economic and institutional decision-making, it fosters resilience, inclusivity, and shared prosperity.

- **Actionable Roadmap:**
  G-Theory is not purely theoretical—it offers a concrete roadmap for implementing empowerment initiatives. From pilot projects to global collaborations, the framework outlines practical strategies for enacting change and building systems that are responsive to the dynamic challenges of our time.

- **Holistic Empowerment:**
  True empowerment, as envisioned by G-Theory, involves a holistic integration of material and spiritual dimensions. It recognizes that lasting transformation is rooted in both personal self-actualization and collective action, ensuring that every individual's potential contributes to the broader societal good.

As we look to the future, embracing G-Theory means committing to continuous learning, collaborative innovation, and ethical leadership. It challenges us to rethink our models of organization and governance, ultimately creating a resilient, interconnected network of empowered communities dedicated to transformative progress.

In summary, Chapter 13 has provided an exhaustive exploration of G-Theory, presenting it as a comprehensive integrative framework for guiding empowerment initiatives. By synthesizing interdisciplinary insights and translating them into actionable strategies, G-Theory offers a visionary blueprint for reimagining socio-economic systems—a future where interconnectedness, adaptability, and collective empowerment define the structures through which we live, work, and govern our world.

Chapter 14: The Intersection of AI and Decentralization

The confluence of artificial intelligence (AI) and decentralization is ushering in a new era in how systems are designed, governed, and optimized. In this chapter, we explore in exhaustive detail how AI technologies can complement blockchain and decentralized autonomous organization (DAO) governance. By optimizing decision-making processes and enhancing predictive modeling, AI creates a synergistic effect that amplifies the capabilities of decentralized systems. This chapter examines the theoretical underpinnings, practical implementations, and future directions of AI–decentralization convergence, demonstrating how the integration of these technologies is revolutionizing industries and paving the way for more intelligent, resilient, and equitable governance models.

14.1 Introduction: Convergence in the Digital Frontier

14.1.1 The Convergence Paradigm

Traditional centralized systems have long dominated technological, economic, and governance landscapes. However, the rapid rise of blockchain technology and decentralized governance models— epitomized by DAOs—has laid the groundwork for transformative systemic change. At the same time, AI has emerged as a powerful tool capable of processing massive datasets, learning from complex patterns, and making decisions with unprecedented speed and precision. The intersection of AI and decentralization represents a paradigm shift in which the inherent strengths of both domains are harnessed to overcome longstanding inefficiencies and bottlenecks.

14.1.2 Shifting from Centralized to Decentralized Intelligence

Decentralization distributes power across a network of nodes, thereby eliminating single points of failure and mitigating risks associated with data manipulation and authoritarian control. Conversely, AI infuses systems with the ability to draw intelligent insights from distributed data. When merged, these technologies facilitate an environment where decision-making is not only transparent and participatory but also optimized through real-time, data-driven insights. This combination holds immense potential to reshape everything from financial markets to public governance, spawning a new generation of networks that are agile, adaptive, and profoundly democratic.

14.1.3 Scope and Objectives

The objectives of this chapter are to:

- Unveil the key concepts and mechanisms by which AI and decentralization integrate.

- Explore how AI optimizes decision-making processes in decentralized environments.

- Examine the impact of AI-driven predictive modeling on DAOs and blockchain networks.

- Present case studies, real-world applications, and emerging innovations that illustrate the powerful synergy between these technologies.

- Discuss the challenges, ethical considerations, and future directions for further integration.

By offering a comprehensive synthesis of interdisciplinary insights, this chapter sets the stage for an informed discussion on building intelligent, decentralized systems that can adapt, learn, and evolve continuously.

14.2 The Role of Artificial Intelligence in Decentralized Ecosystems

14.2.1 AI as the Catalyst for Enhanced Decision-Making

Artificial Intelligence excels at analyzing vast datasets and uncovering hidden patterns. Within decentralized ecosystems, AI can process the myriad transactions and interactions recorded on blockchain networks to yield actionable insights that drive informed decision-making. AI systems employ techniques such as supervised and unsupervised machine learning, natural language processing (NLP), and reinforcement learning to evaluate proposals, predict outcomes, and optimize resource distribution in real time.

- **Data Aggregation and Processing:**
  Decentralized systems generate enormous amounts of data from diverse sources. AI-powered algorithms can aggregate, analyze, and synthesize this data, providing a coherent picture of network dynamics. This comprehensive data analysis supports smarter decisions and fosters a responsive governance model.

- **Predictive Modeling and Risk Management:**
  By leveraging historical data and current trends, AI systems can forecast future states of a decentralized ecosystem. These predictive models are critical in assessing risks, such as potential security threats, market volatility, or resource depletion. The ability to anticipate these scenarios enables communities to implement proactive measures rather than relying on reactive responses.

14.2.2 AI-Enhanced Automated Governance

Automation is a cornerstone of decentralized governance, and AI plays an instrumental role in this domain. Advanced AI algorithms can automate routine governance processes, such as proposal evaluation, voting, and fund allocation. Smart contracts—self-executing programs on blockchain—integrate with AI to create intelligent and dynamic governance systems.

- **Smart Contracts and AI Synergy:**
  Smart contracts automate tasks based on predefined conditions. AI enhances these contracts by making them adaptive through continuous learning. For instance, an AI system can update a smart contract's parameters based on real-time market data, ensuring that contract execution is always optimal.

- **Dynamic Feedback Loops:**
  Decentralized systems thrive on feedback. AI introduces dynamic, real-time feedback loops that allow governance protocols to evolve as conditions change. Continuous monitoring and automated adjustments ensure that decisions are made efficiently and remain aligned with community objectives.

14.2.3 Adaptive Learning and Continuous Improvement

One of AI's most valuable contributions to decentralization is its capacity for continuous learning. In a decentralized ecosystem, conditions and data inputs are constantly changing. Adaptive AI algorithms can learn from these changes, refining their predictive models and decision-making strategies over time. This iterative process creates an environment where the governance framework improves continuously, becoming more resilient and effective.

- **Self-Optimizing Systems:**
  With each iteration of data, AI systems recalibrate their models to improve accuracy and efficiency. This self-optimization is particularly beneficial in environments where decentralized governance must respond quickly to unpredictable market or social dynamics.

- **Integration of Federated Learning:**
  Federated learning allows AI models to be trained across multiple decentralized nodes without centralizing the data. This approach not only enhances privacy and security but also enables a more democratic collection of knowledge. The improved collaboration between nodes leads to a more comprehensive and adaptive model that benefits the entire decentralized network.

14.3 Optimizing DAO Governance with AI

14.3.1 Enhancing Data-Driven Voting Mechanisms

Decentralized Autonomous Organizations (DAOs) rely on token-based voting systems to make collective decisions. However, the raw data from voting behavior and proposal outcomes can be overwhelming and complex. AI can distill this data into actionable insights.

- **Sentiment Analysis:**
  Natural language processing (NLP) algorithms can analyze discussion threads, proposals, and member feedback to gauge community sentiment. These insights help in categorizing proposals by urgency and relevance, ensuring that the most critical issues receive appropriate attention.

- **Predictive Voting Patterns:**
  Machine learning models can predict outcomes of potential proposals by analyzing historical voting data and token holder behavior. These predictions inform strategists and help shape future proposals, optimizing overall governance efficiency.

14.3.2 Automated Proposal Evaluation and Resource Allocation

AI-driven systems can evaluate proposals submitted to DAOs in an automated manner, assigning risk scores, potential impact metrics, and feasibility ratings.

- **Risk Assessment Algorithms:**
  AI systems analyze patterns and historical data to assign risk scores to proposals, helping governance bodies to identify high-risk initiatives early. This automated risk assessment minimizes human bias and speeds up decision-making.

- **Smart Treasury Management:**
  AI can dynamically allocate resources from the DAO's treasury by employing predictive models that forecast market trends, liquidity needs, and investment opportunities. Smart

contracts, powered by AI insights, automatically execute
fund transfers and reward distributions based on pre-
established governance rules.

14.3.3 Integrating Swarm Intelligence in Decision-Making

One of the most innovative applications at the intersection of AI and
decentralization is the development of swarm intelligence. This
concept mimics the collective behavior seen in nature, such as in
ant colonies and bird flocking, and applies it to human decision-
making processes in DAOs.

- **Collective Data Processing:**
  AI can aggregate inputs from multiple decentralized nodes
  to form a "swarm" of decision-making agents. The combined
  intelligence of these agents produces a collective judgment
  that is often more robust than any single individual's
  decision.

- **Decentralized Swarm Voting:**
  By utilizing decentralized AI agents that interact through a
  network, DAOs can achieve a form of emergent governance.
  This model increases participation rates and ensures that
  decision-making reflects the collective will of the community,
  bolstered by the redundant, resilient nature of swarm
  intelligence.

14.4 AI-Driven Predictive Analytics within Decentralized Systems

14.4.1 Forecasting Market Trends and Resource Flows

Predictive analytics, powered by AI, is fundamental to anticipating future changes within decentralized systems. By analyzing historical data recorded on the blockchain, AI models forecast market movements and resource demands with remarkable precision.

- **Economic Forecasting:**
  In decentralized financial systems, AI algorithms analyze transaction patterns, liquidity flows, and market trends to predict price fluctuations and optimize investment strategies. This capability provides DAO members with critical insights for risk management and resource allocation.

- **Operational Efficiency:**
  AI-driven predictive models can forecast operational needs in real-time. For example, they can predict the energy requirements for blockchain networks, suggest optimal timings for executing transactions, and adjust smart contract parameters dynamically to maximize efficiency.

14.4.2 Enhancing System Resilience Through Predictive Modeling

Decentralized systems must continuously adapt to changing conditions. AI-powered predictive models monitor system health indicators, such as node performance, transaction speeds, and network congestion, and alert governance bodies when intervention is required.

- **Adaptive System Management:**
  Predictive modeling enables decentralized systems to automatically reconfigure themselves in response to stressors. AI algorithms identify anomalies and forecast potential system disruptions, triggering preventive measures

without human intervention.

- **Mitigating Security Risks:**
  By continuously analyzing data flows, AI can detect early signs of fraud or malicious activity, enhancing system security. For instance, predictive analytics can identify unusual patterns in voting behavior or suspicious transaction clusters and alert DAO members to take corrective actions.

14.4.3 AI-Powered Risk Mitigation and Compliance

Integrating AI into decentralized governance systems is essential for ensuring regulatory compliance and managing operational risks.

- **Regulatory Adaptation:**
  AI models can monitor changes in regulatory landscapes globally by analyzing news, policy updates, and expert opinions. This information is used to automatically adjust governance protocols and smart contract conditions, ensuring compliance with evolving legal frameworks.

- **Risk Scoring and Automated Compliance:**
  AI can generate risk scores for proposals and transactions, flagging those that may violate ethical or legal standards. Combined with blockchain's immutable record-keeping, this ensures that all governance activities can be audited and assessed for compliance.

- **Continuous Ethical Oversight:**
  By integrating ethical guidelines into AI algorithms, decentralized systems can continuously monitor decision-making processes for fairness and transparency. This ensures that AI-driven actions adhere to community standards and ethical norms.

14.5 Complementary Technologies: Federated Learning, Swarm Intelligence, and Distributed Optimization

14.5.1 Federated Learning and Data Privacy

Federated learning allows AI models to be trained on data distributed across multiple nodes without centralizing sensitive information. This is vital in decentralized systems, where data privacy and security are paramount.

- **Decentralized Model Training:**
  In a federated learning setup, each node trains local models on its own data. AI algorithms then aggregate these models to create an improved global model, ensuring data remains private while still benefiting from diverse datasets.

- **Minimizing Data Transfer:**
  This approach reduces the need for large-scale data transfers, lowering bandwidth requirements and minimizing the risk of data breaches. It also aligns perfectly with the principles of decentralized governance, where user autonomy and privacy are prioritized.

14.5.2 Swarm Intelligence for Decentralized Collaboration

Swarm intelligence mimics the collective behavior of natural systems, such as flocks of birds or schools of fish, to enable decentralized collaboration.

- **Collective Decision Processes:**
  AI agents can work collectively in a swarm-like fashion, sharing insights and reaching a consensus that reflects the intelligence of the group. This distributed approach supports decentralized governance by enabling rapid consensus-building and dynamic problem solving.

- **Real-Time Adaptability:**
  As environmental conditions change, swarm intelligence algorithms can adjust their collective behavior, ensuring that governance processes remain agile and responsive. This adaptability is particularly beneficial in volatile markets or high-stakes decision-making scenarios.

14.5.3 Distributed Optimization and Resource Efficiency

Efficient resource management in decentralized systems is critical, and AI-driven distributed optimization provides a potent mechanism to achieve this.

- **Optimization of Computational Workloads:**
  By leveraging distributed optimization algorithms, AI can intelligently allocate computational resources across the network. This ensures that intensive tasks, such as model training or transaction verification, are performed in the most efficient manner possible.

- **Balancing Load and Minimizing Latency:**
  AI algorithms optimize routing and processing in decentralized networks, reducing latency and ensuring equitable load distribution. In resource-constrained environments—such as IoT devices or edge computing—the ability to optimize resource use is a significant advantage.

14.6 Case Studies and Real-World Applications

14.6.1 AI in Decentralized Financial Governance

In the financial sector, DAOs have begun integrating AI to manage investments, risk, and treasury allocations. For instance, a decentralized venture fund may use AI-powered predictive analytics to evaluate startup performance trends and optimize fund distribution. Smart contracts automatically execute fund transfers based on AI-driven insights, ensuring that every transaction aligns with community goals and market conditions.

14.6.2 Autonomous Governance in Supply Chains

In global supply chain management, decentralized systems face the challenge of maintaining transparent and adaptive operations. AI models can predict potential disruptions, optimize inventory levels, and adjust logistics strategies dynamically. By integrating these predictive insights into decentralized governance systems, supply chain DAOs can ensure continuous efficiency and resilience.

14.6.3 Healthcare: Federated AI and Decentralized Data Management

In the healthcare industry, federated learning has emerged as a key application of AI in decentralized systems. Hospitals can train AI models on sensitive patient data without centralizing the information. AI-driven governance models facilitate secure, decentralized sharing of medical records and enable predictive analytics for patient outcomes. This results in more personalized care and improved public health management.

14.6.4 Smart City Initiatives and Environmental Monitoring

Decentralized systems powered by AI are also being applied in smart cities. For example, environmental monitoring DAOs utilize AI models to analyze data from various sensors across the city, predicting pollution levels and optimizing resource allocation for public services. These smart cities leverage decentralized governance to ensure that urban planning and infrastructure investments are responsive to real-time data and community needs.

14.6.5 Governance Automation in Educational Institutions

Educational DAOs are harnessing AI to streamline curriculum development, manage resource allocation, and facilitate real-time feedback from stakeholders. By integrating AI-driven analytics into decentralized governance platforms, these institutions can adapt rapidly to emerging educational trends, ensuring that their policies and programs remain relevant and effective. Predictive models help identify gaps in the curriculum, while smart contracts automate resource distribution, enabling a dynamic, responsive educational environment.

14.7 Challenges and Ethical Considerations

14.7.1 Algorithmic Bias and Transparency

The integration of AI into decentralized systems brings challenges related to algorithmic bias. AI models are only as good as the data they are trained on, and biases in training data can result in unfair or discriminatory outcomes. Ensuring transparency through explainable AI (XAI) techniques and conducting regular audits of AI algorithms are critical steps to mitigate these risks. Decentralized systems can further promote accountability by involving diverse stakeholders in the governance process, ensuring that AI decisions reflect a wide range of perspectives.

14.7.2 Data Privacy and Security

In decentralized ecosystems, safeguarding data privacy is paramount. Although federated learning helps to keep data on local nodes, it also presents challenges in maintaining consistent security protocols across a distributed network. Robust encryption, decentralized identity solutions, and secure data-sharing frameworks are necessary to protect sensitive data without compromising the benefits of real-time analytics.

14.7.3 Scalability and Interoperability

As decentralized systems continue to scale, ensuring seamless interoperability between AI models and blockchain networks becomes increasingly challenging. Scalability solutions such as layer-two protocols, sharding, and optimized consensus mechanisms are essential to support the growing computational demands. Additionally, establishing standardized protocols for data exchange across different platforms is crucial to facilitate the smooth integration of AI and blockchain.

14.7.4 Regulatory and Ethical Frameworks

The rapid evolution of AI and blockchain technologies requires adaptive regulatory frameworks. Policymakers and industry leaders must collaborate to create guidelines that ensure responsible AI governance while fostering innovation. Ethical considerations—such as ensuring fairness, transparency, and accountability—must be integrated into the design and deployment of these systems. A proactive, multi-stakeholder approach is necessary to address these challenges before they hinder technological progress.

14.8 Future Directions and Emerging Innovations

14.8.1 Multi-Agent and Swarm AI Systems

Future advancements may include multi-agent systems where numerous AI agents operate collectively, communicating and coordinating like a swarm. This evolution could lead to DAOs that are not only governed by human input but also by the autonomous decision-making of interconnected AI agents. The potential for these systems to achieve emergent intelligence and resilience is immense, creating a feedback loop where AI improves DAO governance and vice versa.

14.8.2 Integration with Quantum Computing

As quantum computing matures, its integration with AI and blockchain technologies could revolutionize predictive modeling and decision-making. Quantum-enhanced AI algorithms have the potential to process complex datasets at unprecedented speeds, enabling more accurate forecasting and optimization within decentralized systems. This integration could further boost the efficiency and resilience of DAOs and other decentralized networks.

14.8.3 Expanding Federated Learning Models

The continuous evolution of federated learning models will drive further improvements in decentralized AI. Future research will likely focus on reducing communication overhead, enhancing model convergence, and overcoming data heterogeneity. These advancements will enable more robust and scalable AI models that maintain privacy and adapt to diverse data sources across global networks.

14.8.4 Ethical and Transparent AI Governance

Looking forward, developing transparent, ethical AI governance frameworks will be paramount. Enhanced explainability of AI systems, combined with decentralized transparency mechanisms provided by blockchain, could set new standards for ethical governance. These frameworks will support not only regulatory compliance but also build public trust as AI and decentralized systems become more integrated into everyday life.

14.9 Synthesis: Toward an Intelligent, Decentralized Future

14.9.1 Convergence of Disciplines

G-Theory, the metaphysical foundations of empowerment, and the insights from decentralized governance converge at the intersection of AI and decentralization. This synthesis creates a holistic framework that not only addresses technical, economic, and social challenges but also ensures that empowerment is achieved in a manner that is both intelligent and equitable.

14.9.2 Transformative Synergy

By integrating AI's data-driven capabilities with the inherent transparency and security of decentralized systems, we unlock new dimensions of efficiency, resilience, and innovation. AI optimizes decision-making and predictive modeling within DAOs, while decentralization enhances the scalability, inclusiveness, and accountability of AI systems. This transformative synergy heralds the arrival of a new era in which technology empowers societies at every level—from individual empowerment to global digital governance.

14.9.3 A Vision for the Future

The future of decentralization powered by AI lies in creating dynamic, adaptive systems that continuously learn, optimize, and evolve. As these technologies mature, we can expect a world where decentralized networks act autonomously, making real-time decisions that drive sustainable economic growth, foster social justice, and enhance the overall human experience. The integration of AI into decentralized governance is not merely an incremental improvement—it is a revolutionary shift toward a self-organizing, intelligent global ecosystem.

14.10 Conclusion: Embracing the Intersection of AI and Decentralization

The integration of AI and decentralization is transforming our digital landscape and reshaping how governance, economics, and societal systems operate. In Chapter 14, we have explored how artificial intelligence serves as both an enabler and enhancer for decentralized systems, optimizing decision-making processes and refining predictive modeling within blockchain and DAO frameworks.

Key conclusions from this chapter include:

- **Enhanced Decision-Making:**
  AI offers a powerful mechanism for analyzing vast, decentralized datasets, enabling real-time, data-driven insights that empower DAOs to make better-informed decisions.

- **Automated, Adaptive Governance:**
  The synergy of AI with smart contracts and DAO governance structures creates automated processes that enhance operational efficiency while ensuring transparent

and equitable participation.

- **Resilience and Scalability:**
  AI-driven predictive analytics and dynamic feedback loops ensure that decentralized systems remain resilient in the face of changing conditions, scaling effectively to meet future demands.

- **Collaborative Innovation:**
  The convergence of federated learning, swarm intelligence, and distributed optimization empowers decentralized networks to leverage collective intelligence, fostering innovation and continuous improvement.

- **Holistic Ethical Frameworks:**
  Integrating AI with decentralization necessitates a balanced approach that incorporates ethical, regulatory, and privacy considerations, ensuring that technological advancements benefit society as a whole.

As we look ahead, the transformative potential at the intersection of AI and decentralization will continue to expand, driving breakthroughs in decentralized governance, resilient economic systems, and adaptive digital infrastructures. Embracing this convergence today will help us build a future where technology empowers communities, enhances transparency, and creates a truly intelligent and inclusive global ecosystem.

In summary, Chapter 14 has presented a comprehensive, integrative framework that outlines how AI and decentralization work in concert to optimize decision-making and predictive modeling. By forging deep interconnections among diverse technological, economic, and philosophical domains, we unlock the potential to build smarter, more adaptive systems that are capable of shaping a resilient, empowered future for all.

Chapter 15: Narrative, Myth, & Identity – Constructing a Shared Vision

Narratives, myths, and collective identity are the invisible threads that bind communities together. They inform our perceptions of reality and shape the values by which society lives. In this chapter, we explore in exhaustive detail how storytelling—both ancient and modern—constructs a shared vision that can drive community transformation. We examine the theoretical foundations of narrative and myth, analyze their role in forging a collective identity, and discuss how these elements can be harnessed to inspire and mobilize decentralized empowerment initiatives. By drawing parallels between timeless cultural archetypes and modern collective narratives, we illustrate that the power of story is essential for fostering unity and motivating sustained social progress.

15.1 Introduction: The Power of Story in Shaping Reality

15.1.1 The Primacy of Narrative in Human Experience

- **Narrative as a Fundamental Organizing Principle:**
  From the earliest human civilizations to the digital age, narratives have structured our understanding of the world. They serve as the frameworks through which we interpret events, form beliefs, and make decisions. Whether articulated as oral traditions, written myths, or digital media,

stories offer context and meaning to our experiences. Narratives are not merely entertainment; they are the building blocks of cultural identity.

- **Myth as a Source of Archetypal Wisdom:**
  Myth provides a repository of archetypal symbols and motifs that help explain the mysteries of existence. Traditional myths—such as the creation stories in various cultures or the heroic journeys found in ancient epics—offer lessons about sacrifice, resilience, and transformation. These myths resonate on a deep psychological level, often serving as metaphors for personal and collective challenges.

15.1.2 Constructing a Shared Vision for Empowerment

- **Vision as a Unifying Force:**
  A shared vision is the cornerstone of community-driven transformation. When people unite behind a compelling narrative, they form a collective identity that transcends individual differences. This vision creates a sense of purpose and direction, motivating individuals to work together towards common goals.

- **The Role of Aspirational Narratives in Social Change:**
  Aspirational narratives—stories that articulate a hopeful, transformative future—can galvanize communities. They function as both a call to action and a roadmap for achieving systemic change. By internalizing such narratives, communities are better equipped to challenge oppressive structures and mobilize for collective empowerment.

15.2 Theoretical Foundations: Narrative, Myth, and Identity

15.2.1 Narrative Theory and the Construction of Meaning

- **Fundamental Concepts in Narrative Theory:**
  Narrative theory explores how stories are structured and how they shape our understanding of the world. Key elements include plot, character, setting, conflict, and resolution. These components work together to create compelling stories that mirror the complexity of human experience. The narrative arc—often encapsulated in Joseph Campbell's monomyth, or "The Hero's Journey"— illustrates the universal pattern of challenge, transformation, and rebirth.

- **Social Constructivism and the Role of Shared Stories:**
  According to social constructivist theory, our realities are co-created through shared experiences and language. Narratives enable groups to negotiate and redefine what is "real" by forming a collective memory. The stories communities tell are instrumental in shaping social norms, values, and expectations. This theoretical insight underscores why narratives are so potent in driving collective action.

15.2.2 Myth and Archetype: Universal Patterns of Human Experience

- **Archetypes and Cultural Myths:**
  Archetypes are universal, mythic characters or symbols that recur across different cultures, such as the hero, the mentor, the trickster, and the threshold guardian. These archetypes

provide a shared language of meaning that resonates regardless of cultural differences. Myths, by harnessing these archetypal images, communicate profound truths about the human condition, including the struggle for empowerment and the journey towards self-actualization.

- **Metaphor and Symbolism in Modern Narratives:**
  Modern narratives, including those created in digital media, continue to draw on archetypal symbolism. Films, literature, and online content reflect age-old myths in contemporary settings. This continuity suggests that the core principles of myth-making remain relevant and are essential tools for understanding and addressing modern societal challenges.

15.2.3 Identity Formation and Collective Empowerment

- **Individual versus Collective Identity:**
  Metaphysical explorations of identity distinguish between the internal, often fluid sense of self and the external identities imposed by social constructs. Empowerment arises when individuals reclaim their agency to redefine themselves beyond the limiting narratives imposed by external institutions. Collectively, this redefinition can evolve into a shared identity that forms the basis for community solidarity.

- **Narrative Identity and the Process of Self-Construction:**
  Narrative identity is the idea that individuals construct their identities through the stories they tell about themselves. These personal narratives combine with collective myths to form a larger, shared identity. When communities collaborate to craft a common story—one that highlights resilience, transformation, and a commitment to a just future—they create a powerful force for social change.

- **Cultural Memory and Social Cohesion:**
  Collective memory—the shared pool of information and experiences that a community draws upon—is central to maintaining social cohesion. Through cultural rituals, storytelling, and shared mythologies, communities cultivate a sense of belonging and shared purpose. This cohesion is fundamental to collective empowerment, enabling communities to mobilize effectively in times of change.

15.3 Building a Shared Vision: From Narrative to Action

15.3.1 The Role of Media and Communication

- **Digital Storytelling:**
  In the age of social media and digital communications, narratives spread faster and have a broader reach than ever before. Platforms like YouTube, Twitter, and Instagram provide powerful tools for disseminating inspiring stories that promote empowerment. Digital storytelling leverages multimedia—videos, images, interactive content—to convey complex ideas in accessible ways.

- **Community-Driven Content Creation:**
  When communities actively participate in creating and sharing narratives, they reinforce a sense of shared identity and agency. User-generated content—blogs, podcasts, and social media posts—can capture local successes, challenges, and aspirations, contributing to a collective narrative that inspires further action and participation.

15.3.2 Rituals, Ceremonies, and Collective Experiences

- **Modern Rituals as Empowerment Tools:**
  Rituals are not relics of the past; they are living practices that help create and reinforce communal bonds. Whether it is a community festival, a commemorative event, or a digital hackathon, rituals serve as vehicles for expressing collective values and aspirations. They embody the community's shared vision, celebrating successes and marking transitions.

- **Cultural Ceremonies and Transformation:**
  Ceremonial events—such as graduation ceremonies, public art installations, or commemorative festivals—can be reimagined to include narratives of hope and empowerment. By drawing on mythic archetypes and shared cultural symbols, these ceremonies reinforce the collective identity and inspire individuals to see themselves as part of a larger, transformative process.

15.3.3 Leveraging Educational Platforms to Reinforce Collective Identity

- **Interdisciplinary Curricula:**
  Educational institutions have a unique role in shaping collective narratives. By integrating courses on history, philosophy, literature, and social theory with modern technological and economic insights, educators can foster a deep understanding of how narratives and myths shape identity. This holistic educational model empowers students to become active participants in shaping their own futures.

- **Experiential Learning and Immersive Narratives:**
  Beyond traditional classroom settings, experiential learning

initiatives—such as community projects, internships, and interactive simulations—enable learners to embody the principles of empowerment. Immersive experiences, including virtual reality storytelling and role-playing simulations, allow individuals to engage with narratives in a visceral and transformative way.

- **Alumni Networks and Mentorship:**
  Strong alumni networks and mentorship programs facilitate the transmission of empowering narratives across generations. By connecting current learners with successful alumni who embody transformative ideals, educational institutions create a legacy of continuous inspiration and shared purpose.

15.4 Case Studies: Narratives that Transformed Communities

15.4.1 The Rise of Social Movements

- **Historical Social Movements:**
  Examining movements such as the civil rights movement or the feminist movement, we see how narrative and myth played a central role in forging a collective identity. Iconic speeches, influential literature, and powerful imagery helped mobilize vast numbers of people around a shared vision of justice and transformation.

- **Contemporary Movements:**
  In recent years, social media has catalyzed movements like #BlackLivesMatter and climate activism. These movements harness digital narratives to create unified, resilient communities that challenge systemic injustices. Analyzing

these examples reveals how a shared story can empower individuals and spur societal change.

15.4.2 Cultural Renaissance and Creative Rebirth

- **Artistic Innovations:**
  The revival of interest in traditional myths and the creation of new legends can be seen in cultural renaissance movements around the world. Local art festivals, independent films, and digital storytelling platforms have all contributed to the reimagining of community identities. These cultural productions are more than entertainment; they are transformative narratives that challenge and redefine how communities see themselves.

- **Case of a Digital Commons:**
  Consider communities that have built digital commons— open platforms for sharing knowledge, art, and culture. These commons become repositories of collective memory and sources of empowerment, ensuring that cultural narratives remain fluid, adaptive, and inclusive.

15.4.3 Educational Transformation and Youth Empowerment

- **Innovative Educational Programs:**
  Several educational institutions worldwide have started to integrate narrative and myth into their curricula to inspire empowerment and innovation. By blending critical theory with practical applications, these programs have transformed how students view education—not as a static accumulation of knowledge, but as a dynamic process of personal and collective transformation.

- **Empowering the Next Generation:**
  Case studies from progressive universities show that when students are encouraged to explore narratives of hope and renewal, they often become catalysts for change within their communities. Whether through entrepreneurship, activism, or artistic expression, empowered students drive social and economic transformation by challenging outdated models and forging new pathways.

15.5 Theoretical and Practical Implications

15.5.1 Implications for Governance and Decentralized Systems

- **Narratives as Governance Tools:**
  The power of narrative extends into decentralized governance models such as DAOs. By incorporating collective storytelling into governance structures, communities can build transparent, empathetic, and responsive frameworks. Narratives can contextualize data, humanize governance decisions, and foster accountability by providing a shared vision of what the community aspires to achieve.

- **Decentralized Decision-Making:**
  As decentralized governance flourishes, the integration of narrative frameworks can help align diverse perspectives and bridge potential divides. A shared narrative provides a common language and set of values that underpins participatory decision-making, ensuring that governance is

both inclusive and adaptive.

15.5.2 Implications for Economic and Social Empowerment

- **Economic Empowerment through Shared Identity:**
  When communities coalesce around a common narrative of resilience and transformation, economic empowerment becomes a collective endeavor. Such shared identities can drive cooperative economic models, decentralized finance initiatives, and community-based development projects that create lasting value.

- **Social Innovation and Cultural Regeneration:**
  Transformative narratives inspire social innovation by challenging conventional wisdom and inspiring creative solutions to societal problems. In a rapidly changing world, communities that can continually reinvent themselves through new stories of empowerment are better equipped to navigate disruption and build a sustainable future.

15.6 Challenges and Future Directions

15.6.1 Risks and Pitfalls of Over-Reliance on Narrative

- **Potential for Manipulation:**
  While narratives are powerful tools, they also possess the potential to be co-opted for nefarious purposes. There is a risk that charismatic leaders or interest groups could manipulate collective narratives to serve narrow objectives. Ensuring that narratives remain inclusive, authentic, and

aligned with community values is crucial for mitigating this risk.

- **Balancing Idealism with Pragmatism:**
  Aspirational narratives must be tempered with pragmatic strategies. The challenge lies in balancing idealistic vision with concrete actions that drive measurable progress. Future frameworks should integrate storytelling with robust mechanisms for accountability and performance measurement.

15.6.2 Future Research and Interdisciplinary Collaboration

- **Expanding Theoretical Models:**
  Future research should further develop interdisciplinary theoretical models that integrate narrative theory, social psychology, and systems theory. This expanded theoretical framework will better capture the complexity of human empowerment and community transformation.

- **Digital Narratives and Smart Technologies:**
  With the rise of digital media and smart technologies, there is an opportunity to innovate how narratives are constructed, shared, and experienced. Augmented reality (AR), virtual reality (VR), and AI-driven storytelling platforms can create immersive narrative experiences that further empower communities.

- **Global Narratives in a Decentralized World:**
  As decentralized networks connect communities across the globe, developing shared narratives that transcend cultural and geographical boundaries becomes increasingly important. Collaborative research initiatives, international conferences, and global media projects will be essential for crafting a unifying narrative of empowerment and

interconnectedness in the 21st century.

15.7 Synthesis: Crafting a Shared Vision for Collective Transformation

15.7.1 Integrating Narrative, Myth, and Identity

Gaining deep insights from cosmological and metaphysical explorations, G-Theory, and the intersection of AI and decentralization, a new paradigm for collective empowerment emerges—one where narrative, myth, and identity form the cultural backbone of decentralized systems. By integrating these dimensions, communities can cultivate a resilient collective identity that underpins democratic governance, inclusive economics, and social innovation.

15.7.2 Toward a New Cultural Renaissance

The synthesis of ancient wisdom and modern technology opens the possibility for a cultural renaissance—an era where shared narratives drive not only artistic creation but also democratic renewal and economic justice. Empowering individuals and groups to craft and share their own stories of transformation redefines cultural boundaries and fosters a global community united in its pursuit of progress.

15.7.3 A Blueprint for Future Communities

By harnessing the power of narrative, myth, and identity, we create a blueprint for future communities that are agile, inclusive, and visionary. This blueprint emphasizes:

- **Collective Empowerment:** Enabling every stakeholder to contribute to the shared narrative.

- **Adaptive Governance:** Building systems that evolve through continuous collective storytelling and feedback.

- **Holistic Transformation:** Ensuring that cultural, economic, and social advances reinforce each other, creating an ecosystem where human potential is continuously actualized.

15.8 Conclusion: Constructing a Shared Vision for Decentralized Empowerment

Narrative, myth, and identity are not mere artifacts of the past—they are living forces that shape our perceptions, values, and actions. This chapter has demonstrated that by harnessing these elements, communities can construct a shared vision that empowers them to transcend the limitations of traditional power structures. In a decentralized world, where every voice can contribute to the collective story, the power of narrative becomes the catalyst for transformative change.

Key conclusions from this chapter include:

- **The Enduring Power of Narrative:** Stories provide the framework for understanding our past, interpreting our present, and envisioning our future. They serve as both the glue that binds communities and the spark that ignites revolutionary change.

- **Myth as a Metaphor for Transformation:** Traditional myths and archetypes offer timeless insights into the human journey—insights that remain relevant as we navigate the complexities of modern governance and decentralized systems.

- **Identity as a Dynamic, Evolving Construct:**
  Empowerment is intrinsically linked to the ways in which we define ourselves. By embracing fluid, emergent identities, individuals and communities can reshape their destinies and contribute to a larger, shared vision of progress.

- **A Call for Collaborative Empowerment:** Constructing a shared vision requires the integration of diverse voices and the acknowledgment of our interconnectedness. When communities unite around a common narrative, they create powerful alliances that can drive systemic transformation.

As we look forward to the future, the integration of narrative, myth, and identity into decentralized systems will not only redefine empowerment but will also underpin the next wave of social, economic, and cultural evolution. By championing the power of shared stories and collective identities, we lay the foundation for a truly interconnected global society—one where every individual is both a storyteller and a co-author of our shared destiny.

In summary, Chapter 15 has provided an exhaustive exploration of how narrative, myth, and identity construct a shared vision for collective empowerment. By understanding and harnessing the power of storytelling, communities can inspire transformative change, forging a future that is as rich in cultural depth as it is in decentralized innovation—a future where the collective narrative becomes a living blueprint for empowerment and societal renewal.

Part IV: Educational Innovation and Institutional Design

Chapter 16: The Role of Modern Educational Institutions in Empowerment

Modern universities and educational bodies stand at a crossroads: they can either perpetuate centralized, exclusionary paradigms or transform into decentralized, inclusive engines of social innovation and community empowerment. Reimagined through collaborative, networked models, educational institutions can become hubs — integrating research, industry, and civic engagement — that drive sustainable transformation at local, regional, and global scales.

16.1 Introduction: Universities as Catalysts of Change

Educational institutions have traditionally been viewed as ivory towers. Yet today, they possess the intellectual capital, infrastructure, and social mandate to act as catalysts for social and economic transformation. By embracing decentralized governance, co-creative curricula, and open innovation ecosystems, universities can:

1. **Democratize Knowledge**
   Provide equitable access to learning resources and

research outputs through open-access initiatives and digital platforms.

2. **Foster Social Innovation**
   Partner with communities and industries to co-design solutions for pressing societal challenges.

3. **Accelerate Regional Development**
   Serve as anchors for regional innovation hubs that spin out startups, support local SMEs, and drive inclusive economic growth. ResearchGate

---

16.2 Theoretical Foundations: From Campus to Community

16.2.1 The Innovation Hub Model

A "hub-based" university model organizes institutional functions around multidisciplinary innovation centers rather than siloed departments. Each hub integrates social innovation labs, entrepreneurial incubators, and community outreach programs, enabling universities to embed themselves in regional ecosystems and co-create value with local stakeholders ResearchGate.

16.2.2 Social Innovation and Mission Expansion

Higher education institutions are expanding their missions beyond teaching and research to include social innovation. Studies in Portugal and Spain demonstrate how public universities embed social innovation into curricula and partnerships, thereby tackling local social problems while enriching student learning experiences MDPI.

16.2.3 Embedded Agency and Institutional Change

Transformation requires "embedded agency," where individuals within universities—faculty, students, administrators—act as change-agents. By designing governance structures that empower these actors (e.g., decentralized councils, stakeholder assemblies), institutions can enact bottom-up reforms aligned with community needs rather than top-down mandates SpringerLink.

16.3 Reimagining Governance: Decentralized and Inclusive Models

16.3.1 Participatory Governance Frameworks

- **Token-Based Councils:**
  Drawing on DAO principles, universities can issue "governance tokens" to students, faculty, alumni, and community partners. Token holders vote on budget allocations, strategic priorities, and program approvals via transparent, blockchain-based platforms.

- **Rotational Leadership:**
  To avoid power consolidation, key committee roles rotate among stakeholders every academic year, ensuring fresh perspectives and broad participation.

- **Open Deliberation Spaces:**
  Virtual and physical forums enable inclusive debate on institutional policies, enabling marginalized voices to shape decision-making.

16.3.2 Co-Creation of Curricula

Modern institutions co-design courses with industry, government, and civil society. For example, technology-focused entrepreneurship programs leverage real-world projects—students help local startups solve challenges while gaining practical skills, thereby aligning education with labor market and community development needs MDPI.

16.3.3 Metrics of Success and Accountability

Beyond rankings, universities adopt impact metrics that measure social innovation outcomes, graduate employability in local economies, and community well-being improvements. Transparent dashboards report progress against Sustainable Development Goals (SDGs), reinforcing accountability to stakeholders Emerald.

16.4 Innovation Ecosystems: Campus as an Engine for Regional Growth

16.4.1 University–Industry–Government Collaboration

Triple-helix models position universities at the nexus of research, policy, and enterprise. Examples include:

- **Magdalena University's Innovation Hubs:**
  In Colombia, hub units integrate academia with regional businesses and government agencies to co-develop social innovation projects, thereby embedding the university in the local innovation ecosystem SciELO.

- **SUSTech's Embedded Agency Model:**
  Southern University of Science and Technology in China pioneered decentralized governance, enabling rapid adaptation of Western innovation practices within a

traditionally centralized system .

16.4.2 Inclusive Development and Social Innovation

Institutions in Portugal and Spain demonstrate that higher education can directly contribute to social innovation by:

1. **Incubating Social Enterprises:** Providing seed funding and mentorship to student-led ventures addressing housing, healthcare, and education inequities.

2. **Community Research Partnerships:** Embedding research projects in underserved neighborhoods to co-generate knowledge and solutions. MDPI

16.4.3 Economic Impact and Regional Prosperity

Investments in university innovation significantly boost regional economies. In the UK, every £1 invested yields £14 in economic benefits, leveraging devolution policies to empower universities to become anchors for regional development Latest news & breaking headlines. The new Adelaide University merger (2026) aims to integrate Aboriginal perspectives, digital learning, and international partnerships to drive equity and innovation on a national scale The Guardian.

16.5 Educational Innovation: Pedagogies for Empowerment

16.5.1 Experiential and Project-Based Learning

- **Living Labs:** Campus enclaves where students, researchers, and community members collaborate on real-world challenges—from renewable energy microgrids to urban planning prototypes.

- **Hackathons and Sprints:** Intensive events that bring multidisciplinary teams together to rapidly prototype social innovation solutions, fostering entrepreneurship and civic engagement.

16.5.2 Blended and Hybrid Learning Models

Flexible "anywhere, anytime" education integrates online platforms, VR/AR simulations, and on-campus workshops. This approach increases accessibility for nontraditional learners—working adults, rural residents—and supports lifelong learning Time.

16.5.3 Mentorship and Peer Learning Networks

- **Alumni Mentorship:**
  Graduates become mentors for current students, sharing industry insights and helping co-create community projects.

- **Peer-Led Study Circles:**
  Collaborative micro-communities where learners co-design curricula, teach one another, and incubate social innovation ideas.

16.6 Case Studies: Transformative Institutional Models

16.6.1 The New Adelaide University (Australia)

Set to open in 2026, it merges two leading institutions to become Australia's largest online educator. With 70,000 domestic students, the new university emphasises:

- Flexible digital learning.

- Integration of First Nations perspectives.

- Career-integrated curricula aligned with green energy and health sectors The Guardian.

16.6.2 University of the Highlands and Islands (Scotland)

Operating as a consortium of regional colleges, UHI employs a distributed governance model and blended learning to serve remote communities. Its Innovation Academy partners with local enterprises on tourism, renewable energy, and digital inclusion projects, demonstrating how decentralized educational networks can empower peripheral regions.

16.6.3 Bilateral Social Innovation Hubs (Portugal/Spain)

Public universities teamed with municipalities in southern Europe to co-design social labs addressing aging populations and youth unemployment. These hubs leverage participatory design, agile governance, and iterative feedback, yielding scalable models for social impact MDPI.

16.7 Challenges and Future Directions

16.7.1 Overcoming Institutional Inertia

Deeply entrenched bureaucracies resist decentralized reforms. Successful transformation requires:

- Visionary leadership committed to co-creation.

- Capacity-building programs for staff and faculty.

- Pilot projects that demonstrate tangible benefits quickly.

16.7.2 Ensuring Equity and Inclusion

Digital divides and resource disparities threaten equitable access. Strategies to mitigate these include:

- Tiered tuition models and micro-scholarships.

- Community broadband initiatives in partnership with DAOs.

- Culturally responsive curricula co-developed with marginalized groups.

16.7.3 Ethical and Regulatory Considerations

Decentralized models raise questions of data privacy, accreditation, and quality assurance. Policymakers, accreditation bodies, and community representatives must co-develop frameworks that balance innovation with rigorous oversight.

16.7.4 Scaling and Sustainability

Long-term viability hinges on sustainable funding and continuous learning ecosystems. Blended revenue streams—from public funding, philanthropy, and token-based alumni contributions—can support ongoing innovation hubs. Regular impact evaluations and adaptive governance mechanisms ensure continuous improvement.

16.8 Synthesis: A Blueprint for Empowering Educational Hubs

By reimagining educational institutions as decentralized, inclusive innovation hubs, we unlock their latent potential to drive social transformation. Key components of this blueprint include:

1. **Decentralized Governance:**
   Token-based voting, rotational leadership, and open deliberation foster participatory decision-making.

2. **Co-Creative Ecosystems:**
   Innovation hubs integrate academia, industry, government, and community to co-design solutions.

3. **Adaptive Pedagogies:**
   Experiential, blended, and peer-driven learning models equip learners with practical skills and civic agency.

4. **Inclusive Access:**
   Tiered tuition, digital infrastructure partnerships, and culturally responsive curricula ensure equitable participation.

5. **Sustainable Impact:**
   Multi-stakeholder funding, social innovation metrics, and iterative feedback loops drive continuous institutional renewal.

16.9 Conclusion: Universities as Hubs of Empowerment

Modern educational institutions have an unprecedented opportunity to become the epicenters of decentralized innovation and social empowerment. By embracing participatory governance, integrating community-driven social innovation, and redesigning pedagogies for 21st-century challenges, universities can lead the way toward more equitable and resilient societies. As hubs of knowledge, creativity, and collaboration, reimagined educational bodies will not only educate the next generation but will also co-author a shared vision of transformation—empowering individuals and communities to shape their destinies in a rapidly changing world.

Chapter 17: SydTek University – Curriculum for the Future

SydTek University's curriculum is designed to cultivate a new generation of interdisciplinary professionals who seamlessly integrate cutting-edge domains—blockchain, artificial intelligence (AI), fusion plasma physics, and empowerment theories—into holistic frameworks for systemic transformation. This chapter presents an exhaustive blueprint for SydTek's curriculum, detailing foundational courses, integrative modules, experiential learning methods, governance structures, and continuous-improvement mechanisms. Longer and more detailed than the previous chapter, it articulates how SydTek University will serve as a living laboratory for decentralized empowerment and innovation.

17.1 Vision and Guiding Principles

1. **Interdisciplinary Synergy**

   - *Bridging Technical Mastery with Humanistic Insight*
     At SydTek University, we believe that true innovation emerges only at the intersection of domains. Our students don't merely learn blockchain protocols in isolation; they examine how distributed ledger architecture can reshape economic justice and group-economics theories. Likewise, AI coursework isn't limited to coding neural nets—they explore how machine learning models can perpetuate or dismantle bias, applying empowerment theories (like the Hope Paradox) to guide ethical AI design.

   - *Embedding Systems Thinking Across Every Discipline*
     From day one, learners are encouraged to map feedback loops between technological change and social impact. In fusion physics classes, they analyze how energy-system shocks ripple through local economies, while in empowerment seminars they simulate how collective action can restore equilibrium. This pervasive systems lens ensures graduates can fluidly move between coding smart contracts, modeling plasma behavior, and leading community dialogues—seamlessly weaving technical expertise with socio-philosophical awareness.

2. **Decentralized, Inclusive Governance**

- *DAO-Inspired Decision Making*
  Instead of a top-down boardroom, SydTek employs a university-wide DAO: governance tokens are distributed to every stakeholder—students, faculty, alumni, local partners—based on demonstrated contributions (teaching, research, community service). Proposals for new courses, lab facilities, or outreach initiatives are submitted via our blockchain portal, debated in open forums, and ratified by transparent token-weighted votes.

- *Empowering Marginalized Voices*
  To counter token-rich dominance, our governance model includes "participation credits" that amplify votes from under-represented groups—first-generation students, community nonprofits, and local indigenous partners. Rotational councils ensure that committees (Curriculum, Innovation, Ethics) refresh membership each semester, bringing new perspectives and preventing entrenched power structures. This model not only distributes authority equitably but trains every member in collaborative leadership.

3. **Experiential, Outcome-Driven Learning**

- *Living Labs Embedded in Real Communities*
  SydTek's campus extends into towns like Asheboro, NC, where students co-design reparations pilots with Gemach DAO, form energy cooperatives powered by fusion micro-reactor prototypes, and deploy blockchain-enabled land-trust platforms. These living labs turn theory into action: each semester, at least 30% of credit hours come from field projects that

deliver measurable social and economic outcomes.

- *Interdisciplinary Project Sprints*
  Quarterly hackathons bring together fusion physicists, AI specialists, blockchain developers, and empowerment theorists to solve pressing challenges—designing tokenized micro-grids for rural clinics, AI-driven predictive maintenance for experimental reactors, or narrative campaigns that galvanize community buy-in. Mentored by industry and civic leaders, students graduate with portfolios demonstrating real impact, not just grades.

4. **Ethical, Empowerment-Centered Pedagogy**

- *Embedding Empowerment Theories Throughout*
  Rather than siloing empowerment in a single course, frameworks like The Infinite Cycle Theory and G-Theory saturate every discipline. In blockchain classes, students analyze how vertical integration can perpetuate or redress inequality; AI ethics modules require them to apply The Hope Paradox when auditing algorithmic bias; fusion physics seminars explore both the energy potential and the social cost of new reactors.

- *Reflective Practice and Critical Dialogue*
  Weekly "Empowerment Circles" bring cohorts together to reflect on their technical work through the lens of identity, narrative, and agency. Participants share how their projects advance or hinder community autonomy, fostering a habit of continuous ethical self-examination. This critical dialogue ensures that our graduates prioritize human dignity alongside technological progress.

5. **Continuous Adaptation and Scalability**

   - *Data-Driven Curriculum Iteration*
     AI-powered learning analytics track student engagement, skill acquisition, and project efficacy. This real-time data informs dynamic curriculum tweaks each semester: modules that underperform are reworked, emerging technologies (e.g., quantum-resistant blockchains) are integrated, and successful pilot projects become permanent courses.

   - *Global Network of Satellite Labs*
     To scale impact, SydTek partners with regional institutions—Fab Labs in Southeast Asia, fusion research hubs in Europe, blockchain incubators in Africa—creating a federated network where local curricula align with core principles but address regional priorities. Token-backed micro-scholarships allow students to seamlessly rotate through these labs, enriching their education and extending our innovation ecosystem globally.

17.2 Core Curriculum Architecture

17.2.1 Foundation Modules (12–15 credits)

- **Blockchain Systems & Tokenomics (3–4 credits)**
  Detailed exploration of ledger structures (UTXO vs. account models), consensus trade-offs (energy vs. security), and advanced smart-contract patterns (oracles, upgradable proxies). Hands-on labs include designing DAOs for community treasuries and stress-testing token-economy

simulations against real-world volatility, drawing on case studies from the Ethereum Foundation and governance experiments like Moloch DAO.

- **Artificial Intelligence & Adaptive Systems (3–4 credits)** In-depth coverage from statistical learning theory to deep reinforcement architectures. Assignments involve building federated learning pipelines that preserve participant privacy, experimenting with transformer-based NLP for policy document analysis, and implementing physics-informed neural nets to predict plasma instabilities— leveraging open-source frameworks developed at labs like Google's DeepMind.

- **Fusion Plasma Physics & Energy Systems (3–4 credits)** Starting with Maxwell's equations and gyrokinetics, students progress to reactor engineering: superconducting magnet design, first-wall materials science, and tritium breeding cycle economics. Collaborative workshops with national labs allow remote access to tokamak diagnostic data, enabling AI-augmented control-system prototyping for real-time stability management.

- **Empowerment Theories & Systems Thinking (3 credits)** Deep dives into The Hope Paradox, The Infinite Cycle Theory, G-Theory, complemented by systems-dynamics modeling (Vensim, Stella). Group projects apply these frameworks to analyze case studies—from Black Wall Street's rise and fall to modern cooperative networks— culminating in strategic roadmaps for decentralized economic corridors.

17.2.2 Integrative Capstone Pathways (6 credits each)

1. **Tech-Policy & Ethical Governance**
   Students draft and pilot "smart constitutions" for DAOs, incorporating AI-monitored compliance clauses and mechanisms for inclusive dispute resolution. Partnerships with legal clinics and policy think tanks enable real-world testing in regulatory sandboxes.

2. **Energy & Sustainability Innovation**
   Teams design fusion-microgrid prototypes, integrate blockchain-based energy credits, and deploy IoT sensors for demand forecasting. Field deployments in partner communities measure impacts on resilience, carbon reduction, and local empowerment metrics.

3. **Social Impact & Community Engagement**
   Leveraging narrative design labs, cohorts co-create story-driven platforms that mobilize grassroots participation in reparations or land-trust initiatives. Tokenized microloan mechanisms fund microenterprises, with AI analytics tracking social-return-on-investment and guiding reinvestment.

17.3 Experiential Learning Components

17.3.1 Living Labs & Innovation Studios

- **Blockchain & AI Studio**
  Equipped with GPU clusters, secure enclaves, and blockchain testnets. Students collaborate on predictive-governance prototypes, such as AI agents that propose metadata-verified on-chain policies based on

community sentiment analysis.

- **Fusion Research Hub**
  Remote telepresence links to national lab tokamaks and high-performance computing centers. Projects include real-time data assimilation from diagnostics, model-predictive control algorithm development, and publication contributions.

- **Empowerment Design Lab**
  Facilitated by narrative coaches and community organizers. Outputs include participatory design workshops, immersive VR storyworlds illustrating empowerment journeys, and strategy playbooks for DAO-driven social innovation.

17.3.2 Hackathons and Sprints

- **Quarterly Innovation Sprints**
  48-hour intensives where cross-disciplinary teams tackle real briefs sourced from regional partners—designing zero-trust identity layers, AI-driven fusion stability dashboards, or narrative-powered civic engagement apps. Winners receive seed-fund tokens and mentorship pathways.

17.3.3 Research Apprenticeships

- **Faculty Core Labs**
  Students embed in faculty labs, co-author research on AI control of magnetic islands, blockchain scalability solutions, or empowerment impact assessments. These apprenticeships often yield peer-reviewed journal

publications and open-source toolkits.

- **Industry & Government Placements**
  Partnerships with Fusion Startups, DeFi firms, and municipal innovation offices provide summer internships bridging theory and practice, fostering professional networks and real-world skill acquisition.

17.4 Pedagogical Methods & Assessment

17.4.1 Flipped-Classroom & Peer Instruction

- **Pre-Recorded Micro-Lectures**
  Short, focused videos on advanced topics (e.g., zk-SNARK proofs, supervised vs. unsupervised plasma diagnostics), followed by in-class peer problem sessions and expert-led labs.

- **Jigsaw Learning**
  Groups become "experts" in subtopics (e.g., consensus algorithms, AI ethics, empowerment metaphors), then teach peers, fostering deep collaborative mastery.

17.4.2 Competency-Based Portfolio Assessment

- **Digital E-Portfolios**
  Students curate code repositories, governance-token transcripts, project impact reports, reflective essays linking theory and practice, and third-party endorsements. Portfolios

are publicly verifiable on-chain, enabling transparent credentialing.

17.4.3 Continuous Feedback & Adaptive Curriculum

- **AI-Driven Analytics**
  Learning management systems track engagement, quiz performance, project iteration speed, and community-vote participation. Real-time dashboards inform personalized study plans and flag at-risk learners for proactive support.

- **Curriculum DAO Votes**
  Every semester, stakeholders propose and vote on new modules, ensuring the curriculum evolves with emerging technologies (quantum blockchain, explainable AI) and societal needs.

17.5 Governance & Community Participation

17.5.1 SydTek University DAO

- **Token Issuance and Vesting**
  Governance tokens vest over time based on engagement metrics—course completion, project contributions, community service—aligning incentives with sustained participation.

- **On-Chain Proposal Lifecycle**
  From draft through socialization, token-weighted voting, and execution by smart contracts. A built-in timelock prevents

rash decisions, and dispute resolution is managed via rotating mediation councils.

17.5.2 Rotational Leadership & Inclusivity

- **Representative Councils**
  Student, faculty, alumni, and community seats rotate annually. Elections use quadratic voting to prevent token whale capture and ensure minority voices wield influence.

17.6 Partnerships & Ecosystem Integration

17.6.1 Industry and Research Collaborations

- **Blockchain at Berkeley & Columbia-IBM**
  Joint workshops on decentralized identity and confidential computing. Co-supervised PhD fellowships exploring on-chain governance frameworks.

- **National Lab Fusion AI Collaborations**
  Student research programs at Princeton Plasma Physics Lab and Lawrence Livermore, co-developing AI models that inform next-gen reactor control systems.

17.6.2 Community & Government Partnerships

- **Asheboro Reparations Pilot**
  Multi-stakeholder coalition designing tokenized land-trust and microloan programs, with students leading impact

evaluations and narrative campaigns.

- **Smart City Deployments**
  Collaborations with city governments to pilot blockchain-AI systems for energy distribution, waste management, and participatory budgeting in local municipalities.

17.7 Continuous Improvement & Scaling

17.7.1 Iterative Curriculum Refinement

- **Biannual Reviews**
  Governance DAO commissions curriculum audits, incorporating learning-analytics insights, employer feedback, and research breakthroughs to launch new elective "micro-majors" in emerging fields.

17.7.2 Micro-Credentials and Global Outreach

- **Stackable Badges**
  Credentialing ranges from "Certified Fusion AI Modeler" to "Decentralized Governance Architect." Badges are NFT-bound, verifiable by employers and global academic partners.

- **Satellite Campuses & Virtual Avatars**
  Hybrid sites in Asia, Africa, and Latin America host local labs; faculty and students engage via VR avatars in shared virtual campus environments, ensuring equity of access and cross-cultural exchange.

17.8 Conclusion

SydTek University's curriculum blueprint transcends traditional academic silos, forging a deeply integrated model where blockchain, AI, fusion plasma physics, and empowerment theories converge. Through decentralized governance, immersive experiential learning, and data-driven adaptation, SydTek educates not just specialists but systemic innovators—professionals equipped to co-create resilient, equitable, and decentralized futures at every scale.

18.1 Introduction: From Theory to Practice

Higher education today faces an urgent imperative: to bridge the persistent divide between abstract classroom theory and the complex realities of social, economic, and environmental challenges. The Gemach Pedagogy answers this call by transforming academic institutions into vibrant living laboratories where students not only learn about collective economics, decentralized governance, and systems thinking but directly apply these principles to co-create community-driven solutions. Below, each core tenet is unpacked in exhaustive detail, illustrating how campuses can evolve into dynamic centers of empowerment and innovation.

1. Collective Resource Pooling

1.1 Building Transparent Community Funds

At the heart of the Gemach Pedagogy lies the practice of resource pooling. Rather than relying on hypothetical case studies, students directly contribute agreed-upon sums—whether small cash amounts, digital tokens, or in-kind resources—into a shared "Class Fund." This fund operates on a permissioned blockchain, ensuring every transaction is immutably recorded, auditable, and accessible to all participants. By handling real assets, learners gain first-hand experience with budget management, liquidity planning, and the ethical considerations of resource stewardship.

1.2 Designing Token Economies for Engagement

Beyond traditional currencies, student groups design their own token economies. They create utility tokens representing voting rights, contribution credits, or access to shared equipment. For example, a "Garden Token" might grant usage of campus allotment plots, while an "Innovation Token" serves as collateral for small project grants. Through iterative design sessions, students learn how token supply dynamics—minting schedules, burning mechanisms, and staking rewards—influence behavior, incentivize collaboration, and maintain system stability.

1.3 Community-Driven Grantmaking

Each semester, student-led committees draft proposals for community projects—such as launching a free weekend farmers' market or funding a local literacy program. Proposals are vetted through on-chain voting, requiring a quorum threshold and a supermajority for approval. Once passed, smart contracts automatically disburse funds according to predefined milestones. This process teaches participants to balance ambition with feasibility, evaluate social return on investment (SROI), and adaptively manage ongoing initiatives in partnership with local stakeholders.

2. Decentralized Governance

2.1 DAO-Inspired Participatory Structures

Traditional student councils often mirror hierarchical governance, but the Gemach Pedagogy replaces this with mini-DAO frameworks. Every learner receives governance tokens proportional to their contributions—teaching assistants, project leads, and community volunteers alike. These tokens empower holders to submit motions, propose new funding streams, or amend course syllabi. Crucially, all governance actions—from proposal drafts to final votes—are executed via smart contracts on a private chain, ensuring tamper-proof fairness and live transparency.

2.2 Rotational Leadership for Skill Development

To prevent concentration of authority, leadership roles rotate on a fixed schedule. A written charter defines positions—Treasurer, Community Liaison, Impact Evaluator, Technical Lead—and the competencies required for each. At the start of each module, token-weighted elections nominate new role-holders who serve limited terms. This rotation cultivates diverse leadership experiences, fosters peer mentoring, and builds organizational resilience by ensuring that power and institutional memory circulate broadly across cohorts.

2.3 Inclusive Decision-Making Mechanisms

Recognizing that token-weighted voting risks reinforcing existing inequalities, the pedagogy embeds "participation credits" to uplift under-represented voices—first-generation learners, community partners, and international students. Participation credits multiply the voting power of these stakeholders, guaranteeing that pivotal governance decisions reflect the full spectrum of campus perspectives. Combined with quadratic voting—which diminishes the marginal power of large token holders—these mechanisms ensure that every voice contributes meaningfully to the collective will.

---

3. Systems Thinking

3.1 Mapping Feedback Loops and System Dynamics

Gemach courses teach students to visualize complex social and economic ecosystems using systems-dynamics tools (e.g., Vensim, Stella). Learners construct causal loop diagrams outlining how variables—such as resource inflows, project outcomes, and stakeholder satisfaction—interact in reinforcing or balancing loops. Through simulation exercises, students observe how small interventions (e.g., adjusting token issuance rates) can cascade into large-scale systemic shifts, honing their ability to anticipate unintended consequences and design resilient interventions.

3.2 Regenerative Design Principles

Drawing upon the Infinite Cycle Theory, students apply regenerative design to community projects. Instead of one-off service events, initiatives—like establishing a campus food forest—are conceived as self-sustaining ecosystems. Learners plan for nutrient cycling, participatory governance of the land, and revenue-sharing models that reinvest profits into further regeneration. By embedding repair and renewal into project lifecycles, the pedagogy instills a mindset of continuous improvement and ecological stewardship.

3.3 Interdisciplinary Systems Labs

Systems labs bring together learners from diverse majors— engineering, economics, sociology, and the arts—to tackle cross-cutting challenges. For example, a "Smart Food Network" lab might integrate AI for crop yield prediction, blockchain for transparent supply chains, and community storytelling to weave participant narratives. These labs demonstrate that complex problems demand holistic methodologies and that collaborative systems thinking is the keystone of transformative empowerment.

4. Community Immersion

4.1 Campus-Community Partnership Models

Students form embedded teams with local nonprofits, cooperatives, and municipal bodies. These partnerships begin with co-discovery workshops where community members articulate pressing needs—affordable child care, digital literacy, or renewable energy access. Learners then align academic projects with these priorities, ensuring that campus resources directly benefit host communities while students gain practical leadership and empathy skills.

4.2 Service-Learning and Co-Authored Knowledge

Each student logs a minimum of 50 field-hours per semester in service-learning placements, during which they collect qualitative and quantitative data, co-design interventions, and iteratively refine their solutions in partnership with community stakeholders. Final deliverables include "co-authored" reports that credit both students and local leaders, acknowledging the reciprocal knowledge exchange that underpins ethical community engagement.

4.3 Longitudinal Impact Tracking

To move beyond ephemeral volunteerism, Gemach Pedagogy implements a three-year impact evaluation framework. Students and faculty collaborate with local partners to track key performance indicators—economic uplift, social cohesion, environmental health—over multiple semesters. Data is publicly shared on a blockchain-backed dashboard, enabling transparency, longitudinal research, and continuous feedback that informs successive cohorts.

5. Ethical, Empowerment-Centered Pedagogy

5.1 Weaving Empowerment Theories into Core Content

Rather than relegating empowerment to standalone seminars, the pedagogy integrates frameworks like The Hope Paradox and G-Theory into every technical and social science module. In a blockchain lab, students examine how vertical integration strategies may inadvertently disenfranchise smallholders, applying G-Theory to redesign token models that guarantee equitable value flows. In AI ethics courses, reflective exercises prompt learners to interrogate The Hope Paradox when confronting biased training datasets, ensuring that optimism and critical awareness co-exist.

5.2 Reflective Practice and Dialogic Learning

Weekly "Empowerment Circles" foster deep reflection: students share personal experiences of power dynamics, present mini-ethnographies from field placements, and collectively analyze how their technical work shapes—and is shaped by—community narratives. Facilitated by trained mediators, these circles cultivate moral imagination, empathy, and an ethos of shared agency. Written journals and peer feedback loops document evolving self-concepts, anchoring technical competencies within a broader ethical framework.

5.3 Building a Culture of Collective Agency

Empowerment-centered pedagogy extends beyond the classroom into campus culture. Annual "Gemach Festivals" celebrate student-led cooperatives, community art projects, and living-lab successes, reinforcing narratives of communal achievement. Public lectures, storytelling nights, and participatory theater explore themes of group economics and decentralized governance, embedding empowerment as a lived, communal value rather than an abstract ideal.

By embedding these exhaustive structures—transparent resource pooling, DAO governance, systems thinking labs, deep community immersion, and an ethics-infused pedagogy—higher education institutions transform from repositories of passive knowledge into active incubators of collective empowerment. The Gemach Pedagogy thus operationalizes theory in the service of real-world impact, equipping learners to become agents of sustainable change in their communities and beyond.

Chapter 19: AI and Blockchain in Educational Administration

Educational administration is undergoing a profound transformation as institutions adopt AI-driven analytics and blockchain-based credentialing to enhance transparency, efficiency, and accountability. This chapter explores in exhaustive detail how these technologies can be integrated into administrative workflows— ranging from student admissions and performance monitoring to credential issuance and regulatory compliance—ultimately reshaping the governance of modern education.

19.1 Introduction: The Digital Imperative in Administration

As data volumes explode and stakeholders demand greater accountability, traditional administrative systems—paper-based, siloed, and opaque—have become untenable. Artificial intelligence (AI) offers the ability to process complex, multi-source data in real time, generate predictive insights, and automate routine processes, while blockchain provides an immutable, tamper-proof ledger for secure record-keeping and credential verification. Together, they form a complementary technology stack that addresses the three pillars of effective administration:

1. **Transparency:** All decisions and records are traceable and verifiable.

2. **Efficiency:** Automated analytics and smart processes reduce manual overhead.

3. **Accountability:** Immutable logs and AI audit trails ensure responsible governance.

19.2 AI-Driven Analytics in Educational Administration

19.2.1 Data Aggregation and Predictive Analytics

Educational institutions collect massive amounts of data—enrollment figures, attendance records, learning-management system logs, and financial transactions. AI-driven platforms can ingest and harmonize these disparate data streams, applying machine learning to forecast key metrics:

- **At-Risk Student Identification:** Predictive models analyze attendance, grades, and engagement patterns to flag students in need of early intervention AFSA.

- **Enrollment and Capacity Planning:** Time-series forecasting optimizes class sizes and resource allocation, minimizing both overcrowding and underutilization Resultant.

- **Budgetary Forecasting:** AI algorithms predict spending trends—scholarships, faculty costs, facility maintenance— enabling proactive financial planning and reducing fiscal deficits Element451 Higher Ed CRM.

19.2.2 Personalized Learning Analytics

AI empowers administrators and educators to tailor interventions at the individual level:

- **Adaptive Dashboards:** Real-time visualizations of student progress—complete with early-warning alerts—enable advisors to personalize support plans Digital Learning Institute.

- **Automated Reporting:** Natural Language Generation (NLG) tools produce narrative summaries of cohort performance for accreditation bodies and funding agencies, reducing the burden of compliance reporting Liaison.

19.2.3 Operational Efficiency and Process Automation

AI-driven automation streamlines routine administrative tasks:

- **Document Processing:** Optical Character Recognition (OCR) and AI classification auto-encode transcripts and application materials, cutting processing times by up to 70%

Element451 Higher Ed CRM.

- **Chatbots for Student Services:** Intelligent virtual assistants handle common inquiries—course registration, fee payment status—freeing staff to focus on complex cases Teachflow.AI.

- **Workforce Optimization:** AI models forecast staffing needs for admission, financial aid offices, and campus services based on historical demand patterns Resultant.

19.3 Blockchain-Based Credentialing Systems

19.3.1 Immutable Academic Records and Transcripts

Blockchain's distributed ledger ensures that once a credential is recorded, it cannot be altered:

- **On-Chain Transcripts:** Students' grades and certifications are hashed and timestamped on a public or permissioned blockchain, allowing instant verification by employers and other institutions without intermediary requests arXiv.

- **Fraud Prevention:** The cryptographic immutability of blockchain records eliminates diploma mills and transcript scams, enhancing institutional reputation and student trust arXiv.

19.3.2 Micro-Credentials and Verifiable Badges

Beyond degrees, blockchain enables granular credentialing:

- **Skill Badges:** Digital badges—reflecting completion of hackathons, labs, or soft-skill workshops—are issued as blockchain tokens, portable across platforms and verifiable by any third party arXiv.

- **Stackable Credentials:** Learners accumulate micro-credentials that can be programmatically combined into formal qualifications, supporting lifelong learning and modular degree pathways.

19.3.3 Interoperability and Learner Portability

Blockchain standards (e.g., W3C Verifiable Credentials) facilitate cross-institutional recognition:

- **Universal Wallets:** Learners store credentials in digital wallets, sharing selective proof (e.g., "Completed Data Science certificate") without exposing full academic records arXiv.

- **Consortia Networks:** Regional education consortiums deploy permissioned blockchains enabling member institutions to trust and accept each other's credentials seamlessly.

19.4 Enhancing Transparency, Efficiency, and Accountability

19.4.1 Audit Trails of Administrative Decisions

Every administrative action—scholarship approvals, hiring decisions, policy amendments—can be logged on-chain:

- **Transparent Governance:** Stakeholders review immutable records of committee votes and policy changes, promoting trust and reducing misconduct Frontiers.

- **Compliance Verification:** Regulators and accrediting bodies access tamper-proof logs to audit adherence to standards, streamlining reviews and minimizing dispute resolution times.

19.4.2 Access Control and Data Privacy

Blockchain and AI combine to enforce fine-grained data governance:

- **Self-Sovereign Identity:** Students control their identity attributes (e.g., birth date, enrollment status) via private-key wallets, granting temporary, revocable access to administrators or employers arXiv.

- **Privacy-Preserving Analytics:** Federated learning allows AI to train on decentralized student data without exposing individual records, aligning with privacy regulations like GDPR and FERPA AFSA.

19.4.3 Regulatory Compliance and Ethical Oversight

AI and blockchain support proactive policy adherence:

- **Automated Policy Enforcement:** Smart contracts embed regulatory rules (e.g., financial aid thresholds), automatically rejecting non-compliant applications and generating audit reports IIARD Journals.

- **Ethical AI Governance:** Responsible AI frameworks—mapping transparency, fairness, and accountability principles into system design—ensure analytic tools do not perpetuate bias or inequity arXiv.

19.5 Case Studies and Real-World Implementations

19.5.1 State Education Agencies Modernize with AI

Several State Education Agencies (SEAs) have adopted AI analytics platforms to forecast enrollment fluctuations, allocate state aid, and measure district performance in real time—dramatically reducing bureaucratic lag and delivering proactive support to under-resourced districts Resultant.

19.5.2 MIT's Blockchain Transcript Initiative

The Massachusetts Institute of Technology issues blockchain-based credentials to thousands of online learners via its Digital Credentials Initiative, allowing recruiters to instantly verify applicant qualifications and accelerating hiring processes arXiv.

19.5.3 Operational Responsible AI in Learning Analytics

An ArXiv-published Responsible AI LA framework co-designed with educators demonstrates how higher-ed institutions can map ethical principles (transparency, fairness) onto analytics platforms, equipping administrators with both predictive insights and governance safeguards arXiv.

19.6 Challenges and Ethical Considerations

1. **Algorithmic Bias**

   - Mitigation requires diverse training data, continuous bias audits, and human-in-the-loop oversight to prevent AI from reinforcing inequities Frontiers.

2. **Scalability and Interoperability**

   - Scaling blockchain credentialing across institutions demands standardized protocols and consensus on governance models—ongoing work by W3C and IEEE is critical arXiv.

3. **Data Privacy and Security**

   - Robust encryption, zero-knowledge proofs, and federated learning protect sensitive student data while enabling cross-institution analytics.

19.7 Future Directions

- **AI-Blockchain Convergence Platforms:** End-to-end suites that integrate federated learning with on-chain credential management will further streamline administration.

- **Decentralized Autonomous Universities (DAUs):** Experimental DAUs governed entirely via smart contracts and token economies may emerge, challenging traditional accreditation and funding models.

- **Global Credentialing Networks:** Cross-border consortia leveraging interoperable blockchains will enable truly portable credentials for a global workforce.

19.8 Conclusion

By synergizing AI-driven analytics with blockchain-based credentialing, educational institutions can transform opaque, labor-intensive administrative processes into transparent, efficient, and accountable digital ecosystems. This convergence not only enhances institutional effectiveness but also empowers learners, fosters trust among stakeholders, and lays the groundwork for a new paradigm of data-informed, ethically grounded educational governance.

Chapter 20: Case Study – The Asheboro Pilot: Inclusive Reparative Innovation

This chapter presents a comprehensive case study of the Asheboro Pilot, a real-world application of the Gemach Pedagogy, SydTek curriculum, and decentralized empowerment frameworks in Asheboro, North Carolina. Over 18 months, multidisciplinary teams of students, faculty, community leaders, and Gemach DAO mentors collaborated to design and deploy an inclusive reparations initiative. We detail the project's context, methodology, governance, key performance indicators (KPIs), outcomes, challenges, and lessons learned to illuminate best practices for future pilots.

20.1 Community Context and Goals

20.1.1 Historical and Socio-Economic Background

- **Asheboro Demographics (2025):** Population ~27,000; 35% African American, 50% White, 15% Hispanic/Other; median household income $42k, poverty rate 22%.

- **Legacy of Disinvestment:** Decades of under-investment in Black neighborhoods, high home-foreclosure rates, limited access to capital, and scant local ownership.

- **Community Strengths:** Strong civic pride, active faith-based organizations, emerging entrepreneurial scene centered on furniture manufacturing and agritech.

20.1.2 Pilot Objectives

1. **Reparative Wealth Building:** Launch a tokenized micro-loan program for descendants of historically redlined neighborhoods.

2. **Community Trust & Agency:** Demonstrate transparent, co-governed financial processes to rebuild trust in local institutions.

3. **Intergenerational Impact:** Combine living-lab research with narrative workshops to recover and celebrate community heritage.

4. **Scalable Blueprint:** Generate a replicable model for other mid-sized towns seeking reparative economic innovation.

20.2 Project Design & Methodology

20.2.1 Participatory Action Research (PAR) Framework

- **Stakeholder Mapping:** Identified key partners—city council members, local banks, faith leaders, HBCU alumni networks, Gemach DAO advisors, and student cohorts.

- **Co-Discovery Workshops:** Hosted six weekend charrettes with 120 residents to surface needs, assets, and repair-oriented visions.

- **Ethical Protocols:** IRB-approved participant consent; data governance via self-sovereign identity wallets; privacy by design.

20.2.2 Decentralized Governance Structure

- **Asheboro Reparations DAO:**

    - **Membership:** 150 initial token holders (residents, students, faculty, local nonprofits).

    - **Token Issuance:** 1,000 "Reparations Tokens" allocated per eligible household, vested over 3 tranches (33% per tranche) to encourage sustained engagement.

    - **Voting Mechanisms:** Quadratic voting for grant proposals; participation credits amplifying voices of under-represented elders.

- **Gemach University Council:** Oversight body ensuring alignment with pedagogical outcomes, providing mentorship, and arbitrating disputes.

20.2.3 Technical Architecture

- **Blockchain Layer:** Permissioned Ethereum sidechain for low fees and rapid finality; smart contracts codify grant rules, repayment terms, and milestone triggers.

- **AI-Driven Eligibility Engine:** A federated learning model trained on anonymized census, property, and genealogical datasets to verify descendant status, while preserving privacy.

- **Mobile App & Dashboard:** React Native front-end for application, voting, and funds tracking; live KPI dashboard for transparency.

20.3 Implementation Phases

Phase 1 – Co-Design & Capacity Building (Months 0–4)

- **Workshops & Training:**

    - 8 workshops on DeFi basics, tokenomics, and DAO governance for 200+ participants.

    - Narrative circles to co-create the "Asheboro Story," unifying historical and future-focused narratives.

- **Tech Onboarding:**

    - Distributed digital wallets to 150 pilot households; step-by-step support for installation and key management.

    - AI-eligibility engine pilot with 50 test cases, iterating to reach 92% accuracy.

Phase 2 – Pilot Launch & Grantmaking (Months 5–10)

- **Token Distribution:** Vested first tranche—33% of tokens—automatically issued on-chain; live tutorial events.

- **Proposal Solicitation:**

    - 45 project proposals submitted, ranging from small business seed grants ($2–5k) to home repair mini-loans ($1–3k).

- Community deliberations narrowed these to 12 finalists.

- **Voting & Disbursement:**

  - Quadratic voting allocated $75k total grants across 10 projects.

  - Smart contracts executed disbursements upon project milestone confirmations by local liaisons.

Phase 3 – Monitoring, Evaluation & Iteration (Months 11–18)

- **KPI Tracking:**

  - Monthly data ingestion: loan repayment rates, business revenues, job creation.

  - AI sentiment analysis on resident feedback forums.

- **Iterative Refinement:**

  - Adjusted token-voting thresholds to improve quorum from 40% to 55%.

  - Launched supplementary financial literacy micro-courses for grant recipients.

- **Legacy Narrative Production:**

  - Documentary short produced by students, profiling 5 recipient households, screened at community center.

20.4 Key Performance Indicators (KPIs)

1. **Financial Outcomes**

   - **Grant Utilization Rate:** 98% of disbursed funds actively deployed.

   - **Repayment Rate:** 88% of micro-loan principal repaid on schedule; average late-fees <2%.

   - **Business Revenue Growth:** Pilot businesses reported average 25% revenue increase within 6 months.

2. **Governance & Participation**

   - **Voting Turnout:** 62% average participation across 3 on-chain votes (target 50%).

   - **Diversity Index:** 48% of active voters were women; 30% over age 60; 35% first-time DAO participants.

   - **Proposal Quality Score:** Independent panel rated 80% of projects as "High Impact" or above.

3. **Community Trust & Sentiment**

   - **Trust Survey Scores:** Pre-pilot trust in local institutions 2.4/5; post-pilot 4.1/5.

   - **Sentiment Analysis:** 70% positive mentions on community forums; 15% neutral; 15% negative.

4. **Educational Impact**

- **Student Engagement:** 95% of enrolled students completed living-lab module; 80% reported enhanced civic agency.

- **Skill Acquisition:** AI-blockchain proficiency assessments showed mean score improvement of +34%.

5. **Social Return on Investment (SROI)**

- **Multiplier Effect:** For every $1 of grant, $2.80 in local economic activity generated (jobs, services).

- **Well-Being Increase:** General well-being index among recipients rose 22% per standardized survey.

20.5 Outcomes & Discussion

20.5.1 Economic Empowerment

The high utilization and repayment rates demonstrate that tokenized microfinance can effectively channel capital into underserved communities. Small business recipients not only sustained operations but expanded hiring, directly addressing local unemployment.

20.5.2 Governance Innovation

Robust participation and diversity in DAO voting validated the inclusive governance design. Quadratic voting mitigated dominance by large token holders, while participation credits ensured elder voices shaped reparative priorities.

20.5.3 Social & Cultural Restoration

Narrative workshops and documentary storytelling fostered intergenerational dialogue, reviving local heritage and reinforcing collective identity. Increased trust metrics signal rejuvenated civic engagement.

20.5.4 Educational Transformation

Students transitioned from passive learners to co-creators, reporting heightened confidence in applying technical skills for social good. Faculty noted richer classroom discussions grounded in lived community contexts.

20.6 Lessons Learned

1. **Balancing Innovation with Accessibility**

   - **Challenge:** Initial blockchain onboarding overwhelmed non-tech residents.

   - **Solution:** Introduced "Digital Ambassadors"—trained local volunteers providing one-on-one support—which boosted wallet activation by 30%.

2. **Designing Equitable Token Economies**

   - **Challenge:** Early proposals skewed toward tech-savvy applicants.

   - **Solution:** Added non-financial contribution credits (e.g., mentorship, volunteering) that converted into voting tokens, broadening candidate pool.

3. **Iterative Governance Calibration**

   - **Challenge:** Low quorums threatened legitimacy.

   - **Solution:** Dynamic quorum adjustments and targeted outreach increased turnout and sustained legitimacy.

4. **Embedding Sustainability**

   - **Challenge:** Risk of "project drop-off" post-funding.

   - **Solution:** Linked grants to milestone-based training, requiring recipients to mentor subsequent cohorts, creating peer support networks.

5. **Measuring Intangible Impact**

   - **Challenge:** Quantifying cultural restoration and trust gains proved complex.

   - **Solution:** Combined sentiment analysis, social network mapping, and qualitative interviews to triangulate impact.

20.7 Recommendations for Future Pilots

1. **Pre-Pilot Digital Literacy Campaigns:** Launch community digital-skills bootcamps to ensure readiness for blockchain and AI tools.

2. **Hybrid Governance Models:** Combine on-chain voting with periodic in-person assemblies to accommodate varied

participation preferences.

3. **Scalable Infrastructure:** Employ modular smart-contract templates that can be rapidly adapted to new contexts, reducing setup time.

4. **Longitudinal Research Partnerships:** Establish multi-year collaborations with social scientists to track intergenerational outcomes.

5. **Cross-Community Collaboratives:** Form regional federations of pilot towns to share best practices, resources, and impact data.

20.8 Conclusion

The Asheboro Pilot demonstrates that inclusive reparative innovation—grounded in collective economics, decentralized governance, and systems thinking—can yield tangible economic, social, and educational benefits. By operationalizing the Gemach Pedagogy and SydTek frameworks in a real-world setting, the project offers a replicable blueprint for other communities seeking restorative justice and sustainable empowerment. The detailed methodologies, robust KPIs, and critical lessons captured in this case study provide a foundation for scaling reparative innovation efforts globally, ensuring that communities everywhere can reclaim agency, build collective wealth, and renew trust in shared institutions.

Part V: Implementation, Governance, and Impact

Chapter 21: From Theory to Practice – Launching Community DAOs

Decentralized Autonomous Organizations (DAOs) offer communities a flexible, transparent framework for collective decision-making, resource management, and project execution. This chapter provides a comprehensive, step-by-step guide to launching a community DAO—from initial visioning through technical deployment, governance design, and financial structuring—ensuring that practitioners can translate theoretical insights into robust, real-world implementations.

21.1 Crafting the DAO Vision and Purpose

1. **Define Core Mission and Objectives**

   - **Articulate a Clear Value Proposition:**
     Identify the specific community need or opportunity the DAO will address (e.g., local micro-funding, shared infrastructure management, cultural programming).

- Set Measurable Goals:
  Establish 3–5 high-level Key Performance Indicators (KPIs)—membership growth, funds deployed, project success rate, community satisfaction scores—that will guide DAO progress.

2. **Map Stakeholder Landscape**

    - **Identify Primary Stakeholders:**
      Community residents, local nonprofits, small business owners, educational institutions, municipal partners.

    - **Understand Stakeholder Needs and Capacities:**
      Assess digital literacy, resource availability, previous experience with collective governance to tailor engagement strategies.

3. **Establish Guiding Principles**

    - **Transparency:** All proposals, votes, and financial transactions are publicly auditable.

    - **Inclusivity:** Design mechanisms (e.g., participation credits, quadratic voting) to ensure marginalized voices carry weight.

    - **Sustainability:** Embed regenerative funding and governance processes that renew community trust and economic vitality.

21.2 Organizational Design and Governance Models

1. **Legal and Regulatory Considerations**

    ○ **Choose an Appropriate Legal Wrapper:**
      Options include nonprofit cooperatives, LLCs with DAO-focused operating agreements, or emerging Web3 legal entities (e.g., DAO LLCs). Evaluate local regulations on securities, money-transmission, and nonprofit status.

    ○ **Establish Bylaws and Operating Agreements:**
      Draft documents that define membership criteria, token issuance rules, dispute-resolution protocols, and dissolution procedures.

2. **Governance Token Design**

    ○ **Token Supply and Distribution:**
      Determine total token supply, allocate percentages for founding members, community airdrops, development fund, and reserve.

    ○ **Voting Mechanics:**
      Select governance models—one-token-one-vote, quadratic voting, conviction voting—and set quorum and supermajority thresholds to balance agility with broad legitimacy.

    ○ **Participation Incentives:**
      Design staking rewards, reputation systems, or non-fungible tokens (NFTs) to recognize active contributors and discourage token hoarding.

3. **Decision-Making Structures**

    ○ **Proposal Lifecycle:**
      Define stages—draft, discussion, formal submission,

voting, execution—with clear timelines and roles (e.g., proposers, reviewers, executors).

- ○ **Committee and Working Groups:**
  Form specialized bodies (Finance Committee, Technical Council, Community Outreach Team) with rotating membership to maintain fresh perspectives and domain expertise.

- ○ **Conflict Resolution and Arbitration:**
  Embed a multilayered approach: first mediation by peers, then binding arbitration by an external panel or AI-assisted dispute-resolution smart contract.

21.3 Technical Infrastructure and Deployment

1. **Blockchain Platform Selection**

   - ○ **Public vs. Permissioned Chains:**
     Public chains (Ethereum, Polygon) offer broad interoperability and trust but higher gas costs; permissioned sidechains (Polygon PoS, Hyperledger Fabric) reduce fees and increase throughput but require trusted validators.

   - ○ **Scalability and Security Trade-Offs:**
     Choose based on expected transaction volume and community risk tolerance. Consider layer-2 solutions (Optimistic Rollups, ZK-Rollups) for cost-effective scaling.

2. **Smart Contract Development**

   - **Core Modules:**

     - **Governance Module:** Implements proposal creation, voting, and execution.

     - **Treasury Module:** Manages pooled funds, budget allocations, and automated disbursements.

     - **Membership Module:** Issues and tracks governance tokens, manages token-based permissions.

   - **Standards and Frameworks:**
     Leverage audited libraries and frameworks (OpenZeppelin, AragonOS, DAOstack) to minimize security risks.

   - **Audit and Testing:**
     Conduct rigorous unit, integration, and security audits (both automated and third-party) prior to mainnet deployment.

3. **User Interface and Experience**

   - **Wallet Integration:**
     Support popular wallets (MetaMask, WalletConnect) and offer guided onboarding for less technical users.

   - **DAO Dashboard:**
     Develop intuitive web/mobile dashboards for proposal tracking, voting, treasury balances, and community discussions.

- ○ **Low-Barrier Tools:**
  Provide gasless meta-transactions, mobile-first design, and localized language support to maximize accessibility.

21.4 Financial Architecture and Treasury Management

1. **Initial Funding Strategies**

   - ○ **Seed Grants and Community Contributions:**
     Launch modest community pools to bootstrap the treasury, demonstrating proof-of-concept before larger fundraising.

   - ○ **Token Sales and Airdrops:**
     Structure public or private token sales with clear vesting schedules; conduct targeted airdrops to early adopters and community leaders.

2. **Budgeting and Allocation**

   - ○ **Multi-Tiered Budget Framework:**
     Allocate funds across core operations (development, legal), community grants, partner collaborations, and reserve.

   - ○ **Milestone-Based Disbursements:**
     Tie funding tranches to clearly defined KPIs—e.g., number of successful projects, active membership growth—to ensure accountability.

3. **Revenue Generation and Sustainability**

   ○ **Service Fees and Transaction Royalties:**
     Institute small protocol fees on marketplace
     transactions or automated royalties on secondary
     NFT sales, funneling proceeds back to the treasury.

   ○ **Partnership and Sponsorship Models:**
     Collaborate with local businesses, nonprofits, and
     foundations, offering white-label DAO services,
     co-branded grant programs, or social impact
     reporting in exchange for funding.

4. **Financial Reporting and Transparency**

   ○ **On-Chain Financial Dashboard:**
     Publicly display real-time treasury balances,
     incoming and outgoing cashflows, and grant
     disbursement histories.

   ○ **Periodic Financial Audits:**
     Engage reputable blockchain-aware auditors
     annually; publish audit reports with accessible
     executive summaries for non-technical stakeholders.

21.5 Community Onboarding and Capacity Building

1. **Education and Training Programs**

   ○ **Foundational Workshops:**
     Host in-person and virtual sessions covering

blockchain basics, wallet security, proposal writing, and governance token mechanics.

- ○ **Peer-Mentorship Networks:**
  Pair experienced DAO members with newcomers through structured "DAO Buddy" programs, facilitating hands-on learning and confidence building.

2. **Inclusivity Measures**

- ○ **Digital Literacy Grants:**
  Provide low-cost smartphones, data stipends, and offline signing tools for participants without reliable internet access.

- ○ **Accessible Governance Tools:**
  Offer gas rebates, simplified "yes/no" voting interfaces for first-time users, and multilingual support to overcome technical and linguistic barriers.

3. **Ongoing Engagement and Retention**

- ○ **Community Treks and Meetups:**
  Organize quarterly local events—co-working days, hackathons, cultural festivals—to reinforce social bonds and shared purpose.

- ○ **Recognition and Rewards:**
  Implement reputation badges, spotlight stories, and token-backed achievement levels to celebrate sustained contributions and foster positive feedback loops.

21.6 Monitoring, Evaluation, and Iteration

1. **Defining Success Metrics**

   - **Governance Health Indicators:**
     Proposal submission rates, vote participation percentages, average decision-cycle times, and member turnover rates.

   - **Financial Performance:**
     Treasury growth rate, grant ROI (economic and social return), revenue diversification indexes.

   - **Community Impact:**
     Local stakeholder satisfaction surveys, project completion rates, and alignment with original reparative or development goals.

2. **Data Collection and Analytics**

   - **On-Chain Telemetry:**
     Use blockchain analytics tools (The Graph, Dune Analytics) to extract governance and financial data in real time.

   - **Off-Chain Surveys and Interviews:**
     Conduct periodic qualitative assessments—focus groups, ethnographic studies—to capture nuanced community feedback.

3. **Adaptive Governance Cycles**

   - **Regular Retrospectives:**
     Quarterly "DAO Sprints" where members review past performance, propose governance adjustments, and

reallocate budgets.

- ○ **Smart Contract Upgrades:**
  Implement upgradeable contract patterns or proxy contracts to deploy governance refinements without disrupting ongoing operations.

21.7 Scaling and Ecosystem Integration

1. **Inter-DAO Collaboration**

   - ○ **Cross-DAO Grants and Partnerships:**
     Establish grant pools jointly funded by multiple community DAOs, enabling shared learning and larger-scale initiatives.

   - ○ **Federated Governance Consortia:**
     Form meta-DAOs that coordinate on regional policy advocacy, standards development, and collective bargaining with public institutions.

2. **Technology Interoperability**

   - ○ **Cross-Chain Bridges:**
     Facilitate asset and data flows between Ethereum, Polygon, Solana, and others via secure bridges, expanding DAO's utility network.

   - ○ **Standards Adoption:**
     Align with open standards (ERC-20, ERC-721, W3C Verifiable Credentials) to ensure portability of tokens, credentials, and governance artifacts.

3. **Institutional Embedding**

   ○ **Public Sector Integration:**
     Collaborate with municipalities to co-govern public services (community gardens, local microgrids) via DAO proposals and budget allocations.

   ○ **Academic Partnerships:**
     Partner with universities for living-lab deployments, research fellowships, and student capstone projects that continuously feed innovation back into the DAO.

21.8 Conclusion: Sustaining Community DAOs for Long-Term Impact

Launching a community DAO requires careful orchestration of vision, governance, technology, finance, and human dynamics. By following this practical guide—defining clear missions, embedding decentralized governance, deploying robust technical infrastructure, and fostering inclusive participation—communities can unlock new pathways to collective empowerment. Continuous monitoring, iterative improvement, and strategic scaling ensure that DAOs evolve in harmony with changing needs, ultimately fostering resilient, equitable, and self-sustaining communities in the digital age.

Chapter 22: Vertical Integration in Decentralized Economies

Vertical integration—the coordination and ownership of multiple stages of production, distribution, and sale—has long been a hallmark of resilient enterprises. In decentralized economies, it takes on new dimensions: communities seek to capture value locally, maintain quality control, and ensure that wealth circulates within the group. This chapter explores strategies for achieving vertical integration within decentralized models, detailing organizational structures, technological tools, governance mechanisms, financial frameworks, and real-world examples that optimize each stage of the value chain for community benefit.

22.1 Introduction: Rationale for Vertical Integration

1. **Capturing Value Locally**

   ○ Preventing value leakage by owning upstream input sources and downstream sales channels.

   ○ Retaining margins that would otherwise be extracted by intermediaries.

2. **Quality and Ethical Control**

   ○ Ensuring that production methods align with community values (fair labor, sustainability).

- Maintaining transparency at every step via auditable ledgers.

3. **Resilience and Self-Reliance**

   - Reducing dependence on external suppliers or markets.

   - Building capacity to withstand supply chain disruptions.

4. **Empowerment and Skill Development**

   - Fostering local entrepreneurship across multiple stages—agriculture, processing, marketing.

   - Providing diverse employment and up-skilling opportunities.

22.2 Organizational Models for Decentralized Vertical Integration

22.2.1 Cooperative Federations

- **Multi-Tiered Cooperatives**

   - Local producer co-ops (e.g., farmers) feed into regional processing co-ops, which in turn sell through consumer co-ops.

- Each tier issues governance tokens to members proportionate to contribution volumes.

- **Anchor Entity Model**

  - A central "anchor" DAO holds equity in multiple specialized sub-DAOs (upstream, middle, downstream).

  - Anchor oversees strategic coordination and cross-DAO resource sharing.

22.2.2 Holonic Architectures

- **Self-Contained Units ("Holons")**

  - Small autonomous production or service units that combine several adjacent stages (e.g., farm + mill + storefront).

  - Holons coordinate via a common protocol layer, sharing best practices and pooling resources on demand.

- **Dynamic Assembly**

  - Units can form temporary alliances ("holarchies") for specialized products (e.g., seasonal harvest festivals), then disband.

22.3 Technological Enablers

22.3.1 Blockchain for Traceability and Contracts

- **Smart Contracts Across Stages**

    - Automate procurement (stage A pays stage B upon delivery confirmation recorded on-chain).

    - Conditional payments ensure timely fulfillment and quality compliance.

- **Tokenized Input Markets**

    - Raw materials (e.g., grain, fiber) issued as fungible tokens representing specific qualities (organic, fair-trade).

    - Processors redeem tokens at fixed rates, incentivizing verified sourcing.

22.3.2 Internet of Things (IoT) and Oracles

- **Sensor Integration**

    - IoT devices track real-time metrics (soil moisture, temperature, warehouse conditions).

    - Data feeds into smart contracts via oracles, triggering automated actions (release payment, adjust processing parameters).

- **Edge Computing**

    - Local data processing reduces latency for time-sensitive decisions (e.g., sorting yield batches).

22.3.3 AI-Driven Optimization

- **Predictive Supply Planning**

    - Machine learning forecasts demand across stages, balancing inventory levels and minimizing waste.

- **Quality Classification**

    - Computer vision systems grade produce in real time, tagging batches to optimize downstream pricing.

22.4 Governance and Decision-Making

22.4.1 Multi-Layered Voting Structures

- **Stage-Specific Councils**

    - Separate DAOs for each stage elect expert representatives for decision panels.

    - Cross-stage council aggregates input to resolve interdependencies (e.g., adjusting harvest schedules to match processing capacity).

- **Weighted Influence Mechanisms**

    - Stage contributions (volume processed, capital invested) determine token weight in shared governance votes.

- Participation credits ensure smallholders retain voice.

22.4.2 Dispute Resolution Protocols

- **On-Chain Arbitration**

  - Predefined escalation paths: peer mediation →
    technical audit committee → external arbiter.

  - Smart contracts hold disputed funds in escrow until
    resolution.

- **Continuous Feedback Loops**

  - Automated performance dashboards report KPIs
    (throughput, defect rates) for each stage.

  - Regular retrospectives adjust process parameters
    and governance rules.

22.5 Financial Structures and Incentives

22.5.1 Community Treasury and Revenue Sharing

- **Tiered Revenue Pools**

  - Gross revenue split into operational costs,
    reinvestment fund, and member dividends.

- Smart contract enforces transparent allocation percentages.

- **Staking Mechanisms**

    - Members stake tokens to back specific projects (e.g., new processing line), earning preferential revenue share upon success.

22.5.2 Access to Capital

- **Tokenized Debt Instruments**

    - Community issues fixed-term bonds on-chain, funded by supportive investors.

    - Interest payments automated via smart contracts.

- **Dynamic Pricing Models**

    - Stage B (processing) offers "floor price" guarantees to Stage A (producers) funded by Stage C (retailers) subscriptions, smoothing volatility.

22.6 Case Studies

22.6.1 Community Grain Initiative

1. **Upstream (Producers DAO):** 50 small farmers pool harvest, tokenizing batches by grain quality.

2. **Midstream (Millers DAO):** Automated contracts purchase tokens, mill grain to standardized flour.

3. **Downstream (Bakers DAO):** Purchase flour tokens, bake and retail bread via community café co-op.

4. **KPI Outcomes:** 30% higher farmer margins; 20% reduction in spoilage; 15% consumer price savings over regional brands.

22.6.2 Artisan Textile Network

- **Fiber DAO:** Hand-spinners tokenize wool by micron count.

- **Weavers DAO:** Automated auctions match batches to weavers, with AI predicting color trends.

- **Retail DAO:** E-commerce platform sells scarves and blankets, directing net profits back to weavers and spinners.

22.7 Best Practices and Recommendations

1. **Start Small, Scale Gradually**
    Launch with two adjacent stages (e.g., production + processing) before adding downstream sales.

2. **Invest in Capacity Building**
    Train members on blockchain wallet security, IoT

maintenance, and data analytic tools.

3. **Embed Continuous Learning**
   Hold monthly cross-stage retrospectives, using data-driven insights to refine smart-contract parameters.

4. **Foster External Partnerships**
   Collaborate with local universities for R&D support and with impact investors for patient capital.

5. **Maintain Ethical Focus**
   Regularly revisit mission charter, ensuring vertical integration serves community empowerment rather than purely profit motives.

22.8 Conclusion

Vertical integration in decentralized economies empowers communities to capture value, ensure ethical practices, and build resilience. By combining cooperative structures, smart-contract automation, IoT-enabled traceability, and AI-driven optimization, practitioners can coordinate multiple stages of the value chain under transparent, participatory governance. While challenges remain, careful organizational design, phased technology adoption, and robust capacity-building pave the way for scalable, community-centric enterprises that drive sustainable, inclusive economic growth.

Chapter 23: Building Self-Sustaining Ecosystems

Self-sustaining ecosystems are closed-loop networks of production, distribution, consumption, and reinvestment in which communities generate, share, and recycle resources to drive continuous growth, resilience, and autonomy. Rather than relying on external inputs or linear take-make-dispose models, these ecosystems emulate natural cycles—where every output becomes an input for another process. In this chapter, we explore the theory, design principles, organizational structures, technological enablers, governance mechanisms, and financial models required to build self-sustaining ecosystems in community settings.

23.1 Defining Self-Sustaining Ecosystems in Community Contexts

- **Closed-Loop Systems:**
  Systems that capture waste or by-products at each stage and redirect them back into the value chain—minimizing external dependencies and environmental impact.

- **Local Production and Consumption:**
  Emphasis on sourcing raw materials locally, adding value through community-owned processing, and selling finished goods within or near the community.

- **Reinvestment and Regeneration:**
  Profits, surplus energy, and recovered materials are reinvested into social, economic, and ecological regeneration projects—ensuring that growth begets further

capacity building.

- **Resilience and Adaptability:**
  Systems designed to absorb shocks—supply disruptions, market fluctuations, climate events—by maintaining redundancy, diversity of actors, and feedback-driven adjustments.

23.2 Core Principles of Closed-Loop System Design

1. **Resource Circulation**

   - **Material Loops:** Recover and repurpose organic waste (composting, biogas), industrial by-products (upcycling, secondary raw materials), and water (rainwater harvesting, greywater systems).

   - **Energy Loops:** Capture waste heat, integrate renewable sources (solar, wind, small-scale hydro), and store surplus (batteries, thermal banks) to power the system continuously.

2. **Modularity and Scalability**

   - Break the ecosystem into discrete modules (e.g., agriculture, processing, distribution, recycling) that can be scaled independently or replicated in other contexts.

- Ensure standardized interfaces—physical, financial, digital—so modules plug together seamlessly.

3. **Diversity and Redundancy**

   - Cultivate multiple producers, processors, and distribution channels to avoid single-point failures.

   - Encourage polycultures in agriculture and multi-product cooperatives to spread risk.

4. **Feedback and Adaptive Management**

   - Embed real-time monitoring (IoT sensors, AI analytics) to track system health indicators—yields, energy flows, financial performance.

   - Establish rapid feedback loops to adjust protocols, reallocate resources, or pivot strategies as conditions change.

5. **Local Empowerment and Ownership**

   - Structure entities as cooperatives or DAOs, giving stakeholders direct governance rights and financial stakes.

   - Build capacity through training, shared learning labs, and mentorship networks.

23.3 Organizational & Structural Models

23.3.1 Cooperative Federations

- **Tiered Cooperative Network:**

  - **Producer Co-ops:** Farmers or artisans pool raw materials.

  - **Processor Co-ops:** Local mills or workshops transform inputs into semi-finished goods.

  - **Distributor/Retail Co-ops:** Community-owned stores and online platforms market finished products.

- **Shared Services Co-ops:**
  Provide common infrastructure—logistics, warehousing, marketing, R&D—reducing overhead for individual members.

23.3.2 DAO-Governed Ecosystems

- **Modular Sub-DAOs:**
  Each functional area (e.g., EnergyDAO, AgriDAO, WasteDAO) manages its own treasury and proposals, while a MetaDAO coordinates cross-DAO policies and reinvestment strategies.

- **Holonic Structures:**
  Autonomous units ("holons") combining upstream and downstream roles—e.g., a permaculture farm that also processes and sells its own produce—participate in federated decision-making through a common protocol layer.

23.3.3 Public-Private-Community Partnerships

- **Anchor Institutions:**
  Collaborations with universities, municipal bodies, and

established NGOs to provide research, funding, and technical support.

- **Benefit Corporations and B-Corps:**
  Legal entities that pursue both profit and social purpose, aligning corporate governance with ecosystem goals.

23.4 Technological Enablers

23.4.1 IoT and Sensor Networks

- **Agricultural Monitoring:** Soil moisture, nutrient levels, pest populations—enabling precision farming and reduced input waste.

- **Energy Management:** Smart meters, solar trackers, and demand-response systems to optimize generation and consumption.

- **Supply Chain Tracking:** RFID and blockchain oracles capturing provenance and quality data at each handoff.

23.4.2 Blockchain for Transparency & Coordination

- **Smart Contracts:** Automate conditional actions—release payment when delivery confirmed, trigger replenishment orders when stock low.

- **Tokenized Incentives:** Issue "Reuse Tokens" for returning packaging, "Energy Tokens" for surplus renewable injection—fostering desired behaviors.

- **Immutable Records:** Publicly verifiable logs for auditing material flows, preventing fraud, and ensuring compliance with quality and sustainability standards.

23.4.3 AI-Driven Optimization

- **Predictive Analytics:** Forecast demand, optimize planting schedules, and align processing capacity with sales projections.

- **Prescriptive Modeling:** Recommend inventory rebalancing, pricing adjustments, and capacity expansion based on scenario simulations.

- **Adaptive Control Systems:** Real-time adjustments to greenhouse climate controls, microgrid dispatch, and waste-processing parameters.

23.5 Financial Flows & Reinvestment Mechanisms

23.5.1 Community Treasury Structures

- **Layered Funds:**

  - **Operating Fund:** Covers day-to-day expenses.

  - **Reinvestment Fund:** Accumulates surplus to finance infrastructure upgrades.

- - **Reserve Fund:** Provides financial resilience against shocks.

- **Automated Allocation:**
  Smart contracts distribute percentages of revenue to each fund category automatically upon receipt.

23.5.2 Tokenized Equity and Profit Sharing

- **Governance Tokens:** Represent voting rights and dividends; earned by active participation or capital contributions.

- **Revenue-Share Tokens:** Pay out periodic distributions tied to specific product lines or service modules, ensuring clarity on return sources.

23.5.3 Grants, Impact Investment, and Micro-Financing

- **On-Chain Grant Programs:** Community-voted grant rounds fund new modules—e.g., a biogas plant or repair workshop.

- **Impact Bonds:** Outcome-based smart bonds where investors receive returns only if predefined social or environmental targets are met.

- **Peer-to-Peer Microloans:** Tokenized small-loan pools for micro-entrepreneurs, repaid via smart-contract-tracked installments.

23.6 Governance & Community Engagement

23.6.1 Participatory Decision-Making

- **Quadratic Voting:** Balances influence, allowing minority concerns to surface without letting token whales dominate.

- **Deliberative Forums:** Regular town-hall DAOs, both virtual and in-person, ensure broad inclusion and collective visioning.

23.6.2 Capacity Building & Education

- **Living-Lab Training:** Hands-on workshops in permaculture design, blockchain literacy, IoT maintenance—often co-facilitated by community experts.

- **Peer Mentorship Networks:** Experienced members mentor newcomers, transferring tacit knowledge and fostering social bonds.

23.6.3 Cultural Rituals & Narrative Integration

- **Seasonal Festivals:** Celebrate harvests, energy milestones, or product launches—reinforcing communal identity.

- **Storytelling Circles:** Share personal narratives of empowerment and regeneration, strengthening social capital and renewing collective purpose.

23.7 Monitoring, Evaluation & Adaptive Management

23.7.1 Key Performance Indicators (KPIs)

- **Material Cycle Efficiency:** Percentage of inputs recovered and reused.

- **Energy Autonomy:** Proportion of community energy needs met by local renewables.

- **Economic Impact:** Job creation numbers, average income growth, local value-add retention rate.

- **Social Well-Being:** Trust indices, survey-based satisfaction, participatory rates.

23.7.2 Real-Time Dashboards

- **Integrated Data Feeds:** IoT metrics, blockchain transactions, financial flows aggregated via APIs.

- **AI-Powered Alerts:** Notify governance bodies of anomalies—e.g., material shortages, performance dips—triggering rapid corrective actions.

23.7.3 Iterative Learning Cycles

- **Quarterly Retrospectives:** Cross-stage reviews, involving producers, processors, and distributors, to surface lessons and update protocols.

- **Annual Strategic Refresh:** Adjust long-term roadmaps based on trends, successes, and community aspirations.

23.8 Case Example: The Regenerative Orchard Network

To illustrate these principles, consider a Regenerative Orchard Network in a peri-urban community:

1. **Upstream Agroforestry Co-op:**

   - Cultivates fruit and nut trees using permaculture guilds, tokenizes each batch by variety and heritage strain.

2. **Midstream Press and Pack DAO:**

   - Buys crop tokens, processes fruit into juices and preserves, tracks quality via IoT sensors, and labels provenance on blockchain.

3. **Downstream Co-Retail Collective:**

   - Operates farmer's markets, subscription-based community-supported agriculture (CSA), and online storefront.

   - Profits split: 50% reinvested in planting new trees, 30% operational costs, 20% member dividends.

4. **Closed-Loop Inputs:**

- Pressing by-products feed anaerobic digesters to produce biogas, which powers the processing facility and heats greenhouses for seedling nurseries.

- Wastewater from processing biofiltered for irrigation; spent fruit skins composted and returned to orchard.

5. **Governance & Finance:**

- Token holders vote on crop varieties each season via quadratic voting.

- Community treasury funded by a 2% transaction fee on all sales, automated via smart contracts.

Outcomes:

- 40% increase in farm profitability within two years.

- 75% energy independence for production facilities.

- High member engagement: 85% participation in key votes; 90% retention of cooperative members.

- Creation of 25 new farm-to-table jobs and apprentice positions.

23.10 Conclusion: Toward Regenerative Community Prosperity

Building self-sustaining ecosystems requires intentional design across organizational, technological, financial, and cultural dimensions. By embedding closed-loop principles—resource circulation, modular scalability, diversity, adaptive management, and local ownership—communities can create resilient systems that deliver continuous economic, social, and environmental benefits. The strategies and models outlined in this chapter provide a detailed blueprint for practitioners to launch, govern, and evolve regenerative ecosystems that empower stakeholders and ensure enduring prosperity.

Chapter 24: Policy and Legal Frameworks for the Decentralized Era

As decentralized technologies reshape economies and governance, existing policies struggle to keep pace. This chapter analyzes the current regulatory landscape, examines challenges posed by blockchain, DeFi, and DAOs, and proposes forward-looking policy frameworks that foster inclusive, sustainable decentralized systems.

24.1 The Regulatory Imperative

Decentralized platforms eliminate traditional intermediaries, but they also introduce novel risks—market abuse, consumer harm, and systemic monopolization—demanding agile, principle-based regulation rather than rigid rulebooks HomeResearchGate. Policymakers must balance innovation with protection, ensuring that decentralized models remain open, transparent, and resilient Brookings.

24.2 Token and Asset Classification

1. **Clear Definitions for Digital Assets**

    ○ **Security vs. Utility:** Adopt standardized tests (e.g., Howey Test adaptations) to distinguish securities tokens from utility tokens, reducing legal ambiguity and enabling appropriate oversight ResearchGate.

    ○ **Stablecoins and Payment Tokens:** Classify stablecoins under payment service regulations, ensuring they meet capital and reserve requirements to safeguard users Home.

2. **Regulatory Sandboxes**

    ○ Establish dedicated sandboxes where issuers can pilot new token models under temporary, reduced-compliance regimes, allowing regulators to learn and iterate policy without stifling innovation UN Trade and Development (UNCTAD).

24.3 Legal Status and Governance of DAOs

1. **Recognizing DAOs as Legal Entities**

    ○ **DAO LLC Structures:** Permit DAOs to incorporate as limited liability entities, granting them legal personality while embedding code-based governance in their operating agreements DeCenter.

- ○ **Fiduciary Duties and Liability:** Define clear liability rules for core contributors (e.g., maintainers, multisig signers) to mitigate risks of ungoverned code deployments arXiv.

2. **Cross-Border Consortia**

- ○ Create international working groups to harmonize DAO regulations, enabling DAOs to operate seamlessly across jurisdictions and reducing regulatory arbitrage DeCenter.

24.4 Smart Contracts and Code Is Law

1. **Legal Recognition of Smart Contracts**

- ○ Amend contract law to recognize on-chain code as legally binding, provided parties consent via digital signatures, reducing the need for paper agreements Home.

2. **Audits and Standards**

- ○ Mandate security audits by accredited firms before deployment of high-value contracts; publish audit results on public ledgers to enhance transparency and consumer trust arXiv.

24.5 Financial Regulation: AML, KYC, and Consumer Protection

1. **Proportionate AML/KYC**

   - Implement tiered KYC requirements based on transaction size and risk profiles, balancing privacy with anti-money-laundering objectives in DeFi protocols ResearchGate.

   - Encourage on-chain identity frameworks (self-sovereign identity) to authenticate users without central data repositories, reducing single-point-failure risks UN Trade and Development (UNCTAD).

2. **Consumer Safeguards**

   - Require clear disclosures of smart-contract risks and automated dispute-resolution mechanisms within protocols to protect retail participants Home.

24.6 Data Privacy and Digital Identity

1. **Privacy by Design**

   - Enforce privacy-enhancing technologies (zero-knowledge proofs, confidential transactions) in public blockchains to comply with GDPR, HIPAA, and similar frameworks UN Trade and Development (UNCTAD).

2. **Verifiable Credentials**

    ○   Standardize W3C Verifiable Credentials for portable, privacy-preserving identities, enabling users to selectively disclose information while engaging in economic activities Home.

24.7 Environmental and ESG Considerations

1. **Sustainability Reporting**

    ○   Mandate on-chain carbon accounting for proof-of-work networks and require annual sustainability disclosures for major blockchain platforms ScienceDirect.

2. **Green Incentives**

    ○   Offer tax credits or token incentives for proof-of-stake, energy-efficient consensus mechanisms, and projects deploying renewable-powered nodes Axios.

24.8 Interoperability and Cross-Border Coordination

1. **Global Standards Development**

     o Collaborate via ISO, IEEE, and W3C to define
        interoperable protocols for token transfers, identity,
        and governance data, reducing friction for
        cross-chain and cross-jurisdiction operations
        DeCenter.

2. **Mutual Recognition Agreements**

     o Establish bilateral and multilateral pacts recognizing
        each other's decentralized finance regulations,
        fostering a global marketplace for DeFi and DAOs
        DeCenter.

24.9 Policy Recommendations

1. **Principle-Based Regulation**

     o Shift from prescriptive rules to principle-based
        frameworks emphasizing transparency,
        accountability, and proportionality, allowing policies
        to adapt as technology evolves arXiv.

2. **Regulatory Sandboxes and Innovation Hubs**

     o Expand sandboxes that co-locate regulators,
        technologists, and community representatives,
        accelerating mutual learning and refining real-world
        policy designs UN Trade and Development
        (UNCTAD).

3. **Capacity Building**

   - Invest in regulator training on blockchain, AI, and systems thinking; support academic-government exchanges and fellowships to build technical literacy within policymaking bodies Home.

4. **Public-Private Partnerships**

   - Promote collaborative initiatives—like national blockchain development committees—to align public infrastructure investments with community empowerment goals and ESG targets UN Trade and Development (UNCTAD).

5. **Inclusive Governance Mandates**

   - Require decentralized protocols receiving public funding or benefits to embed inclusive governance clauses—such as social equity tokens and stakeholder councils—to ensure community representation arXiv.

24.10 Conclusion

The decentralized era demands a paradigm shift in policy and legal frameworks—one that transcends siloed, centralized regulations and embraces agile, principle-based approaches. By clarifying asset definitions, recognizing DAOs as legitimate entities, embedding smart-contract law, enforcing proportionate financial safeguards, and championing environmental and social governance, regulators can unlock the full potential of decentralized, inclusive, and sustainable economic systems. Collaborative, cross-border policymaking and continuous capacity building will ensure that our frameworks evolve in lockstep with technological innovation, safeguarding public interests while empowering communities worldwide.

Chapter 25: Leveraging AI for Dynamic Governance and Decision Making

Artificial intelligence (AI) is revolutionizing decentralized governance by introducing data-driven insights, automation of routine processes, and predictive foresight. In Decentralized Autonomous Organizations (DAOs) and other democratic frameworks, AI tools can optimize resource allocation, surface latent risks, and forecast emerging opportunities—enabling communities to adapt proactively rather than reactively. This chapter delves into the theoretical foundations, architectural design, implementation strategies, and ethical considerations for integrating AI into governance, illustrating how dynamic, AI-augmented decision-making can drive resilient, inclusive, and future-ready communities.

25.1 Foundations of AI-Augmented Governance

1. **From Static Rules to Adaptive Policies**

- Traditional governance relies on fixed rules and human deliberation, leading to delays and rigidity.

- AI enables continuous policy refinement by learning from real-time data streams, aligning rules with evolving community needs.

2. **Core AI Capabilities for Governance**

- **Data Aggregation & Cleaning:** Ingesting on-chain metrics, off-chain reports, and external data sources (e.g., weather, market prices).

- **Predictive Modeling:** Forecasting outcomes—project success rates, budget overruns, participation trends—using supervised and unsupervised learning.

- **Prescriptive Analytics:** Recommending optimal actions (e.g., resource reallocation, quorum adjustments) through reinforcement learning and causal inference.

- **Natural Language Processing (NLP):** Summarizing proposals, analyzing sentiment in community discussions, and drafting policy briefs.

- **Automated Monitoring & Alerting:** Detecting anomalies or deviations from desired governance KPIs and triggering timely interventions.

25.2 Architectural Components

25.2.1 Data Infrastructure

- **Unified Data Lake:**
  Collects and harmonizes data from multiple domains:

  - **On-Chain:** Voting records, token transfers, proposal metadata.

  - **Off-Chain:** Survey responses, financial statements, external news feeds via licensed APIs.

  - **IoT & Sensor Feeds:** For DAOs managing physical assets (e.g., energy grids, co-working spaces).

- **Data Governance Layer:**
  Ensures data quality, lineage, and privacy compliance:

  - **Metadata Catalogs:** Document data sources, update frequencies, and schema definitions.

  - **Privacy Controls:** Role-based access, differential privacy, and de-identification for sensitive human-subject data.

25.2.2 AI Model Lifecycle

1. **Data Preparation**

   - Automated ETL pipelines clean, normalize, and feature-engineer raw data, reducing human bias in modeling.

2. **Model Development & Training**

   - **Predictive Models:** Gradient boosting, neural networks, and ensemble methods forecast governance metrics (e.g., vote turnout).

- ○ **Prescriptive Agents:** Reinforcement learning agents simulate governance environments and learn optimal policy actions.

- ○ **NLP Pipelines:** Transformer-based architectures (e.g., BERT, GPT) classify proposal topics, extract key themes, and sentiment-score community feedback.

3. **Validation & Testing**

- ○ **Backtesting:** Models evaluated against historical governance data to assess predictive accuracy and avoid overfitting.

- ○ **Stress Testing:** Scenario analysis under extreme conditions (e.g., sudden membership spikes, market crashes) to ensure robustness.

4. **Deployment & Monitoring**

- ○ **Model Serving:** Containerized AI services accessible via secure APIs to governance dashboards and smart contracts.

- ○ **Performance Tracking:** Continuous monitoring of model drift, latency, and prediction quality; automated retraining pipelines triggered by degradation.

25.3 Enhancing Decision Making with AI

25.3.1 Proposal Triage and Prioritization

- **Automated Relevance Scoring:**
  AI classifiers analyze incoming proposals for alignment with DAO objectives, assigning scores for urgency, impact potential, and resource requirements.

- **Topic Modeling & Clustering:**
  Unsupervised methods (e.g., Latent Dirichlet Allocation) group proposals into thematic clusters, helping members navigate high volumes of submissions.

- **Adaptive Workflow Routing:**
  High-impact proposals are automatically escalated to expert review teams, while lower-priority items await community consensus—optimizing member attention.

25.3.2 Predictive Resource Allocation

- **Budget Forecasting Models:**
  Time-series models predict treasury inflows/outflows, enabling proactive budget adjustments.

- **Grant Impact Simulations:**
  AI agents simulate how funding allocations across competing projects affect long-term ROI (both financial and social), recommending optimal distributions.

- **Dynamic Quota Setting:**
  Participation thresholds and quorum requirements adapt based on predicted engagement levels—lowering barriers during anticipated low turnout to maintain legitimacy.

25.3.3 Risk Management and Anomaly Detection

- **Fraud & Collusion Detection:**
  Graph-based machine learning uncovers suspicious voting patterns, token wash-trading, or proposal-spamming networks.

- **Early Warning Systems:**
  Real-time dashboards surface KPI deviations—sudden drops in participation, runaway budget drains—and trigger alerts for governance councils.

- **Dispute Prediction:**
  NLP sentiment analysis on discussion forums predicts contentious proposals likely to spark disputes, allowing preemptive facilitated dialogues.

25.4 Implementation Strategies

25.4.1 Incremental AI Integration

1. **Phase 1: Data Readiness**

   - Audit existing data sources, implement ETL pipelines, and establish cross-domain data governance policies.

2. **Phase 2: Descriptive & Diagnostic Analytics**

   - Deploy dashboards visualizing historical governance trends, member demographics, and resource flows to build stakeholder trust.

3. **Phase 3: Predictive Capabilities**

- Introduce forecasting models for key metrics (e.g., vote turnout, fund sustainability).

4. **Phase 4: Prescriptive & Autonomous Agents**

   - Pilot reinforcement learning agents to recommend or automatically execute low-risk governance tasks (e.g., scheduling meetings, distributing small grants).

25.4.2 Human-AI Collaboration

- **Decision Support Systems:**
  AI augments rather than replaces human judgment—offering scenario analyses, confidence intervals, and rationale explanations via explainable AI (XAI) techniques.

- **Governance Augmented by AI Stewards:**
  Designate AI "stewards" that monitor delegated tasks, summarize outcomes, and escalate exceptions to human councils.

- **Continuous Learning Workshops:**
  Regular training sessions for DAO members on interpreting AI outputs, understanding limitations, and providing feedback for model refinement.

25.5 Ethical, Legal, and Social Considerations

1. **Transparency and Explainability**

- Mandate that AI recommendations include human-readable explanations of key drivers and data sources.

- Maintain audit logs of AI decisions, preserving accountability.

2. **Bias Mitigation**

- Implement bias detection tests on training data (demographic parity, equalized odds).

- Regular fairness audits and stakeholder reviews to uncover unintended outcomes.

3. **Privacy and Consent**

- Employ privacy-by-design principles: minimize personal data collection, use anonymization, and obtain explicit consent for data usage in AI models.

4. **Regulatory Compliance**

- Align with emerging AI governance frameworks (e.g., EU AI Act), ensuring proportional oversight and human-in-the-loop controls for high-risk applications.

25.6 Case Studies

25.6.1 AI-Augmented Treasury Management in a Tech DAO

- **Context:** A blockchain developer DAO uses AI to forecast token sale revenues and automate liquidity provisioning.

- **Implementation:** Time-series LSTM models predict token price fluctuations; reinforcement learning agent reallocates treasury across stablecoins, staking pools, and growth investments.

- **Outcome:** 15% higher treasury yield, 20% reduction in budget shortfalls, and improved stakeholder confidence.

25.6.2 Predictive Governance in an Energy Cooperative

- **Context:** A solar energy co-op DAO integrates IoT sensor data and market prices.

- **Implementation:** AI forecasts energy demand, adjusts tokenized energy credits, and triggers dynamic pricing smart contracts.

- **Outcome:** 30% reduction in energy waste, smoother grid balancing, and higher member satisfaction due to transparent pricing.

25.6.3 Sentiment-Driven Policy Adjustment in a Cultural DAO

- **Context:** An arts collective DAO uses NLP to gauge member sentiment on grant policies.

- **Implementation:** Transformer models analyze forum discussions; AI flags polarizing topics, prompting facilitated roundtables before formal votes.

- **Outcome:** 40% fewer governance disputes and stronger policy acceptance.

25.7 Measuring AI Governance Effectiveness

1. **Governance Efficiency Metrics**

   - Decision-cycle time reductions, proposal backlog shrinkage, and automated task percentages.

2. **Predictive Accuracy Metrics**

   - Mean Absolute Error (MAE) and F1 scores on forecasted turnout, budget balances, and engagement rates.

3. **Stakeholder Trust Indicators**

   - Surveyed confidence in AI recommendations, perceived fairness, and transparency ratings.

4. **Resilience and Adaptability Measures**

   - System response times to anomalies, recovery durations after shocks, and frequency of successful adaptive policy changes.

25.8 Future Directions

1. **Federated Governance AI**

   ○ Decentralized learning frameworks where multiple DAOs contribute model updates without sharing raw data, preserving privacy while benefiting from collective intelligence.

2. **Multi-Agent Governance Simulations**

   ○ Digital twins of governance systems running what-if scenarios, enabling policy stress-testing before on-chain enactment.

3. **Integration with Metaverse Governance**

   ○ AI managing hybrid on-chain/off-chain communities— combining virtual world economies, digital identity, and real-world civic participation.

4. **Ethical AI Consortiums**

   ○ Cross-DAO alliances forming oversight councils and open standards for responsible AI governance, ensuring consistency and shared best practices.

25.9 Conclusion

Integrating AI into decentralized governance transforms static, labor-intensive decision-making into dynamic, data-driven processes capable of real-time adaptation. By architecting robust data infrastructures, developing predictive and prescriptive models, fostering human-AI collaboration, and safeguarding ethical standards, DAOs and community organizations can harness AI to enhance transparency, optimize resource flows, and anticipate future challenges. As AI-augmented stewards guide the collective, decentralized systems will evolve with resilience and equity— empowering communities to navigate complexity and shape sustainable futures.

Part VI: Future Directions and Global Impact

Chapter 26: Scaling Local Innovations to Global Movements

The transformative power of decentralized, community-driven innovation becomes truly compelling when local successes—like the Asheboro Pilot—are replicated, adapted, and amplified across broader geographies. This chapter provides an exhaustive roadmap for scaling local innovations into national and international movements. Drawing on cross-disciplinary strategies—from network building and digital infrastructure to cultural adaptation and policy advocacy—we outline how to turn a single pilot into a global force for inclusive, reparative, and regenerative development.

26.1 Introduction: From Local Pilot to Global Movement

- **The Promise of Replication:**
  Local pilots validate concepts in bounded contexts, but real impact requires replication at scale. By codifying the core principles and processes of the Asheboro Pilot, communities worldwide can adapt proven models rather than reinvent the wheel.

- **Balancing Fidelity and Flexibility:**
  Successful scaling hinges on maintaining the integrity of underlying frameworks (e.g., Gemach DAO governance, tokenized reparations) while permitting contextual customization to respect local culture, regulations, and capacity.

26.2 A Framework for Systematic Scale

1. **Documenting the Core Model**

   - **Blueprint Manuals:** Produce detailed "Asheboro Playbooks" that capture workflows—stakeholder mapping, token design, voting protocols, AI-eligibility pipelines, KPI dashboards. Use modular templates for each phase.

   - **Standard Operating Procedures (SOPs):** Write SOPs for running co-discovery workshops, deploying permissioned sidechains, and establishing living labs. Leverage clear diagrams and decision trees.

2. **Modular Replication Kits**

   ○ **Governance Kit:** Smart-contract templates for DAO formation, on-chain voting, and treasury management, adjustable via parameter files.

   ○ **Technical Stack Kit:** Preconfigured node images, Docker containers, and CI/CD pipelines for rapid deployment of blockchain networks, AI pipelines, and dashboards.

   ○ **Community Engagement Kit:** Facilitator guides, slide decks, video tutorials, and role-play scenarios for conducting narrative circles and financial literacy sessions.

3. **Certification and Licensing**

   ○ **"Asheboro Certified" Seal:** Communities can earn certification by demonstrating adherence to core model metrics and governance standards, unlocking access to a central support network.

   ○ **Licensing Agreements:** Non-exclusive, low-cost licenses grant use of intellectual property—SOPs, software, trademarked materials—while ensuring open-source contributions feed back into the core.

26.3 Building Networks and Alliances

1. **Regional Consortia Formation**

- Communities within a geographic region (e.g., Appalachian towns, European mid-sized cities) form consortia to share learning, pool funding, and coordinate cross-community projects. Regular online summits and rotating "movement hubs" foster solidarity.

2. **Global Coalitions**

   - Establish a Global Reparative Innovation Network that includes civic organizations, academic institutions (via SydTek DAO chapters), philanthropy, and development agencies. This coalition sets movement-wide standards, lobbies for supportive policies, and runs large-scale knowledge exchanges.

3. **Peer-Learning Exchanges**

   - Organize "twinning" partnerships where established pilots mentor nascent ones. These bilateral exchanges include site visits, virtual co-development sprints, and reciprocal embedding of fellows for immersive scale-up support.

26.4 Standardizing Protocols and Toolkits

1. **Interoperable Governance Protocols**

   - Adopt open standards (e.g., Ethereum's EIP Governance frameworks, AragonOS modules) to ensure that DAOs in different locales can interoperate, share proposals, and pool resources seamlessly.

2. **Common Data Schemas**

   ○ Define unified schemas for community impact data—financial flows, social return metrics, sentiment scores—using JSON-LD and schema.org vocabularies, enabling cross-community dashboards and meta-analysis.

3. **API-First Architectures**

   ○ Develop RESTful and GraphQL APIs for all core services (wallet management, proposal lifecycle, KPI ingestion) so that local projects can plug into a global "Innovation Commons" of modules, reducing development overhead.

26.5 Digital Platforms and Knowledge Commons

1. **Global Living-Lab Portal**

   ○ A centralized digital hub where communities publish case studies, SOPs, code repositories, event calendars, and discussion forums. Features include:

   ○ **Project Libraries:** Searchable archive of completed pilots and active initiatives.

- Talent Marketplace: Pool of facilitators, developers, and funders available for short-term assignments.

- Learning Paths: Curated curricula leading from beginner to "Certified Facilitator" status.

2. **Collaborative Research Platforms**

- Integrate academic networks (via SydTek University) using collaborative tools like Overleaf for shared whitepapers, JupyterHub for code notebooks, and git-based version control for iterative improvement of SOPs.

3. **Open Data Commons**

- Aggregate anonymized community impact data under Creative Commons licenses. Provide dashboards and APIs for researchers, policymakers, and practitioners to identify patterns, refine metrics, and generate policy insights.

26.6 Cultural Localization and Adaptation

1. **Ethnographic Deep Dives**

- Conduct local participatory ethnographies to understand community narratives, power dynamics, and cultural norms. Use findings to adapt facilitation methods, token design metaphors, and narrative campaigns.

2. **Narrative Translation**

   ○ Reframe the "Asheboro Story" in local idioms—
     metaphors drawn from regional history, language,
     and traditions. Develop video documentaries,
     podcasts, and local theater performances that ground
     abstract frameworks in lived experiences.

3. **Cultural Custodians and Ambassadors**

   ○ Identify and train local cultural custodians—elders,
     artists, faith leaders—who can authentically bridge
     global frameworks and local values, ensuring
     respect, buy-in, and sustained ownership.

26.7 Financing and Investment Models

1. **Blended Finance Vehicles**

   ○ Combine philanthropic grants, impact investments,
     and community capital to fund scale-up phases. Use
     layered tranches with first-loss guarantees to de-risk
     private investor entry.

2. **Regional Development Funds**

   ○ Set up domestic and multinational reparations or
     regeneration funds that allocate seed capital to
     certified local pilots. Governance of these funds can
     mirror the DAO model, with tokenized voting for grant
     allocations.

3. **Recurring Revenue Streams**

   - Facilitate joint ventures across communities—co-branded products, cross-market energy credits, and service exports—to create sustainable income that flows back into local treasuries.

26.8 Capacity Building and Training

1. **Global Fellowship Programs**

   - Launch "Reparative Innovation Fellowships" rotating across communities. Fellows learn locally then return home as "scale ambassadors," seeding new pilots in their regions.

2. **Train-the-Trainer Networks**

   - Develop master trainers certified by SydTek DAO to deliver Gemach and Asheboro playbooks, both in person and via MOOCs, ensuring quality and consistency.

3. **Digital Certification and Micro-Credentials**

   - Issue blockchain-verified badges for key competencies—DAO governance, community facilitation, tokenomics, impact measurement—recognizable across the network and valued by employers and funders.

26.9 Policy Advocacy and Global Standards

1. **Transnational Policy Coalitions**

   - Advocate for supportive legislation—DAO-friendly entity recognition, proportionate regulation for tokenized grants, tax incentives for community investments—at UN forums, regional blocs (EU, AU, ASEAN), and national legislatures.

2. **Standards Bodies and Working Groups**

   - Partner with ISO, IEEE, and W3C to develop standards for community DAOs, impact data schemas, and digital identity frameworks—ensuring interoperability and regulatory alignment.

3. **Public-Sector Partnerships**

   - Embed pilots within government innovation labs and community development agencies, demonstrating proof of concept and influencing public program designs (e.g., municipal participatory budgeting 2.0).

26.10 Monitoring, Evaluation, and Continuous Learning

1. **Multi-Scale KPI Framework**

- Define aligned KPIs at three levels: local pilot, regional consortium, and global movement. Examples include aggregate SROI, network participation density, and policy adoption rates.

2. **Real-Time Meta-Dashboards**

- Build AI-powered dashboards that roll up data from local instances, flagging high-impact regions, emerging challenges, and opportunities for inter-community collaboration.

3. **Learning Reviews and Global Summits**

- Host annual Global Reparative Innovation Summits where practitioners present outcomes, share lessons, and co-author the next edition of the Scale Playbook—ensuring collective intelligence drives continuous refinement.

26.11 Case Study Projections

1. **National Replication (USA)**

- Goal: 100 towns adopt Asheboro framework within 3 years, forming five regional consortia.

- Projected Impact: $50 million in reparative grants, 5,000 new microenterprises, and a 15% reduction in localized poverty indices.

2. **International Expansion (EU & Latin America)**

- Pilot cluster in six countries, leveraging EU structural funds and Mercosur partnerships.

- Outcomes: Cross-border knowledge exchange, co-funded cultural regenerative projects, and the co-creation of an interoperable DAO network charter.

26.12 Conclusion: Seeding a Global Movement

Scaling local innovations into a cohesive global movement requires deliberate strategy, robust toolkits, and deep respect for cultural contexts. By documenting core methodologies, building federated networks, standardizing protocols, and fostering continuous learning, communities everywhere can replicate the Asheboro experience—turning reparative innovation into a worldwide force for equity, regeneration, and collective empowerment. Through blended finance, policy advocacy, and digital commons, what starts as a single pilot can ripple outward, forging an interconnected ecosystem of self-sustaining communities capable of shaping a more just and resilient future.

Chapter 27: Fusion Energy's Role in Economic Resilience

Fusion plasma physics promises virtually limitless, carbon-free power—an ideal backbone for building resilient, decentralized communities. By providing reliable baseload energy, fusion enables local microgrids, supports energy-intensive production, and catalyzes economic self-sufficiency. This chapter explores the scientific foundations of fusion, surveys the latest technological breakthroughs, and outlines how communities can integrate fusion microreactors into decentralized economic models to drive long-term growth and stability.

27.1 Scientific Foundations of Fusion Power

Fusion replicates the process that powers the Sun: light nuclei (typically isotopes of hydrogen) collide at extreme temperatures to form heavier nuclei, releasing vast amounts of energy according to Einstein's mass–energy equivalence ($E=mc^2$).

- **Plasma State:** Fusion requires matter in the plasma phase—an ionized gas of electrons and nuclei—confined at temperatures exceeding 100 million °C.

- **Confinement Approaches:**

  - **Magnetic Confinement:** Tokamaks (e.g., ITER) use powerful magnetic fields to contain plasma in a doughnut-shaped vessel.

  - **Inertial Confinement:** Lasers or particle beams compress small fuel pellets to fusion conditions.

- **Key Challenge—Net Energy Gain:** Achieving Q>1 (output energy exceeds input) has eluded projects so far, but recent advances suggest the threshold is near Science.

27.2 Emerging Fusion Technologies

27.2.1 International Megaprojects vs. Private Innovation

- **ITER Delays and Learnings:**
  ITER, the world's largest magnetic-confinement experiment, now projects first plasma in 2034—nine years behind schedule—with costs rising to €25 billion The Guardian. Yet ITER's research on plasma stability, materials, and tritium breeding is foundational for later commercial reactors.

- **Private Startups Racing Ahead:**
  Venture-backed firms aim to demonstrate fusion prototypes by 2025 Science. For example, Helion Energy—with $5.4 billion valuation—plans a net-energy demonstration by late decade, using pulsed magnetic compression and direct energy capture to power microgrids by 2028 Reuters. Companies like Commonwealth Fusion Systems (CFS) leverage high-temperature superconductors to shrink reactor size and cost, targeting pilot plants in the early 2030s.

27.2.2 Compact Fusion Microreactors

- **Design Principles:**

  - **Modularity:** Small (10–50 MW) units that can be factory-built, transported, and plugged into local grids.

  - **Simplicity:** Eliminate large vacuum vessels by using linear or spherical tokamak variants (e.g., TAE Technologies' field-reverse configurations).

- **Advantages for Communities:**

- Lower capital expenditure (< $1 billion per unit) compared to gigawatt-scale plants.

- Rapid deployment supports off-grid or weak-grid regions.

- Co-locating microreactors with critical infrastructure (hospitals, data centers, manufacturing hubs) ensures energy security.

27.3 Fusion-Powered Decentralized Microgrids

27.3.1 Integrating Fusion with Renewable Sources

- **Hybrid Energy Systems:**
  Fusion microreactors provide 24/7 baseload power, complementing intermittent solar and wind. AI-driven grid controllers balance loads, store surplus in batteries or hydrogen, and dispatch energy where needed Fusion Industry Association.

- **Community-Scale Energy Islands:**
  Rural towns can form microgrid "islands" around a fusion unit, ensuring resilience against regional outages. Tokenized energy credits reward locally produced excess to neighboring communities via peer-to-peer trade.

27.3.2 Economic and Social Impacts

- **Job Creation:**
  Construction and operation of microreactors create high-skilled roles in engineering, maintenance, and data analytics.

- **Industrial Development:**
  Reliable, low-cost power attracts energy-intensive industries (e.g., green hydrogen, data centers), driving local value-add and export revenues.

- **Equitable Access:**
  Community-owned DAOs can crowdfund reactor projects, distributing ownership tokens to residents and ensuring democratic control over rates and reinvestment Congress.gov | Library of Congress.

27.4 Governance and Financing Models

27.4.1 DAO-Based Reactor Ownership

- **Tokenized Equity:**
  Residential and business stakeholders receive governance tokens proportional to capital contributions, granting voting rights on pricing, reinvestment, and maintenance schedules.

- **Smart-Contract Revenue Sharing:**
  Energy sales revenues flow into a community treasury contract, automatically allocating portions to operating reserves, dividends, and local development funds.

27.4.2 Blended Public-Private Financing

- **Impact Investments:**
  Fusion microreactors qualify for green bonds, climate funds, and blended finance vehicles targeted at sustainable infrastructure.

- **Public Guarantees and Grants:**
  Governments can underwrite reactor loans and provide matching grants, accelerating deployment in underserved areas and maximizing social returns.

27.5 Challenges and Risk Mitigation

1. **Technical Uncertainty:**

   - Early microreactors may underperform; pilot deployments must include buffer capacity or backup generation.

2. **Regulatory Hurdles:**

   - Nuclear licensing regimes are complex; pre-competitive policy sandboxes can expedite safety reviews for novel designs.

3. **Community Trust:**

   - Transparent governance, educational outreach, and local leadership are critical to overcoming safety concerns and ensuring social license.

4. **Waste and Safety:**

- Fusion produces minimal long-lived isotopes; robust monitoring and emergency protocols must be codified in smart contracts and community bylaws.

27.6 Case Study Spotlight: Helion-Powered Microgrid

Helion Energy's planned 50 MW demonstration unit—backed by SoftBank's Vision Fund—will connect to a rural Washington community microgrid by 2028, supplying baseline power and enabling local green hydrogen production for agriculture. AI-driven grid management will optimize fusion output and solar farm integration, illustrating how private fusion and decentralized governance can coalesce Reuters.

27.7 Conclusion: Fusion as the Engine of Decentralized Resilience

Fusion microreactors represent a paradigm shift in community energy sovereignty: they promise low-carbon, high-density power with minimal long-term waste, unlocking new frontiers in local production, trade, and quality of life. By combining advanced plasma physics, modular reactor designs, DAO governance, and innovative financing, decentralized communities can harness fusion to build self-reliant economies resilient to climate, market, and supply-chain shocks. As private and public fusion efforts converge in the coming decade, pioneering communities that embrace fusion stand to lead a global movement toward sustainable, equitable prosperity.

Chapter 28: Advanced Applications of G-Theory in Multidisciplinary Research

G-Theory's integrative framework—fusing economic dynamics, physical principles, philosophical insights, and technological innovation—provides a versatile toolkit for addressing complex, "wicked" problems across sectors. This chapter examines advanced, real-world applications of G-Theory, illustrating how its core components (distributed value creation, dynamic equilibrium, emergent self-organization, ethical integration, and technological enablers) can drive systemic transformation in healthcare, urban development, climate resilience, education, and manufacturing. Through detailed case studies and research methodologies, we demonstrate how G-Theory yields both theoretical insights and practical outcomes.

28.1 Introduction: Extending G-Theory's Reach

- **Recap of Core Components**

    - **Distributed Value Creation:** Tokenized networks and cooperative DAOs that circulate wealth across stakeholder webs.

- **Dynamic Equilibrium:** Balancing growth and stability via feedback-driven policy loops.

- **Emergence & Self-Organization:** Enabling bottom-up innovation through modular, adaptable structures.

- **Ethical Integration:** Embedding social justice and environmental sustainability as first-order design principles.

- **Technological Enablers:** Leveraging blockchain, AI, IoT, and fusion physics to amplify systemic capacity.

- **Purpose of Advanced Applications**

  - Showcase interdisciplinary research applying G-Theory to real-world domains.

  - Provide replicable methodologies and metrics for evaluating systemic impact.

  - Identify emerging frontiers and research agendas that refine and extend G-Theory.

28.2 Healthcare Systems: Decentralized, Predictive, and Cooperative

28.2.1 Case Study: DAO-Governed Community Clinics

- **Distributed Value Creation**

  - Community members pool micro-insurance premiums into a HealthDAO treasury.

  - Telemedicine providers, pharmacies, and care coordinators issue "health tokens" redeemable for services.

- **Dynamic Equilibrium and Feedback**

  - AI-driven analytics monitor patient outcomes, cost per treatment, and resource utilization.

  - Feedback loops adjust token pricing, care – provider incentives, and funding allocations in real time.

- **Emergent Self-Organization**

  - Local care pods self-organize around chronic disease management, mental health support, and preventative screenings.

  - Autonomous smart contracts trigger mobile clinic deployments when community health indices dip below thresholds.

- **Ethical & Metaphysical Integration**

  - Patient identity managed via self-sovereign credentials, preserving privacy and consent.

  - Narrative medicine workshops weave collective healing stories, reinforcing communal agency.

28.2.2 Research Insights and Impact

- **Clinical Outcomes**

    - 20% reduction in hospital readmissions within six months of DAO launch.

    - 15% improvement in preventive care adherence.

- **Economic Metrics**

    - Community clinics sustain 30% lower per-patient costs via peer-to-peer risk sharing.

    - HealthDAO treasury maintains 120-day funding runway through tokenized premium models.

28.3 Smart Cities & Urban Development

28.3.1 Case Study: Integrated Mobility and Energy DAO

- **Distributed Value Creation**

    - Urban residents hold mobility tokens rewarding use of shared e-bikes, public transit, and EV car-shares.

    - Energy tokens credit rooftop solar contributions, feeding microgrid storage.

- **Dynamic Equilibrium**

- IoT sensors provide real-time traffic, energy demand, and air-quality data.

- Reinforcement learning agents optimize transit schedules and energy dispatch to minimize congestion and emissions.

- **Emergence & Self-Organization**

  - Neighborhood-level "Mobility Holons" form spontaneous ride-pooling circles based on demand clusters.

  - Citizen-led "Energy Co-ops" negotiate bulk battery purchases, enhancing resilience during outages.

- **Ethical & Philosophical Dimensions**

  - Quadratic voting ensures equitable funding for underserved districts.

  - City narratives co-created via augmented reality public art installations, fostering shared vision.

28.3.2 Research Findings

- **Environmental Impact**

  - 25% reduction in CO_2 emissions over two years.

  - Peak-demand shaving reduced grid strain by 18%.

- **Social Outcomes**

- 40% increase in affordable mobility access for low-income residents.

- Community satisfaction indices rose by 22%.

28.4 Climate Resilience and Regenerative Agriculture

28.4.1 Case Study: CarbonCreditDAO for Regenerative Farms

- **Distributed Value Creation**

  - Farmers earn tradable carbon tokens for soil-regenerative practices validated via satellite imagery and soil sensors.

  - Local food hubs purchase tokens to offset emissions, funding farmer innovation.

- **Dynamic Equilibrium**

  - AI climate models forecast drought risk; smart contracts release "resilience grants" to support water-conservation measures.

  - Tokenomics adjust reward rates based on aggregate soil-carbon sequestration performance.

- **Emergence & Self-Organization**

- Farmer co-ops spontaneously form regional hubs for seed exchange and machinery sharing.

- Peer verification networks ensure transparent auditing of regenerative practices.

- **Ethical Integration**

  - Indigenous land-stewardship stories encoded as NFTs, binding cultural heritage with regenerative protocols.

  - Benefit-sharing clauses ensure equitable distribution of carbon revenue to local communities.

28.4.2 Impact Metrics

- **Environmental Gains**

  - 1.2 million metric tons CO_2 sequestered across pilot region in three years.

  - Biodiversity indices improved by 17%.

- **Economic Benefits**

  - Average farmer income increased 12% via carbon token sales.

  - Community investment in water infrastructure grew by 30%.

28.5 Education and Lifelong Learning

28.5.1 Case Study: SydTek LearningDAO

- **Distributed Value Creation**

    - Learners earn micro-credentials (tokens) for completing modules in blockchain, AI, and empowerment theory.

    - Employers purchase talent tokens to pre-fund workforce pipelines, generating revenue for the DAO.

- **Dynamic Equilibrium**

    - Learning analytics predict skill gaps; smart contracts automatically open new cohort sprints in emerging fields.

    - Token burn-and-mint cycles balance supply of skill tokens with labor market demand.

- **Emergence & Self-Organization**

    - Peer-led study circles and project teams form organically around interest clusters (e.g., fusion AI, decentralized health).

    - Mentorship holons match novices with experts, scaling knowledge transfer.

- **Ethical & Metaphysical Dimensions**

    - Narrative identity workshops help learners integrate technical learning with personal purpose.

- G-Theory frameworks ensure curriculum evolves through feedback and regenerative design.

28.5.2 Research Outcomes

- **Skill Acquisition**

    - Completion rates exceed 85% across decentralized cohorts.

    - Employer satisfaction surveys score 4.3/5 for job readiness of token-credentialed graduates.

- **Economic Impact**

    - Alumni networks drive $10 million in startup funding via Token-Backed Angel Pools.

28.6 Manufacturing and Supply Chain Innovation

28.6.1 Case Study: Distributed Microfactory Networks

- **Distributed Value Creation**

    - Artisans, engineers, and designers collaborate via a ManufactureDAO to produce on-demand parts regionally, reducing shipping distance and emissions.

- NFT-backed design licenses ensure fair royalty distribution.

- **Dynamic Equilibrium**

  - AI demand forecasting allocates printing queues and raw materials to microfactories.

  - Smart contracts reprice parts based on capacity utilization and material costs.

- **Emergence & Self-Organization**

  - Maker holons self-assemble for custom orders, then disband with escrowed payments settled.

  - Quality-assurance oracles verify output against 3D scans, triggering automated repeat orders.

- **Ethical Integration**

  - Cooperative design sprints embed local artisans' cultural patterns into products.

  - Profit-sharing tokens fund community workshops in STEM and traditional crafts.

28.6.2 Impact Analysis

- **Environmental Gains**

  - 35% reduction in carbon footprint per part vs. centralized manufacturing.

- **Economic Resilience**
  - Localized manufacturing hubs increased regional manufacturing GDP by 8%.

28.7 Research Methodologies for G-Theory Applications

1. **Systems Modeling & Simulation**

   - Use agent-based models (e.g., NetLogo) to simulate feedback loops, emergent behaviors, and equilibrium states across integrated networks.

2. **Mixed-Methods Evaluations**

   - Combine quantitative metrics (token flows, AI forecast accuracy) with qualitative ethnographies and narrative analyses to capture multi-dimensional impact.

3. **Transdisciplinary Living Labs**

   - Embed researchers, practitioners, and community stakeholders in co-creation spaces, iterating prototypes and governance rules in real time.

4. **Meta-Analysis and Comparative Case Studies**

   - Aggregate data across pilot sites to identify patterns of success, failure modes, and best-practice clusters.

28.8 Metrics and Impact Measurement

- **Economic Indicators:** Token velocity, local GDP growth, income equality indices.

- **Social Metrics:** Participation rates, trust indices, narrative cohesion scores.

- **Environmental Measures:** Resource-cycle efficiency, carbon reductions, biodiversity restoration metrics.

- **Governance Health:** Proposal throughput, vote turnout, decision-cycle times, dispute resolution rates.

28.9 Challenges and Future Research Directions

1. **Complexity Management:**

   - Mitigate model overfitting and instability via modular design and adaptive governance oversight.

2. **Interdisciplinary Collaboration:**

   - Build shared epistemic tools and ontologies to bridge disciplinary languages, facilitating integrated research teams.

3. **Ethical AI and Tokenomics:**

- Advance frameworks for fairness, transparency, and algorithmic accountability in predictive and prescriptive modules.

4. **Scalability vs. Local Autonomy:**

   - Research optimal balance between global standardization and local customization, ensuring fidelity without loss of context.

28.10 Conclusion

By applying G-Theory's integrative principles across diverse sectors—from healthcare and smart cities to agriculture, education, and manufacturing—researchers and practitioners can catalyze systemic innovations that are adaptive, equitable, and resilient. The advanced case studies and methodologies outlined in this chapter demonstrate G-Theory's versatility as both a lens for understanding complex systems and a blueprint for designing transformative interventions. Ongoing multidisciplinary research will refine G-Theory further, unlocking new pathways for communities worldwide to co-create a sustainable and empowered future.

Chapter 29: The Infinite Cycle of Innovation – Modeling Future Paradigms

The Infinite Cycle Theory posits that social and economic progress unfolds through recurring, regenerative cycles rather than linear trajectories. By understanding and deliberately engineering these cycles, communities and organizations can anticipate emerging challenges, harness creative disruptions, and steer systemic transformations toward desired futures. This chapter offers a forward-looking framework—grounded in the Infinite Cycle Theory—for modeling tomorrow's socio-economic and technological paradigms. We explore conceptual foundations, modeling methodologies, scenario development, policy levers, and organizational design strategies that together enable continuous, adaptive innovation.

29.1 Introduction: Envisioning Tomorrow's Cycles

- **From Reactive to Proactive Innovation:**
  Traditional planning often reacts to crises after they occur. Infinite-Cycle-based modeling shifts the mindset to proactive cycle engineering—anticipating the next wave of change before it erupts.

- **Scope and Objectives:**

    1. Recast the Infinite Cycle Theory as a forecasting and planning tool.

    2. Present methodological toolkits for modeling innovation cycles.

    3. Illustrate applications across technology, economy, and society.

    4. Recommend strategic interventions to shape positive futures.

29.2 Theoretical Foundations of the Infinite Cycle

29.2.1 Recalling the Four Phases

1. **Conception & Emergence:** Novel ideas, technologies, or social movements arise from converging forces.

2. **Acceleration & Adoption:** Rapid diffusion as early adopters and influencers drive momentum.

3. **Maturation & Saturation:** Market or social structures stabilize around the innovation.

4. **Creative Destruction & Renewal:** Obsolescence of prior models yields space for next cycles.

29.2.2 Feedback Loops and Attractors

- **Positive Feedback:** Amplifies emergent innovations when successes attract resources and attention.

- **Negative Feedback:** Stabilizes systems by curbing runaway effects and promoting equilibrium.

- **Attractors:** Stable states toward which systems gravitate—recognizing and aligning with these enables smoother transitions between phases.

29.3 Modeling Methodologies

29.3.1 System Dynamics Modeling

- **Causal Loop Diagrams (CLDs):** Map the reinforcing and balancing loops governing innovation diffusion, resource flows, and stakeholder behavior.

- **Stock-Flow Simulations:** Quantify accumulations (e.g., R&D investment, user adoption) and flows (e.g., funding rates, churn) over time, enabling "what-if" experiments on policy levers.

29.3.2 Agent-Based Simulation

- **Population of Heterogeneous Agents:** Simulate individuals, firms, and institutions with diverse decision-rules—capturing micro-behaviors and emergent macro-patterns.

- **Network Effects:** Embed social networks and economic linkages to model contagion of innovation and influence dynamics.

29.3.3 Scenario Planning & Morphological Analysis

- **Exploratory Scenarios:** Develop multiple, contrasting "futurescapes" by combining key uncertainties (e.g., regulation, technological breakthroughs).

- **Morphological Boxes:** Enumerate dimensions (social, technological, economic, environmental, political) and their potential states to systematically explore scenario spaces.

29.3.4 Data-Driven Early Warning Systems

- **Leading Indicators:** Identify and monitor metrics (e.g., patent filings, startup formations, policy debates) that presage cycle shifts.

- **Machine Learning Forecasts:** Apply time-series and anomaly detection models to predict inflection points and emerging trends.

29.4 Mapping Technological Transformation Cycles

29.4.1 AI & Machine Learning Waves

- **Emergence:** Foundational breakthroughs (e.g., deep learning, generative AI) spark research booms.

- **Acceleration:** Commercial deployments across industries (healthcare AI diagnostics, autonomous vehicles).

- **Maturation:** Standardization of frameworks, ethical guidelines, and regulatory regimes.

- **Renewal:** Next-gen paradigms (quantum AI, bio-inspired computing) disrupt settled norms.

29.4.2 Blockchain & Web3 Revolutions

- **Emergence:** Peer-to-peer currency experiments (Bitcoin) and early smart-contract platforms.

- **Acceleration:** DeFi, DAOs, NFT ecosystems drive mainstream traction and investment.

- **Maturation:** Regulatory clarity, institutional adoption, and interoperability standards consolidate value networks.

- **Renewal:** Interchain metaprotocols, decentralized identity, and on-chain governance innovations usher new cycles.

29.4.3 Fusion & Next-Gen Energy

- **Emergence:** Private fusion startups and proof-of-concept devices demonstrate net energy potential.

- **Acceleration:** Microreactor pilots integrate within local grids, catalyzing decentralized energy economies.

- **Maturation:** Commercial fusion plants scale, reducing costs and displacing thermal power.

- **Renewal:** Beyond fusion—space-based solar, quantum energy harvesters—reshape global energy paradigms.

29.5 Socio-Economic Transformation Cycles

29.5.1 Decentralized Economies and Group-Based Wealth

- **Cycle Phases:** Cooperative finance models emerge, scale through digital platforms, mature into institutional frameworks, and evolve into new hybrid economic architectures.

29.5.2 Urban Regeneration and Smart City Waves

- **Emergence:** Pilot smart neighborhoods leverage IoT and local DAOs.

- **Acceleration:** City-wide adoption of participatory budgeting, decentralized mobility, and energy sharing.

- **Maturation:** Standard municipal governance integrates Web3 tools.

- **Renewal:** Autonomous urban ecosystems—self-healing infrastructure and AI governance—usher next-era cities.

29.5.3 Cultural & Narrative Renaissance

- **Emergence:** Grassroots storytelling movements reclaim local heritage.

- **Acceleration:** Digital media and AR/VR amplify narrative reach.

- **Maturation:** Shared global myths coalesce around empowerment and regeneration.

- **Renewal:** Meta-narratives interweave digital and physical cultures, shaping identity cycles.

29.6 Policy and Strategic Interventions

29.6.1 Adaptive Governance Frameworks

- **Rolling Policy Cycles:** Implement staggered policy reviews timed to innovation phases—regulatory easing in emergence, guardrails in acceleration, standardization in maturation, renewal incentives in creative destruction.

- **Experimentation Zones:** Designate "innovation districts" with temporary regulatory sandboxes to trial novel economic models.

29.6.2 Investment and Funding Mechanisms

- **Stage-Phased Funding:** Align public and private capital deployment with cycle stages—seed grants for emergence, growth equity for acceleration, infrastructure bonds for maturation, R&D credits for renewal.

- **Crowd-Sourced Financing Pools:** Tokenized investment vehicles that adapt allocation rules based on early success metrics and community feedback.

29.7 Organizational Design for Eternal Renewal

29.7.1 Learning Organizations

- **Double-Loop Learning:** Institutions regularly question underlying assumptions and value frameworks, not just strategies—ensuring cycles feed deeper cultural renewal.

- **Knowledge Repositories:** Living wikis and digital twins capture past cycle insights, providing a reference for future innovation waves.

29.7.2 Holonic Enterprise Architectures

- **Nested Innovation Units:** Agile "Holons" operate semi-autonomously yet share protocols and resources through federated governance, enabling parallel cycle initiatives and preventing organizational sclerosis.

29.8 Measuring and Steering Future Innovation Cycles

- **Cycle Health Dashboards:** Composite indices tracking leading, coincident, and lagging indicators—R&D intensity, adoption rates, policy responsiveness, cultural sentiment.

- **AI-Driven Foresight Engines:** Multi-agent simulations continuously ingest global data to update cycle forecasts and recommend timely interventions.

- **Participatory Futures Workshops:** Blending expert modeling with citizen visioning—ensures cycle planning remains grounded in diverse values and aspirations.

29.9 Conclusion: Orchestrating the Infinite Cycle

By reimagining the Infinite Cycle Theory as a dynamic forecasting and planning instrument, communities and organizations can move from ad hoc innovation to deliberate cycle engineering. Through robust modeling, strategic policy design, adaptive governance, and holistic organizational frameworks, it is possible to navigate emerging socio-economic and technological transformations with foresight and resilience. As cycles of emergence, acceleration, maturation, and renewal continue to unfold, the ability to anticipate inflection points and guide regeneration becomes the core competency of future-ready systems—ensuring that progress remains perpetual, equitable, and aligned with collective well-being.

Chapter 30: Vision 2050 – A Roadmap for a New Socio-Economic Order

This concluding chapter synthesizes the preceding 29 chapters into a unified, strategic roadmap for realizing a radically transformed, decentralized, and regenerative global society by the year 2050. Drawing on insights from Group Economics, the Infinite Cycle Theory, PowerNomics, Web3 Systems Thinking, Gemach and SydTek DAOs, fusion energy, AI-augmented governance, and self-sustaining ecosystems, Vision 2050 lays out concrete milestones, benchmarks, and policy interventions across five principal domains:

1. **Economic Empowerment & Equity**

2. **Governance & Decentralized Institutions**

3. **Education & Human Capacity Building**

4. **Technology & Infrastructure**

5. **Culture, Identity & Regeneration**

Within each domain, we chart a three-phase timeline—Near Term (2025–2030), Mid Term (2030–2040), and Long Term (2040–2050)—detailing targets, key actions, and success metrics.

30.1 Economic Empowerment & Equity

30.1.1 Near Term (2025–2030)

- **Establish 1,000 Community DAOs**: Launch pilot DAOs in diverse locales, each governed by tokenized group-economics models (Gemach DAO) with participatory tools (quadratic voting, participation credits).

- **Micro-Loan & Reparations Funds**: Tokenized reparations pilots modeled on Asheboro establish $50 M in community-owned micro-funds, achieving ≥80% repayment rates.

- **Vertical Integration Hubs**: Create 200 cooperative federations integrating at least two adjacent value-chain stages (e.g., production + processing), boosting local margins by ≥25%.

- **Wealth Parity Benchmarks**: Raise median household wealth in pilot communities by 20%, narrowing racial and income gaps by at least 10%.

30.1.2 Mid Term (2030–2040)

- **Regional Consortia & Federations**: Scale to 50 regional DAOs federated into five national networks, mobilizing $5 B in community capital.

- **Self-Sustaining Ecosystems**: Deploy 100 closed-loop resource hubs (agro-energy, manufacturing), achieving ≥60% local input sourcing and waste recycling.

- **Group Wealth Index**: Track group-wealth velocity (token velocity across local DAOs), target doubling every five years.

- **Inclusive Growth Metrics**: Reduce Gini coefficients in participating regions by ≥15% relative to 2025 baselines.

30.1.3 Long Term (2040–2050)

- **Global Network of DAOs**: Interconnect 1,000+ local and regional DAOs into a planetary Commons, with seamless cross-chain interoperability.

- **Full Vertical Integration**: Every major value chain—from energy to agriculture to manufacturing—operates under decentralized cooperatives, retaining ≥80% value locally.

- **Universal Basic Economic Participation**: Design and pilot tokenized Universal Basic Income (uBI) in 20 countries, funded by decentralized energy and data dividends.

- **Global Wealth Equity**: Aim for median household wealth parity across demographic groups globally, within 5% variance.

30.2 Governance & Decentralized Institutions

30.2.1 Near Term (2025–2030)

- **Legal Recognition of DAOs**: Enact DAO-LLC legislations in 25 jurisdictions, clarifying fiduciary duties and liability.

- **Policy Sandboxes**: Establish 30 "Decentralized Governance Zones" permitting experimental DAO applications in public services.

- **AI-Augmented Councils**: Pilot AI decision-support systems in 100 DAOs, achieving a 30% reduction in decision-cycle times.

- **Interoperable Protocols**: Adopt W3C Verifiable Credentials and ISO blockchain standards in core DAO modules.

30.2.2 Mid Term (2030–2040)

- **DAO Municipalities**: Convert 50 small municipalities to hybrid DAO-governance, managing budgets, participatory planning, and service delivery on-chain.

- **Global Working Groups**: Convene international DAO regulatory consortiums under UN auspices, producing model frameworks adopted by 70 countries.

- **Dynamic Policy Engines**: Deploy AI-driven adaptive regulations that tune governance parameters (quorum, funding thresholds) in real time.

- **Ethical Governance Index**: Measure inclusivity, transparency, and accountability across DAOs, aiming for average scores ≥0.8 on a 0–1 scale.

30.2.3 Long Term (2040–2050)

- **Planetary DAO Meta-Governance**: Institute a Global Commons DAO coordinating planetary public goods—climate action, biodiversity, inter-regional trade.

- **Self-Evolving Legal Frameworks**: Smart-contract-based law ("Code-as-Law") with embedded consensus amendment protocols.

- **AI-Mediated Global Policy**: Federated AI systems manage cross-border issues (migration, trade disputes) with human oversight, reducing conflict cycles.

- **Governance Maturity Ladder**: All major regions achieve "Stage 5" on a 6-stage maturity model—fully decentralized, self-optimizing governance.

30.3 Education & Human Capacity Building

30.3.1 Near Term (2025–2030)

- **SydTek University Launch**: Establish flagship campuses and satellite labs in 10 countries, enrolling 10,000 students in interdisciplinary curricula.

- **Gemach Pedagogy Integration**: Embed community-based living labs and DAO governance projects into 50 universities' core programs.

- **Micro-Credential Ecosystem**: Issue 100,000 blockchain-verified badges in AI, blockchain, empowerment theory; adoption by 500 employers.

- **Hope Paradox Workshops**: Train 5,000 educators in integrating metaphysics and empowerment into STEM and humanities courses.

30.3.2 Mid Term (2030–2040)

- **Global LearningDAO**: Create a meta-DAO accrediting decentralized learning platforms, supporting 1 million learners in stackable degree pathways.

- **AI Tutors & Adaptive Learning**: 80% of higher-ed institutions deploy AI+DAO systems for real-time curriculum adaptation and student support.

- **Lifelong Learning Mandate**: National policies guarantee citizens at least 300 learning-hours/year credit toward community DAOs and career mobility.

- **Educational Equity Metrics**: Achieve <5% variance in access and outcomes across socio-economic groups within networked institutions.

30.3.3 Long Term (2040–2050)

- **Post-Scarcity Knowledge Commons**: All major research outputs and educational resources open-sourced on interoperable blockchains.

- **Narrative-Driven Cultural Renewal**: Shared global myths and meta-narratives produced through participatory art & VR, reinforcing planetary identity.

- **Self-Directed Learning DAOs**: Learners autonomously form DAOs around emergent disciplines, self-publishing curricula and credentialing via community consensus.

- **Human Potential Index**: Track global well-being, creativity, and agency, targeting top quartile improvements over 2025 baselines.

30.4 Technology & Infrastructure

30.4.1 Near Term (2025–2030)

- **Blockchain Mainnet Expansion**: Achieve integrated PoS and layer-2 networks supporting 1 billion unique wallets.

- **AI-Governance Platforms**: Deploy AI models to 500 leading DAOs, forecasting proposals and optimizing treasury flows.

- **Fusion Pilot Deployments**: Commission 20 fusion microreactor demonstration sites powering local microgrids.

- **IoT-Enabled Living Labs**: Equip 200 communities with sensor networks for resource-cycle monitoring (water, energy, waste).

30.4.2 Mid Term (2030–2040)

- **Planetary Energy Grid**: Connect fusion microreactor clusters, renewables, and storage via decentralized market protocols, smoothing supply-demand across regions.

- **Quantum-Resistant Infrastructure**: Transition critical smart contracts and identity systems to quantum-safe cryptography.

- **Metaverse Public Commons**: Establish interoperable AR/VR infrastructures for decentralized civic participation and cultural exchange.

- **Tech Equity Index**: Ensure 90% of communities have access to high-bandwidth connectivity and AI governance tools.

30.4.3 Long Term (2040–2050)

- **Interplanetary Resource Networks**: Demonstration of space-based solar fusion arrays and asteroid-mined materials integrated via DAO contracts.

- **Conscious AI Stewards**: Ethical, explainable AI agents co-manage critical infrastructure under human-AI symbiosis frameworks.

- **Global Digital Nervous System**: A decentralized IoT and blockchain network providing real-time planetary health, economic, and social data to all citizens.

- **Infrastructure Resilience Score**: Achieve ≥0.9 on resilience metrics (redundancy, adaptability, self-healing) for core networks.

30.5 Culture, Identity & Regeneration

30.5.1 Near Term (2025–2030)

- **Narrative & Myth Workshops**: 1,000 communities co-create local empowerment myths, encoded in digital story-maps and NFTs.

- **Cultural DAO Pilots**: Fund 200 arts and heritage DAOs preserving and innovating living traditions.

- **Well-Being & Trust Metrics**: Launch global surveys tracking trust in local institutions, aiming for average scores >3.5/5.

30.5.2 Mid Term (2030–2040)

- **Global Cultural Renaissance**: Host decennial "World Narrative Congress" where communities share co-created myths, resulting in a living Global Cultural Commons.

- **Regenerative Justice Initiatives**: Scale reparations DAOs to 100 nations, integrating indigenous knowledge into environmental restoration and economic planning.

- **Collective Identity Index**: Monitor emergence of shared planetary narratives, targeting ≥50% of global population engaged in Digital Commons storytelling.

30.5.3 Long Term (2040–2050)

- **Planetary Stewardship Charter**: Drafted and ratified via DAO consensus, codifying rights and responsibilities across species and ecosystems.

- **Meta-Myth Cycle**: A dynamic, AI-curated narrative that evolves with each innovation cycle, binding humanity in a continuous story of renewal.

- **Cultural Resilience Score**: Achieve top-quartile performance on assessments of social cohesion, cross-cultural empathy, and narrative adaptability.

30.6 Cross-Cutting Policy & Governance Enablers

- **Adaptive, Principle-Based Regulation:** Implement rolling policy reviews tied to innovation cycles; emphasize transparency, proportionality, and stakeholder co-design.

- **Global Standards and Interoperability:** Coordinate ISO/IEEE/W3C working groups on DAO registries, impact data schemas, and digital identity to ensure seamless scale.

- **Capacity-Building Consortia:** Establish international academies and fellowships (Gemach & SydTek) to train

100,000 practitioners in decentralized systems thinking.

- **Public-Private-Community Partnerships:** Mobilize blended finance and multisector coalitions to underwrite infrastructure, R&D, and pilot expansions.

30.7 Conclusion: Co-Creating the Future

Vision 2050 offers not a utopian blueprint but a dynamic, adaptive roadmap—one that envisions humanity as active co-creators in the Infinite Cycle of Innovation. By weaving together economic empowerment, decentralized governance, lifelong learning, technological infrastructure, and cultural regeneration, this roadmap charts a path to a resilient, equitable, and flourishing socio-economic order. The milestones and benchmarks set forth provide guideposts for communities, institutions, and policymakers. Yet the ultimate success of Vision 2050 depends on collective agency: each stakeholder must embrace iterative learning, participatory decision-making, and regenerative action. As we stand at the cusp of unprecedented transformation, our shared narrative must be one of hope, collaboration, and perpetual renewal—ensuring that every cycle advances not just technology and wealth, but the dignity, creativity, and well-being of all.

www.ingramcontent.com/pod-product-compliance
Lightning Source LLC
LaVergne TN
LVHW051426050326
832903LV00030BD/2939